STUDIES IN JUDAISM

STUDIES IN JUDAISM

BY

SOLOMON SCHECHTER

Essay Index Reprint Series

 BOOKS FOR LIBRARIES PRESS
FREEPORT, NEW YORK

First Published 1896
Reprinted 1972

Library of Congress Cataloging in Publication Data

Schechter, Solomon, 1847-1915.
    Studies in Judaism.

    (Essay index reprint series)
    Reprint of the 1896 ed.
    Includes bibliographical references.
    1. Judaism--History--Addresses, essays, lectures.
I. Title.
BM160.S3 1972   296   78-38775
ISBN 0-8369-2670-6

PRINTED IN THE UNITED STATES OF AMERICA
BY
NEW WORLD BOOK MANUFACTURING CO., INC.
HALLANDALE, FLORIDA 33009

TO

THE EVER-CHERISHED MEMORY

OF

THE LATE DR. P. F. FRANKL, RABBI IN BERLIN

THESE STUDIES ARE REVERENTLY

DEDICATED

PREFACE

THESE studies appeared originally in their first form in The Jewish Quarterly *and* The Jewish Chronicle. *To the Editors of these periodicals my best thanks are due for their readiness in placing the articles at my disposal for the purposes of the present volume. The Introductory Essay is new. I desire to express my sincere gratitude to Mr. J. G. Frazer, Fellow of Trinity College, Cambridge, and Dr. J. Sutherland Black, of London, for their great kindness in revising the proofs, and for many a valuable suggestion. To Mr. Claude G. Montefiore I am indebted for the English version of the Essay on "Chassidim" — my first literary effort in this country, written at his own suggestion.*

In the transliteration of Hebrew names, I have given the familiar English forms of the authorised version. As regards post-Biblical names, I have with few exceptions followed Zedner's Catalogue of the Hebrew Books in the Library of the British Museum. *A Hebrew word will be found here and there in the text; I have purposely avoided bewildering devices for representing the actual sound of the word, contenting myself with the ordinary Roman alphabet, in spite of its shortcomings.*

vii

The authorities used for the various Essays will be found indicated in the Notes at the end of the volume, where the reader will also find short biographical and bibliographical notices, together with brief explanations of technical terms for which no exact equivalent exists in English.   The index will, it is hoped, facilitate reference.

S. S.

CAMBRIDGE, *February* 1896.

CONTENTS

ix

INTRODUCTION

THE essays published in this volume under the title of *Studies in Judaism* have been written on various occasions and at long intervals. There is thus no necessary connection between them. If some sort of unity may be detected in the book, it can only be between the first three essays — on the Chassidim, Krochmal, and the Gaon — in which there is a certain unity of purpose. The purpose in view was, as may easily be gathered from the essays themselves, to bring under the notice of the English public a type of men produced by the Synagogue of the Eastern Jews. That Synagogue is widely different from ours. Its places of worship have no claims to "beauty of holiness," being in their outward appearance rather bare and bald, if not repulsive; whilst those who frequent them are a noisy, excitable people, who actually dance on the "Season of Rejoicing" and cry bitterly on the "Days of Mourning." But among all these vagaries — or perhaps because of them — this Synagogue has had its moments of grace, when enthusiasm wedded to inspiration gave birth to such beautiful souls as Baalshem, such fine sceptics as Krochmal, and such saintly scholars as Elijah Wilna. The Synagogue of the West is certainly of a more presentable character, and free from excesses; though it is not devoid of an enthusiasm of its own which

finds its outlet in an ardent and self-sacrificing philan-
thropic activity.   But owing to its practical tendency
there is too little room in it for that play of intellectual
forces which finds its extravagant expression in the saint
on the one hand, and the learned heretic on the other.

Eight of these essays are more or less of a theological
nature.   But in reading the proofs I have been struck by
the fact that there is assumed in them a certain conception of the Synagogue which, familiar though it be to the
Jewish student, may appear obscure and even strange to
the general English reader.   For brevity's sake I will call
it the High Synagogue, though it does not correspond in
all details to what one is accustomed to understand under
the term of High Church.   The High Synagogue has a
history which is not altogether without its points of
interest.

Some years ago when the waves of the Higher Criticism
of the Old Testament reached the shores of this country,
and such questions as the heterogeneous composition of
the Pentateuch, the comparatively late date of the Levitical Legislation, and the post-exilic origin of certain Prophecies as well as of the Psalms began to be freely discussed
by the press and even in the pulpit, the invidious remark
was often made : What will now become of Judaism when
its last stronghold, the Law, is being shaken to its very
foundations ?

Such a remark shows a very superficial acquaintance
with the nature of an old historical religion like Judaism,
and the richness of the resources it has to fall back upon
in cases of emergency.

As a fact, the emergency did not quite surprise Judaism.
The alarm signal was given some 150 years ago by an

Italian Rabbi, Abiad Sar Shalom Bazilai, in his pamphlet *The Faith of the Sages*. The pamphlet is, as the title indicates, of a polemical character, reviewing the work of the Jewish rationalistic schools ; and after warming up in his attacks against their heterodox views, Bazilai exclaims : "Nature and simple meaning, they are our misfortune." By "nature and simple meaning" Bazilai, who wrote in Hebrew, understood what we would call Natural Science and Philology. With the right instinct of faith, Bazilai hit on the real sore points. For though he mostly argues against the philosophical systems of Aristotle and his commentators, he felt that it is not speculation that will ever seriously endanger religion. There is hardly any metaphysical system, old or new, which has not in course of time been adapted by able dialecticians to the creed which they happened to hold. In our own time we have seen the glorious, though not entirely novel spectacle, of Agnosticism itself becoming the rightful handmaid of Queen Theology. The real danger lies in "nature" (or Natural Science) with its stern demand of law and regularity in all phenomena, and in the "simple meaning" (or Philology) with its inconsiderate insistence on truth. Of the two, the "simple meaning" is the more objectionable. Not only is it very often at variance with Tradition, which has its own code of interpretation, but it is constantly increasing the difficulties raised by science. For if words could only have more than òne meaning, there would be no objection to reading the first words of Genesis, "In *a* beginning God *evolved*." The difficulties of science would then be disposed of easily enough. Maimonides, who was as bold an interpreter as he was a deep metaphysician, hinted plainly enough that were he as convinced of the eternity of matter as he was satisfied of the impossibility of any corporeal quality in the deity, he would feel as little compunction in explaining (figuratively) the contents of the first chapter of Genesis as he did in allegorising the anthropomorphic passages of the Bible. Thus in the end all the difficulties resolve themselves into the one great difficulty of the "simple meaning." The best way to meet this difficulty was found to be to shift the centre of gravity in Judaism and to place it in the secondary meaning, thus making religion independent of philology and all its dangerous consequences.

This shifting work was chiefly done, perhaps not quite consciously, by the historical school which followed upon that of Mendelssohn and his first successors. The historical school, which is still in the ascendant, comprises many of the best Jewish writers who either by their learning or by their ecclesiastical profession as Rabbis and preachers in great communities have acquired some important position among their brethren. The men who have inaugurated this movement were Krochmal (1785–1841), Rapoport (1790–1867), and Zunz (1794–1886).

It is not a mere coincidence that the first representatives of the historical school were also the first Jewish scholars who proved themselves more or less ready to join the modern school of Bible Criticism, and even to contribute their share to it. The first two, Krochmal and Rapoport, early in the second quarter of this century accepted and defended the modern view about a second Isaiah, the post-exilic origin of many Psalms, and the late date of Ecclesiastes; whilst Zunz, who began (in 1832) with denying the authenticity of Ezekiel, concluded his literary career (1873) with a study on the Bible (*Gesam-*

melte Schriften, i. pp. 217–290), in which he expressed his view "that the Book of Leviticus dates from a later period than the Book of Deuteronomy, later even than Ezekiel, having been composed during the age of the Second Temple, when there already existed a well-established priesthood which superintended the sacrificial worship." But when Revelation or the Written Word is reduced to the level of history, there is no difficulty in elevating history in its aspect of Tradition to the rank of Scripture, for both have then the same human or divine origin (according to the student's predilection for the one or the other adjective), and emanate from the same authority. Tradition becomes thus the means whereby the modern divine seeks to compensate himself for the loss of the Bible, and the theological balance is to the satisfaction of all parties happily readjusted.

Jewish Tradition, or, as it is commonly called, the Oral Law, or, as we may term it (in consideration of its claims to represent an interpretation of the Bible), the Secondary Meaning of the Scriptures, is mainly embodied in the works of the Rabbis and their subsequent followers during the Middle Ages. Hence the zeal and energy with which the historical school applied itself to the Jewish post-biblical literature, not only elucidating its texts by means of new critical editions, dictionaries, and commentaries, but also trying to trace its origins and to pursue its history through its gradual development. To the work of Krochmal in this direction a special essay is devoted in this volume. The labours of Rapoport are more of a biographical and bibliographical nature, being occupied mostly with the minor details in the lives and writings of various famous Jewish Rabbis in the Middle Ages; thus they offer but little opportunity for general theological comment. Of more importance in this respect are the hints thrown out in his various works by Zunz, who was just as emphatic in asserting the claims of Tradition as he was advanced in his views on Bible criticism. Zunz's greatest work is *Die Gottesdienstlichen Vorträge* — an awkward title, which in fact means " The History of the Interpretation of the Scriptures as forming a part of the divine service." Now if a work displaying such wide learning and critical acumen, and written in such an impartial spirit can be said to have a bias, it was towards bridging over the seemingly wide gap between the Written Word (the Scriptures) and the Spoken Word (the Oral Law or Tradition), which was the more deeply felt, as most of Zunz's older contemporaries were men, grown up in the habits of thought of the eighteenth century — a century distinguished both for its ignorance of, and its power of ignoring, the teachings of history. Indeed it would seem that ages employed in making history have no time for studying it.

Zunz accomplished the task he set himself, by showing, as already indicated, the late date of certain portions of the Bible, which by setting the early history of Israel in an ideal light betray the moralising tendency of their authors, and are, in fact, little more than a traditional interpretation of older portions of Scripture, adapted to the religious needs of the time. Placing thus the origin of Tradition in the Bible itself, it was a comparatively easy matter for Zunz to prove its further continuity. Prophecy and Interpretation are with him the natural expressions of the religious life of the nation ; and though by the loss of Israel's political independence the voice of the prophets gradually died away, the voice of God was still heard. Israel continues to consult God through the medium of the Scriptures, and He answers His people by the mouth of the Scribes, the Sages, the Interpreters of the Law; whilst the liturgy of the Synagogue, springing up at the time when Psalms were still being composed, expands in its later stages through the work of the Poets of the Synagogue into such a rich luxuriance "that it forms in itself a treasure of history, poetry, philosophy; and prophecy and psalms are again revived in the hymnology of the Middle Ages." This is in brief the lesson to be learned from Zunz's *Gottesdienstliche Vorträge* as far as it deals with the significance of Tradition; and it is in the introduction to this work that Zunz expresses himself to the following effect: Indispensable is the free Spoken Word. Mankind has acquired all its ideal treasures only by Word of Mouth; an education continuing through all stages of life. In Israel, too, the Word of Instruction transmitted from mouth to mouth was never silenced.

The historical school has never, to my knowledge, offered to the world a theological programme of its own. By the nature of its task, its labours are mostly conducted in the field of philology and archæology, and it pays but little attention to purely dogmatic questions. On the whole, its attitude towards religion may be defined as an enlightened Scepticism combined with a staunch conservatism which is not even wholly devoid of a certain mystical touch. As far as we may gather from vague remarks and hints thrown out now and then, its theological position may perhaps be thus defined: — It is not the mere revealed Bible that is of first importance to the Jew, but the Bible as it repeats itself in history, in other words, as it is interpreted by Tradition. The Talmud, that wonderful mine of religious ideas from which it would be just as easy to draw up a manual for the most orthodox as to extract a vade-mecum for the most sceptical, lends some countenance to this view by certain controversial passages — not to be taken seriously — in which "the words of the scribes" are placed almost above the words of the Torah. Since then the interpretation of Scripture or the Secondary Meaning is mainly a product of changing historical influences, it follows that the centre of authority is actually removed from the Bible and placed in some *living body*, which, by reason of its being in touch with the ideal aspirations and the religious needs of the age, is best able to determine the nature of the Secondary Meaning. This living body, however, is not represented by any section of the nation, or any corporate priesthood, or Rabbihood, but by the collective conscience of Catholic Israel as embodied in the Universal Synagogue. The Synagogue "with its long, continuous cry after God for more than twenty-three centuries," with its unremittent activity in teaching and developing the word of God, with its uninterrupted succession of prophets, Psalmists, Scribes, Assideans, Rabbis, Patriarchs, Interpreters, Elucidators, Eminences, and Teachers, with its glorious record of Saints, martyrs, sages, philosophers, scholars, and mystics; this Synagogue, the only true witness to the past, and forming in all ages the sublimest expression of Israel's religious life, must also retain its authority as the sole true guide for the present and the future. And being in communion with this Synagogue, we may also look hopefully for a safe and rational solution of our present theological troubles. For was it not the Synagogue which even in antiquity determined the fate of Scripture? On the one hand, for example, books like Ezekiel, the Song of Songs, and Ecclesiastes, were only declared to be Holy Writ in virtue of the interpretation put upon them by the Rabbis: and, on the other hand, it was the veto of the Rabbis which excluded from the canon the works that now pass under the name of Apocrypha. We may, therefore, safely trust that the Synagogue will again assert its divine right in passing judgment upon the Bible when it feels called upon to exercise that holy office. It is "God who has chosen the Torah, and Moses His servant, and Israel His people." But indeed God's choice invariably coincides with the wishes of Israel; He "performeth all things" upon which the councils of Israel, meeting under promise of the Divine presence and communion, have previously agreed. As the Talmud somewhere expresses itself with regard to the Book of Esther, "They have confirmed above what Israel has accepted below."

Another consequence of this conception of Tradition is that it is neither Scripture nor primitive Judaism, but general custom which forms the real rule of practice. Holy Writ as well as history, Zunz tells us, teaches that the law of Moses was never fully and absolutely put in practice. Liberty was always given to the great teachers of every generation to make modifications and innovations in harmony with the spirit of existing institutions. Hence a return to Mosaism would be illegal, pernicious, and indeed impossible. The norm as well as the sanction of Judaism is the practice actually in vogue. Its consecration is the consecration of general use, — or, in other words, of Catholic Israel. It was probably with a view to this communion that the later mystics introduced a short prayer to be said before the performance of any religious ceremony, in which, among other things, the speaker professes his readiness to act "in the name of all Israel."

It would be out of place in an introductory essay to pursue any further this interesting subject with its far-reaching consequences upon Jewish life and Jewish thought. But the foregoing remarks may suffice to show that Judaism did not remain quite inactive at the approach of the great religious crisis which our generation has witnessed. Like so many other religious communities, it reviewed its forces, entrenched itself on the field of history, and what it lost of its old devotion to the Bible, it has sought to make up by a renewed reverence for institutions.

In this connection, a mere mention may suffice of the ultra-Orthodox party, led by the late Dr. S. R. Hirsch of Frankfort (1808–1889) whose defiance of reason and criticism even a Ward might have envied, and whose saintliness and sublimity even a Keble might have admired. And, to take an example from the opposite school, we must at least record the name of that devout Jew, Osias Schorr (1816–1895), in whom we have profound learning combined with an uncompromising disposition of mind productive of a typical champion of Radicalism in things religious. These men are, however, representative of two extremes, and their followers constitute mere minorities; the majority is with the historical school.

How long the position of this school will prove tenable is another question. Being brought up in the old Low Synagogue, where, with all attachment to tradition, the Bible was looked upon as the crown and the climax of Judaism, the old Adam still asserts itself in me, and in unguarded moments makes me rebel against this new rival of revelation in the shape of history. At times this now fashionable exaltation of Tradition at the expense of Scripture even impresses me as a sort of religious bimetallism in which bold speculators in theology try to keep up the market value of an inferior currency by denouncing loudly the bright shining gold which, they would have us believe, is less fitted to circulate in the vulgar use of daily life than the small cash of historical interpretation. Nor can I quite reconcile myself to this alliance of religion with history, which seems to me both unworthy and unnatural. The Jew, some writer aptly remarked, was the first and the fiercest Nonconformist of the East, and so Judaism was always a protesting religion. To break the idols, whether of the past or of the present, has always been a sacred mission of Judaism, and has indeed been esteemed by it as a necessary preliminary to the advent of the kingdom of God on earth. One of its daily prayers was and still is: "We therefore hope in Thee, O Lord our God, that we may speedily behold the glory of Thy might, when . . . the idols will be cut off, when the world will be perfected under the kingdom of the Almighty." It bowed before truth, but it had never made a covenant with facts only because they were facts. History had to be re-made and to sanctify itself before it found its way into its sacred annals. Nor did Judaism make a virtue of swallowing down institutions. Such institutions as crept into it in course of time had, when the Synagogue was conscious of their claims to form part of religion, to submit to the laborious process of a thorough adaptation to prophetic notions before they were formally sanctioned. But when this process was deemed impossible or impracti-

cable, Judaism boldly denounced the past in such fierce
language as the prophets used and as still finds its echo
in such passages of the liturgy as "First our ancestors
were worshippers of idols and now God has brought us
near to His service"; or "But of a truth, we and our ancestors have sinned."

However, it would be unfair to argue any further
against a theological system which, as already said, was
never avowed distinctly by the historical school — a
school, moreover, with which speculation is a matter of
minor importance. The main strength of this school lies
in its scientific work, for which Judaism will always be
under a sense of deep gratitude. And living as we do in
an age in which history reigns supreme in all departments
of human thought, we may hope that even its theology,
as far as it goes, will "do" for us, though I neither hope
nor believe that it will do for those who come after us. I
may, however, humbly confess that the sixth essay in this
volume was written in a spirit of rebellion against this all-
absorbing Catholic Israel, with its decently. veiled scepticism on the one hand, and its unfortunate tendency with
many people to degenerate into a soulless conformity on
the other hand. There is, I am afraid, not much to be
said in favour of this essay. It is deficient both in matter
and in style. It proved to be a futile attempt to bring
within the compass of an essay what a whole book could
hardly do justice to. The Hebrew documents bearing
upon the question of dogma which I have collected from
various manuscripts and rare printed books, would alone
make a fair-sized volume. I only venture to offer it to
the public in the absence of anything better; since, so far
as I know, no other attempt has ever been made to treat

the subject even in its meagrest outlines. I even venture to hope that, with all its shortcomings, it will contribute something towards destroying the illusion, in which so many theologians indulge, that Judaism is a religion without dogmas. To declare that a religion has no dogmas is tantamount to saying that it was wise enough not to commit itself to any vital principles. But prudence, useful as it may be in worldly affairs, is quite unworthy of a great spiritual power.

Jewish mysticism in the Middle Ages and in modern times is represented in this volume by two essays ("The Chassidim" and "Nachmanides"). But in order to avoid mistakes which might be implied by my silence, I think it desirable to state that there are also to be found many mystical elements in the old Rabbinic literature. Mysticism, not as a theosophic system or as an occult science, but as a manifestation of the spiritual and as an expression of man's agonies in his struggle after communion with God, as well as of his ineffable joy when he receives the assurance that he has found it, is not, as some maintain, foreign to the spirit of old Rabbinic Judaism. There was no need for the mediæval Rabbi to borrow the elements of such a mysticism from non-Jewish sources. The perusal of the old Homilies on the Song of Songs, and on the Lessons from the Prophets, or even a fair acquaintance with the Jewish liturgy would, in itself, suffice to refute such baseless assertions. Those who are at all familiar with old Rabbinic literature hardly need to be told that "the sea of the Talmud" has also its gulf stream of mysticism which, taking its origin in the moralising portions of the Bible, runs through the wide ocean of Jewish thought, constantly commingling with the icy waters of legalism, and unceasingly washing the desolate shores of an apparently meaningless ceremonialism, communicating to it life, warmth, and spirituality. To draw attention to this fact a humble attempt has been made in the ninth essay, "The Law and Recent Criticism," a subject which I have essayed to expound in a series of essays on "Some Aspects of Rabbinic Theology," now appearing in *The Jewish Quarterly Review*.

The last five essays touch rather on certain social and familiar aspects of Judaism, and need no further comment. They are mere *causeries* and hardly deserve the name of studies. Perhaps it may be useful for those who judge of the heaviness of a work by its bulk to know that there is also a lighter side of Rabbinic literature.

But I shall be better pleased if the more serious side of this volume — Jewish mysticism and Rabbinic theology — should attract the attention of students, and so draw some fellow-workers into a field which is utterly neglected. Notwithstanding the numerous Manuals and Introductions which all more or less touch on the subject of Rabbinic theology, there is, after nearly 250 years, not a single work among them which, either in knowledge of facts or in their interpretation, is a single step in advance of the Cambridge Platonist, John Smith, in his *Select Discourses*. But those who try so hard to determine the miraculous distance of Christianity by the eclipses in Rabbinism, should, if they wish to be just or prove themselves worthy scholars, also endeavour to make themselves acquainted with the numberless bright stars that move in the wide universe of Jewish thought. We are often told that no creed or theological system which has come down to us from antiquity can afford to be judged by any other standard

than by its spiritual and poetic *possibilities:* this indul-
gence Judaism is as justly entitled to claim as any other
religion. The great and saintly Franz Delitzsch who, born
with an intellect of admirable temper, was also endowed
by Heaven with a soul — and a beautiful soul it was —
was one of the few theologians who, partly at least, admitted this claim, and sought earnestly and diligently after
these spiritual and poetic possibilities, and was amply rewarded for his labours.

I

THE CHASSIDIM[1]

THROUGHOUT the whole of that interesting field of Theological Literature which deals with the genesis and course of religious movements, there is probably none whose history, even whose name, is so little known to English students, as that of the Chassidim. And yet it would be difficult to point, in comparatively recent times, to a Dissenting movement more strikingly complete in its development, more suggestive of analogy, more full of interest in its original purpose, more pregnant of warning in its decay.

The Hebrew word "Chassidim"[2] merely means "the Pious," and appears to have been complacently adopted by the early apostles of the sect. But the thing — Chassidism — was, in its inception at all events, a revolt among the Jews of Eastern Europe against the excessive casuistry of the contemporary Rabbis. It was in fact one more manifestation of the yearning of the human heart towards the Divine idea, and of its ceaseless craving for direct communion with God. It was the protest of an emotional but uneducated people against a one-sided expression of Judaism, presented to them in cold and over-subtle disquisitions which not only did they not understand, but which shut out the play of the feelings and the affections, so that religion was made almost impossible to them.

Some account of the sect is the more necessary because, although the Chassidim have not been wholly ignored by historians or novelists, the references to them have generally, for perfectly intelligible reasons, been either biassed or inaccurate. The historians who have treated of them have been almost exclusively men saturated with Western culture and rationalism. To them the rude and uncouth manifestations of an undisciplined religious spirit could not be other than repellent; to them Chassidism was a movement to be dismissed as unæsthetic and irrational.

To the purposes of fiction the romantic side of Chassidism lends itself readily, but the novelists who have used this material have confined themselves to its externals. Indeed, to have done more would have involved a tedious and unremunerative study of difficult Hebrew texts, an undertaking not to be expected from the most conscientious writers of this class. Thus Franzos in his references to the Jews of Barnow describes faithfully the outer signs of the man, his long coat and tangled curls, but the inner life, the world in which the Chassid moved and had his being, was unknown to him and is therefore unrecorded.

As to my treatment of the subject, I confess that there was a time when I loved the Chassidim as there was a time when I hated them. And even now I am not able to suppress these feelings. I have rather tried to guide my feelings in such a way as to love in Chassidism what is ideal and noble, and to hate in it what turned out bad and pernicious for Judaism. How far I have been successful is another question. At least I have endeavoured to write this paper in such a spirit. But of one thing I must warn the reader — the desire to give some clear notion of the leading ideas of Chassidism has compelled me to quote some passages in which the Chassidim have spoken in very offensive terms of their opponents. In justice to these I must remark that unfortunately religious struggles are usually conducted on the most irreligious principles. Thus the Chassidim imputed to their antagonists, the contemporary Rabbis, many vices from which they were free. Certainly, there was, as one can read in every history of Jewish religion, something wrong in the state of Judaism. But I know people who maintain that there is something very wrong in the present state of Judaism, and who despair of a regeneration. But surely this is a silly exaggeration. The Chassidim also exaggerated. It would be better to take but little notice of their accusations and dwell more on that which was spoken in a kind and loving spirit.

As to the literature of the subject, I can only say here that I have made use of every book I could consult, both in English and in foreign libraries. But I cannot pledge myself to be what early Jewish writers called "a donkey which carries books." I exercise my own choice and my own judgment on many points.

As an active force for good, Chassidism was short-lived. For, as I propose to show, there lurked among its central tenets the germs of the degeneracy which so speedily came upon it. But its early purposes were high, its doctrines fairly pure, its aspirations ideal and sublime.

The founder of the sect was one Israel Baalshem,[3] and the story of his parentage, birth, and childhood, and the current anecdotes of his subsequent career play a considerable part in Chassidic literature. But the authentic

materials for his biography are everywhere interwoven
with much that is pure legend and with much more that
is miraculous. This was, perhaps, inevitable, and is certainly not an unfamiliar feature in the personal histories
of religious reformers as presented by their followers and
devotees.

The sayings and doings of Baalshem are an essential
— perhaps the most essential — portion of any account
of the sect. For Baalshem is the centre of the Chassidic
world, and Chassidism is so intimately bound up with
the personality of its founder that any separation between them is well nigh impossible. To the Chassidim
Baalshem is not a man who established a theory or
set forth a system; he himself was the incarnation of a
theory and his whole life the revelation of a system.

Even those portions of his history which are plainly
legendary have their uses in indicating the ideals and in
illustrating the aspirations of the early Chassidim; while
their circulation and the ready credence they received
are valuable evidence of the real power and influence
of Baalshem's personality.

In the tale as told by the sect little is omitted of
those biographical accessories which are proper to an
Avatar. There is all the conventional heralding of a
pre-ordained advent; all the usual signs and portents
of a new dispensation may be recognised in the almost
preternatural virtues of Baalshem's parents, in the miraculous annunciation and exceptional circumstances of his
nativity, and in the early indication of a strong and fearless individuality. Everywhere it seems to be suggested
that Baalshem from his infancy was conscious of a lofty
mission. It is already in tender years that he is made

to give evidence of an indifference to conventional restraints and accepted ideals.

Rabbi Eliezer and his wife, the parents of Baalshem, dwelt, as the story goes, in Moldavia. They are described as a pious and God-fearing couple, who, when they had already reached old age, were still childless. They are accredited with a spotless rectitude, which was unimpaired by a long series of strange vicissitudes and misfortunes.

Ultimately, an angel of God appeared to Eliezer and announced that, as he had successfully withstood all the temptations and sufferings by which he had been tried, God was about to reward him with a son, who was destined to enlighten the eyes of all Israel. Therefore his name should be Israel, for in him the words of Scripture were to be fulfilled, "Thou art my servant, Israel, in whom I will be glorified." In due course the promise was fulfilled, and to the aged couple a son was born, who was named Israel according to the angel's word. The date of Baalshem's birth is about 1700; his birthplace, in Bukowina, in a hitherto unidentified village which the authorities call Ukop, then still belonging to Roumania. The child's mother died soon after he was weaned, and his father did not long survive her. But before Eliezer died he took his child in his arms, and blessing him, bade him fear naught, for God would always be with him.

As Eliezer had been greatly honoured in the community in which he lived, his orphan son was carefully tended and educated. He was early supplied with an instructor in the Holy Law. But though he learned with rare facility, he rejected the customary methods of instruction. One day, while still quite young, his teacher missed him, and on seeking found him sitting alone in the forest that skirted his native village, in happy and fearless solitude. He repeated this escapade so often that it was thought best to leave him to follow his own bent. A little later we find him engaged as assistant to a schoolmaster. His duty was not to teach, but to take the children from their homes to the synagogue and thence on to the school. It was his wont while accompanying the children to the synagogue to teach them solemn hymns which he sang with them. In the synagogue he encouraged them to sing the responses, so that the voices of the children penetrated through the heavens and moved the Divine father to compassion. Satan, fearing lest his power on earth should thereby be diminished, assumed the shape of a werewolf, and, appearing before the procession of children on their way to the synagogue, put them to flight. In consequence of this alarming incident the children's services were suspended. But Israel, recollecting his father's counsel to fear naught, besought the parents to be allowed to lead the children once more in the old way. His request was granted, and when the werewolf appeared a second time Israel attacked him with a club and routed him.

In his fourteenth year Israel became a beadle at the Beth Hammidrash.[4] Here he assiduously but secretly pursued the study of the Law. Yet, being anxious that none should know his design, he read and worked only at night, when the schoolroom was empty and the usual scholars had retired. During the daytime he slept, so that he was popularly believed to be both ignorant and lazy. Despite these precautions, however, his true character was revealed to one person. A certain holy

man, the father of a young student at the college, had
discovered some old manuscripts which contained the
deepest secrets. Before his death he bade his son repair
to Ukop, Israel's birthplace, telling him that he would
find one Israel, son of Eliezer, to whom the precious
documents were to be entrusted. They possessed, so the
old man declared, a certain mystic and heavenly affinity
with Israel's soul. The student carried out his father's
instructions, and at last discovered the object of his
search in the beadle of the Beth Hammidrash. Israel
admitted him to his friendship and confidence on the
condition of secrecy as to his real character. The student,
however, paid dearly for this acquaintance with Israel.
Contrary to Baalshem's advice, he entered upon a dangerous incantation in the course of which he made a mistake
so serious that it cost him his life.

Upon the death of his friend, Baalshem left his native
village and settled as a teacher in a small town near
Brody. Here, although his true mission and character
were still unknown, he became much respected for his
rigid probity, and was frequently chosen as umpire in
disputes among Jews. On one of these occasions he
arbitrated with so much learning and impartiality that
not only did he satisfy both parties, but one of them,
a learned man of Brody, named Abraham, offered him
his own daughter in marriage. Israel, to whom it had
been revealed that Abraham's daughter was his predestined wife, immediately accepted the offer and the act of
betrothal was drawn up. But wishing his true character to
remain unknown he stipulated that Abraham, although a
" Talmid Chacham " (student)[5] himself and therefore pre-
sumably desirous that his daughter should marry a scholar,

should omit from the betrothal-deed all the titles of honour usually appended to the name of a learned bridegroom. While returning to Brody, Abraham died, and Gershon his son, a scholar still greater and more celebrated than his father, was surprised and shocked to find a deed of betrothal among his father's papers, from which it appeared that his sister was to wed a man with apparently no claim to scholarship or learning. He protested to his sister, but she declined to entertain any objections to a marriage which her father had arranged. When the time for the wedding was at hand, Israel gave up his post as teacher, and repaired to Brody. Disguised as a peasant he presented himself before his future brother-in-law, who was then fulfilling some high judicial function. Gershon taking him for a beggar offered him alms, but Israel, refusing the money, asked for a private interview, stating that he had an important secret to reveal. He then, to Gershon's surprise and disgust, explained who he was and that he had come to claim his bride. As the girl was determined to obey her father's will the affair was settled and the day fixed. On the morning of the wedding Israel revealed to his bride his real character and mission, at the same time enjoining secrecy. Evil fortunes would befall them, he said, but a better time would eventually follow.

After the wedding, Gershon, having in vain attempted to instruct his seemingly ignorant brother-in-law, decided to rid himself of his presence. He gave his sister the choice of being separated from her husband, or of leaving the town in his company. She chose the latter, and thereupon the two left Brody and began a life of hardship and suffering. Israel chose for his new home a spot on one of the spurs of the Carpathian Mountains. No Jews lived there, and Israel and his wife were thus separated from the society of their fellows in a life of complete and unchanging solitude. Israel dug lime in the ravines among the mountains, and his wife conveyed it for sale to the nearest town. Their life at this period seems to have been one of great privation, but the harder Israel's outward lot, the more he increased in spiritual greatness. In his solitude he gave himself up entirely to devotion and religious contemplation. His habit was to climb to the summit of the mountains and wander about rapt in spiritual ecstasies. He fasted, prayed, made continual ablutions, and observed all the customary outward and inward exercises of piety and devotion.

After seven years, Gershon, who was well aware of the bitter poverty which his sister endured, relented and brought her and her husband back to Brody. At first he employed Baalshem as his coachman, but as he proved wholly unfit for this work Gershon rented a small inn in a remote village, and there established his sister and her husband. The business of the inn was managed by the wife, while Baalshem passed most of his time in a hut in a neighbouring forest. Here he once more gave himself up to meditation and preparation for his future work, and here, a little later, when nearly forty-two years of age, to a few chosen spirits, afterwards his most fervent disciples, he first revealed his true character and mission.

From this point unfortunately the materials for a continuous biography are wanting; we next hear of Baalshem discharging the functions of an ordinary Rabbi at Miedziboz in Podolia, but for the remainder of his personal history we have to be content with detached anecdotes and fragmentary passages in his life, the sum total of which goes to show that he resided in Podolia and Wallachia, teaching his doctrines to his disciples and "working Wonders." He does not seem to have figured as a public preacher, nor has he left behind him any written work. He appears rather to have used the method, familiar to students of Greek philosophy, of teaching by conversations with his friends and disciples. These conversations, and the parables with which they were largely interspersed, were remembered and stored up by his hearers. By his neighbours the country folk, Baalshem was regarded simply as "a man of God." He was allowed to pursue his course undisturbed by persecution of the serious character which his more aggressive successors provoked. Such of the Rabbis as were aware of his existence despised him and his ways, but the Rabbinical world was at that time too much occupied in the controversy between Eybeschütz and Emden to concern itself with the vagaries of an obscure and apparently "unlearned" eccentric. Baalshem also took part in the disputes which were held in Lemberg, the capital of Galicia (1757?), between the Rabbis and the Frankists,[6] who denounced the Talmud to the Polish Government and wanted to have all the Rabbinical books destroyed. Baalshem suffered from this excitement in a most terrible way. The abrogation of the Oral Law meant for him the ruin of Judaism.

Baalshem, in forming the little band of devoted followers who were destined to spread a knowledge of his creed, travelled considerably about Wallachia. He at one time decided to make a pilgrimage to Palestine, but when he reached Constantinople he felt himself inspired to return and continue his work at home. He died at Miedziboz on the eve of Pentecost, 1761.

After his death his disciples, of whom one Beer of Mizriez was the most prominent, undertook the proselytising mission for which Baalshem had prepared them, but from which he himself appears to have abstained. They preached and taught in all the provinces of Russia where Jews may reside, and in Roumania, and Galicia. The number of the sect at the present day is probably about half a million.

Returning now to Baalshem the founder, it may be noted that his appearance as a teacher and reformer was accompanied and justified by a customary and adequate number of miracles. To one disciple he revealed secrets which could have become known to him only by divine revelation; to another he appeared with a nimbus round his head. On the evidence of the Chassidim we learn that Baalshem performed all the recognised signs and marvels which have ever been the customary minor characteristics of men of similar type in similar environment. When Baalshem desired to cross a stream, he spread forth his mantle upon the waters, and standing thereupon passed safely to the other side. Ghosts evacuated haunted houses at the mere mention of his name. Was he alone in the forest on a wintry night, he had but to touch a tree with his finger tips and flames burst forth. When his spirit wandered through the angelic spheres, as was frequently the case, he obtained access to Paradise for millions of pining souls who had vainly waited without through long thousands of mournful years. These and other miracles need not be examined. Here, as in the case of other such blissful seasons of grace, they were the

ephemeral though important accessories in establishing
the inspired character of his utterances and the authority
of his injunctions.   It is not as a worker of miracles, but
as a religious teacher and reformer, that Baalshem is
interesting.

Properly to understand the nature and special direction
of his teaching, it is necessary in some measure to realise
the character of the field in which he worked; to consider,
in other words, the moral and religious condition of the
Jews in those districts where Chassidism first took root.

In a Hebrew Hymn, written about 1000 A.C., and still
recited in the synagogue on the Day of Atonement, the
poet expresses the strange and bitter fortunes of his race
in touching words of mingled sorrow and exultation.

> Destroyed lies Zion and profaned,
> Of splendour and renown bereft,
> Her ancient glories wholly waned,
> One deathless treasure only left;
>   Still ours, O Lord,
>   Thy Holy Word.

And this Divine Word it was, which a persecuted religion has sought to preserve intact through so many centuries of persecution, and for the sake of which no labour
seemed too severe, no sacrifice too large.   " Bethink
Thee, O God," exclaimed one of our Jewish sages who
flourished about the same period, " bethink Thee of Thy
faithful children who, amid their poverty and want, are
busy in the study of Thy Law.   Bethink Thee of the
poor in Israel who are willing to suffer hunger and desti-
tution if only they can secure for their children the knowledge of Thy Law."   And so indeed it was.   Old and

young, weak and strong, rich and poor, all pursued that
single study, the Torah. The product of this prolonged
study is that gigantic literature which, as a long unbroken
chain of spiritual activity, connects together the various
periods of the Jews' chequered and eventful history. All
ages and all lands have contributed to the development of this supreme study. For under the word Torah
was comprised not only the Law, but also the contributions of later times expressing either the thoughts or
the emotions of holy and sincere men; and even their
honest scepticism was not entirely excluded. As in the
canon of the Bible, Ecclesiastes and the Song of Solomon
found place in the same volume that contains the Law
and the Prophets, so at a later time people did not object
to put the philosophical works of Maimonides and the
songs of Judah Hallevi on the same level with the Code
of the Law compiled by R. Isaac Alfasi, and the commentaries on the Bible by R. Solomon b. Isaac.[7] None
of them was declared infallible, but also to none of them,
as soon as people were convinced of the author's sincerity, was denied the homage due to seekers after truth.
Almost every author was called Rabbi ("my master")
or Rabbenu ("our master"),[8] and nearly every book was
regarded more or less as a contribution to the great bulk
of the Torah. It was called Writ,[9] and was treated with
a certain kind of piety. But, by a series of accidents too
long to be related here, sincerity ceased and sport took
its place. I refer to the casuistic schools commonly
known by the name of Pilpulists [10] (the "seasoned" or the
"sharp" ones), who flourished in the last two centuries
preceding ours. To the authors of this unhappy period,
a few glorious exceptions always allowed, the preceding

Jewish literature did not mean a "fountain of living waters," supplying men with truth and religious inspiration, but rather a kind of armoury providing them with juristic cases over which to fight, and to out-do each other in sophistry and subtlety. As a consequence they cared little or nothing for that part of the Jewish literature that appeals less to the intellect than to the feelings of men. In short, religion consisted only of complicated cases and innumerable ordinances, in which the wit of these men found delight. But the emotional part of it, whose root is the Faith and Love of men, was almost entirely neglected.

But it was precisely these higher religious emotions that were Baalshem's peculiar province, and it was to them that he assigned in his religious system a place befitting their importance and their dignity. And the locality where his ministration lay was curiously adapted for such propaganda. To that universal study of the Law of which I have just spoken there was one exception. That exception was amongst the Jews in the territories which bordered on the Carpathian Mountains, and comprise the principalities of Moldavia, and Wallachia, Bukowina, and the Ukraine.

It is historically certain that the first arrival of the Jews in Roumania was at a very early date, but there is no trace of any intellectual productivity among the immigrants until recent times, and it is admitted that the study of the Law was almost entirely neglected. It was in these districts of mental, and perhaps we might add of even spiritual, darkness that Chassidism took its rise and achieved its first success. "The sect of the Chassidim," says one of the bitterest but most trustworthy of their opponents, "first gained ground in the most uncivilised provinces; in the wild ravines of Wallachia and the dreary steppes of the Ukraine."

Apart from the genius of its founder, Chassidism owed its rapid growth to the intellectual barrenness of these districts as compared with the intellectual fertility of the other regions where Jews most thickly congregated. The Roumanian Jews were to some extent under the jurisdiction of the Rabbis of Poland. Now the Poles were celebrated even in Germany for the elaboration of their casuistry. These over-subtle Rabbis, delighting in the quibbles of their sophistry, and reducing religion to an unending number of juristic calculations and all sorts of possibilities and impossibilities, were but too apt to forget the claims of feeling in their eager desire to question and to settle everything. They may have been satisfactory guides in matters spiritual to the men of their own stamp, but they were of no avail to their Roumanian brethren who failed to recognise religion in the garb of casuistry. It was, therefore, not surprising that a revolt against the excess of intellectualism should have sprung up and flourished in those districts where the inhabitants were constitutionally incapable of appreciating the delights of argument. The field was ready, and in the fulness of time came the sower in the person of Baalshem.

In the above estimate of the Polish Rabbis there undoubtedly lurks a touch of exaggeration. But it represents the view which the Chassidim took of their opponents. The whole life of Baalshem is a protest against the typical Rabbi thus conceived. The essential difference in the ideals of the two parties is perhaps best illustrated in those portions of their biographical literature where legend treads most closely upon the heels of fact.

The hero of Polish Rabbinic biography at five years of age can recite by heart the most difficult tractates of the Talmud; at eight he is the disciple of the most celebrated teacher of the time, and perplexes him by the penetrative subtlety of his questions; while at thirteen he appears before the world as a full-fledged Doctor of the Law.

The hero of the Chassidim has a totally different education, and his distinctive glory is of another kind. The legendary stories about Baalshem's youth tell us little of his proficiency in Talmudic studies; instead of sitting in the Beth Hammidrash with the folios of some casuistic treatise spread out before him, Baalshem passes his time singing hymns out of doors, or under the green trees of the forest with the children. Satan, however, says the Chassid, is more afraid of these innocent exercises than of all the controversies in the Meheram Shiff.[11] It was through external nature, the woods of his childhood, the hills and wild ravines of the Carpathians where he passed many of his maturer years, that Baalshem, according to his disciples, reached his spiritual confirmation. The Chassidic hero had no celebrated Rabbi for his master. He was his own teacher. If not self-taught, it was from angelic lips, or even the Divine voice itself, that he learned the higher knowledge. From the source whence the Torah flowed Baalshem received heavenly lore. His method of self-education, his ways of life, his choice of associates were all instances of revolt; not only did he teach a wholly different theory and practice, but he and his disciples seem to have missed no opportunity of denouncing the old teachers as misleading and ungodly. Among the many anecdotes illustrating this feature, it is told how once, on the evening before the great Day of Atonement,

Baalshem was noticed by his disciples to be, contrary to his usual custom, depressed and ill at ease. The whole subsequent day he passed in violent weeping and lamentations. At its close he once more resumed his wonted cheerfulness of manner. When asked for the explanation of his behaviour, he replied that the Holy Spirit had revealed to him that heavy accusations were being made against the Jewish people, and a heavy punishment had been ordained upon them. The anger of heaven was caused by the Rabbis, whose sole occupation was to invent lying premises and to draw from them false conclusions. All the truly wise Rabbis of the olden time (such as the Tannaim, the Amoraim [12] and their followers, whom Baalshem regarded as so many saints and prophets) had now stood forth as the accusers of their modern successors by whom their words were so grossly perverted from their original meaning. On this account Baalshem's tears had been shed, and his prayers as usual had been successful. The impending judgment was annulled. On another occasion, when he overheard the sounds of eager, loud discussion issuing from a Rabbinical college, Baalshem, closing his ears with his hands, declared that it was such disputants who delayed the redemption of Israel from captivity. Satan, he said, incites the Rabbis to study those portions of Jewish literature only on which they can whet the sharpness of their intellects, but from all writings of which the reading would promote piety and the fear of God he keeps them away. "Where there is much study," says a disciple of Baalshem, "there is little piety." "Jewish Devils" [13] is one of the numerous polite epithets applied to the Rabbis by the friends of Baalshem. "Even the worst sinners are better than they; so blind are they in

c

the arrogance of their self-conceit that their very devotion
to the Law becomes a vehicle for their sin." It will be
found when we deal with the most positive side of Baalshem's teaching that this antagonism to the attitude and
methods of the contemporary Rabbis is further emphasised, and it will readily be seen that his whole scheme
of religion and of conduct in relation to God and man
rendered this acknowledged hostility inevitable. In approaching this part of our subject it should be remembered
that, as stated above, Baalshem himself wrote nothing.
For a knowledge of his sayings we are therefore dependent on the reports of his friends and disciples. And it is
not unfrequently necessary to supplement these by the
teaching of his followers, whom we may suppose in large
measure to have caught the spirit of their master. Unfortunately the original authorities are in a difficult Hebrew patois which often obscures the precise meaning of
whole passages.

The originality of Baalshem's teaching has been frequently impugned, chiefly by the suggestion that he drew
largely from the Zohar (Book of Brightness).[14] This
mystical book, "the Bible of the Cabbalists," whether we
regard its subject-matter or its history and influence, is
unique in literature. Its pretended author is Simeon ben
Yochai, a great Rabbi of the second century, but the real
writer is probably one Moses de Leon, a Spanish Jew, who
lived eleven centuries later. The book is one of the most
interesting literary forgeries, and is a marvellous mixture
of good and evil. A passage of delicate religious fancy
is succeeded by another of gross obscenity in illustration
and suggestion; true piety and wild blasphemy are
strangely mingled together. Baalshem undoubtedly had

studied the Zohar, and he even is reported to have said that the reading of the Zohar had enabled him to see into the whole universe of things. But, for all that, Baalshem was no copyist; and the Zohar, although it may have suggested a hint to him here and there, was not the source whence his inspiration was drawn.

Its attraction for Baalshem is sufficiently explained by the fantastic, imaginative, and emotional nature of its contents. It lent itself more easily than the older Rabbinical literature to new explanations unthought of by its author. But even the Talmud and its early commentaries became apocalyptic to the heroes of Chassidism. Nay, the driest and most legal disquisitions about *meum* and *tuum* could be translated into parables and allegories and symbols full of the most exalted meanings. Baalshem, like every other religious reformer, was partially the product of his age. The influences of the past, the history and literature of his own people, helped to make him what he was. But they do not rob him of his originality. He was a religious revivalist in the best sense; full of burning faith in his God and his cause; convinced utterly of the value of his work and the truth of his teaching.

Although there can be no real doubt of Baalshem's claim to originality, it should be borne in mind that his teaching is not only distinctively Jewish, but that for every part of it parallels and analogies could be found in the older Hebrew literature. Indeed it is not wonderful that in a literature, extending over 2000 years, of a people whose chief thoughts have been religion, and who have come in contact with so many external religious and philosophic influences, the germs can be dis-

covered of almost every conceivable system, and the
outline of almost every imaginable doctrine.

The keynote of all Baalshem's teachings is the
Omnipresence, or more strictly the Immanence, of God.
This is the source from which flows naturally every
article of his creed; the universality of the Divinity is
the foundation of the entire Chassidic fabric. The
idea of the constant living presence of God in all existence permeates the whole of Baalshem's scheme; it is
insisted on in every relation; from it is deduced every
important proposition and every rule in conduct of his
school.

All created things and every product of human intelligence owe their being to God. All generation and all
existence spring from the thought and will of God. It
is incumbent upon man to believe that all things are
pervaded by the divine life, and when he speaks he
should remember that it is this divine life which is
speaking through him. There is nothing which is void
of God. If we imagine for a moment such a thing to
be, it would instantly fall into nothingness. In every
human thought God is present. If the thought be
gross or evil, we should seek to raise and ennoble it by
carrying it back to its origin. So, if a man be suddenly
overwhelmed by the aspect of a beautiful woman, he
should remember that this splendour of beauty is owing
to the all-pervading emanation from the divine. When
he remembers that the source of corporeal beauty is
God, he will not be content to let his thought abide
with the body when he can rise to the inward contemplation of the infinite soul of beauty, which is God. A
disciple of Baalshem has said: Even as in the jewels

of his beloved the lover sees only the beauty of her he loves, so does the true lover of God see in all the appearances of this world, the vitalising and generative power of his divine master. If you do not see the world in the light of God you separate the creation from its Creator. ▪He who does not fully believe in this universality of God's presence has never properly acknowledged God's Sovereignty, for he excludes God from an existing portion of the actual world. The word of God (to Baalshem, a synonym for God himself), which "is settled in heaven" and "established on earth," is still and always speaking, acting, and generating throughout heaven and earth in endless gradations and varieties. If the vitalising word were to cease, chaos would come again. The belief in a single creation after which the Master withdrew from his completed work, is erroneous and heretical. The vivifying power is never withdrawn from the world which it animates. Creation is continuous; an unending manifestation of the goodness of God. All things are an affluence from the two divine attributes of Power and Love, which express themselves in various images and reflections.

This is the doctrine of universality in Chassidism. God, the father of Israel, God the Merciful, God the All-powerful, the God of Love, not only created everything but is embodied in everything. The necessity of believing this doctrine is the cardinal Dogma. But as creation is continuous so also is revelation. This revelation is only to be grasped by faith. Faith, therefore, is more efficacious than learning. Thus it is that in times of persecution, the wise and the foolish, the sinner and the saint, are wont alike to give up their life for their faith. They who could render no answer to the questions of the casuist are yet willing to die the most cruel of deaths rather than deny their faith in the One and Supreme God. Their strength to face danger and death is owing to that divine illumination of the soul which is more exalted than knowledge.

We should thus regard all things in the light of so many manifestations of the Divinity. God is present in all things; therefore there is good, actual or potential, in all things. It is our duty everywhere to seek out and to honour the good, and not to arrogate to ourselves the right to judge that which may seem to be evil. In thinking therefore of a fellow-man, we should above all things realise in him the presence of the spirit of good. Whence we have the Doctrine that each of us, while thinking humbly of himself, should alway be ready to think well, and alway slow to think evil, of another. This explains the Chassidic attitude towards erring humanity. Baalshem viewed human sin and infirmity in a very different light from that of the ordinary Rabbi. Ever conscious of the Divine side of Humanity, he vigorously combated the gratuitous assumption of sinfulness in man which was a fertile subject with contemporary preachers. They, among the Roumanian Jews as in other communities, delighted chiefly to dwell on the dark side of things, and found their favourite theme in elaborate descriptions of the infernal punishments that were awaiting the sinner after death. It is related how on one occasion Baalshem rebuked one of these. The preacher had been denouncing woe to an audience of whom he knew nothing whether for evil or for good. Baalshem, indignant at this indiscriminative abuse and conceited arrogation of the divine office of judgment, turned on him in the following words: "Woe

upon thee who darest to speak evil of Israel! Dost not
know that every Jew, when he utters ever so short a
prayer at the close of day, is performing a great work
before which the angels in heaven bow down?" Great,
as it would seem, was the value set by Baalshem upon the
smallest evidence of the higher nature in man, and few
there were, as he believed, who, if their spirit was not
darkened by pride, did not now and again give proof of
the divine stamp in which God had created them. No sin
so separates us from God that we need despair of return.
From every rung of the moral ladder, no matter how low,
let man seek God. If he but fully believe that nothing is
void of God, and that God is concealed in the midst of
apparent ruin and degradation, he will not fear lest God
be far from him. God is regained in a moment of repentance, for repentance " transcends the limits of space and
time." And he who leads the sinner to repentance causes
a divine joy; it is as though a king's son had been in captivity and were now brought back to his father's gaze.

Baalshem refused to regard any one as wholly irredeem-
able. His was an optimistic faith. God was to be
praised in gladness by the dwellers in this glorious world.
The true believer, recognising the reflection of God in
every man, should hopefully strive, when that reflection
was obscured by sin, to restore the likeness of God in man.
The peculiar detestability of sin lies in this, that man
rejects the earthly manifestations of the Divinity and
pollutes them. One of Baalshem's disciples delighted in
the saying that the most hardened sinners were not to be
despaired of, but prayed for. None knows the heart of
man, and none should judge his neighbour. Let him who
burns with zeal for God's sake, exercise his zeal on him-

self, not others. Baalshem said, " Let no one think himself better than his neighbour, for all serve God; each
according to the measure of understanding which God
has given him."

From this position it is a natural step to Baalshem's
view of prayer. He is reputed to have said that all the
greatness he had achieved was the issue not of study but
of prayer. But true prayer "must move," as Baalshem
phrased it, "in the realms above," and not be concerned
with affairs sublunary. Your prayer should not be taken
up with your wishes and needs, but should be the means
to bring you nigh to God. In prayer man must lay aside
his own individuality, and not even be conscious of his
existence; for if, when he prays, Self is not absolutely
quiescent, the object of prayer is unattainable. Indeed
it is only through God's grace that after true prayer man
is yet alive; to such a point has the annihilation of self
proceeded.

It may be necessary to caution the reader against
ascribing to Baalshem any modern rationalistic notions
on the subject of prayer. The power of prayer, in the
old-fashioned sense, to produce an answer from God was
never doubted by Baalshem for a moment. Baalshem's
deity is not restricted towards any side by any philosophic
considerations. All Baalshem meant was that any reference or regard to earthly requirements was unworthy
and destructive of this communion of man with God.
The wise man, says Baalshem, does not trouble the king
with innumerable petitions about trifles. His desire is
merely to gain admission into the king's presence and to
speak with him without a go-between. To be with the
king whom he loves so dearly is for him the highest good.

But his love for the king has its reward; for the king loves him.

It has already been implied that, with regard to our duty towards our fellow-man, we must not only honour him for the good, and abstain from judging the evil that may be in him, but must pray for him. Furthermore we must work for his spiritual and moral reclamation. In giving practical effect in his own life to this doctrine, Baalshem's conduct was in striking contrast to that of his contemporaries. He habitually consorted with outcasts and sinners, with the poor and uneducated of both sexes, whom the other teachers ignored. He thus won for his doctrines a way to the heart of the people by adapting his life and language to their understanding and sympathies. In illustration of this, as well as of his hatred of vanity and display, it is told how, on the occasion of his being accorded a public reception by the Jews on his arrival at Brody, instead of addressing to them in the conventional fashion some subtle discourse upon a Talmudical difficulty, he contented himself with conversing upon trivial topics in the local dialect with some of the less important persons in the crowd.

This incident is perhaps the more noteworthy because it occurred in Brody, which was at that time a seat of learning and Rabbinic culture, — a place where, for that very reason, Chassidism was never able to gain a foothold. It is probable enough that Baalshem in his visits to this town kept aloof from the learned and the wise, and sought to gather round him the neglected and humbler elements of Jewish society. It is well known that Baalshem consorted a good deal with the innkeepers of the district, who were held in very low repute among their brethren. The

following remark by one of his followers is very suggestive in this respect. Just as only superficial minds
attach a certain holiness to special places, whilst with
the deeper ones all places are alike holy, so that to them
it makes no difference whether prayers be said in the
synagogue or in the forest; so the latter believe that not
only prophecies and visions come from heaven, but that
every utterance of man, if properly understood, contains
a message of God. Those who are absorbed in God will
easily find the divine element in everything which they
hear, even though the speaker himself be quite ignorant
of it.

This line of conduct gave a fair opening for attack to
his opponents, an opportunity of which they were not
slow to avail themselves. Baalshem was pointed at as
the associate of the lowest classes. They avenged themselves for his neglect of and hostility to the learned by
imputing the worst motives to his indifference to appearances. He was accused of idling about the streets with
disreputable characters, and one polemical treatise draws
the vilest inferences from his apparent familiarity with
women. To this charge Baalshem's conduct, innocent in
itself, gave some colour; for his views and habits in relation to women marked a strong divergence from current
customs. The position of women in contemporary circles
was neither debased nor inevitably unhappy, but it was
distinctly subordinate. Their education was almost entirely neglected, and their very existence was practically
ignored. According to the Chassidic doctrine of Universality, woman was necessarily to be honoured. "All
Jews," says one Chassid, "even the uneducated and the
women, believe in God." Baalshem frequently associated

with women, assigning to them not only social equality, but a high degree of religious importance.

His own wife he reverenced as a saint; when she died he abandoned the hope of rising to heaven while yet alive, like Elijah of old, saying mournfully that undivided such translation might have happened, but for him alone it was impossible. Then again in a form of religion utilising so largely the emotions of Faith and Love there was a strong appeal to the female mind. The effect of this was soon evident, and Baalshem did not neglect to profit by it. Among the most devoted of his early adherents were women. One of them was the heroine of a favourite anecdote concerning Baalshem's work of Love and Rescue. It is related that in a certain village there dwelt a woman whose life was so disgraceful that her brothers at last determined to kill her. With this object they enticed her into a neighbouring wood, but guided by the Holy Spirit Baalshem intervened at the critical moment, and dissuading the men from their purpose rescued the sinner. The woman afterwards became a sort of Magdalen in the new community.

Above I have endeavoured to throw together in some order of sequence the doctrines and practical rules of conduct which Baalshem and his early disciples seem to have deduced from their central idea of the omnipresence of God. This was necessary in order to give a connected idea of their creed, but it is right to say that nowhere in Chassidic literature have these deductions been logically co-ordinated. Perhaps their solitary attempt to formulate and condense their distinctive views is confined to a statement of their idea of piety or service of God, and an examination of three cardinal virtues, Humility, Cheerfulness, and Enthusiasm. What the Chassidim held as to true service brings into relief Baalshem's characteristic manner of regarding the Law.

By the service of God was generally understood a life which fulfilled the precepts of the written and oral law. Baalshem understood by it a certain attitude towards life as a whole. For, as God is realised in life, each activity of life when rightly conceived and executed is at once a manifestation and a service of the Divine. All things have been created for the glory and service of God. The smallest worm serves Him with all its power. Thus, while eating, drinking, sleeping, and the other ordinary functions of the body are regarded by the old Jewish moralists as mere means to an end, to Baalshem they are already a service of God in themselves. All pleasures are manifestations of God's attribute of love; and, so regarded, they are at once spiritualised and ennobled. Man should seek to reach a higher level of purity and holiness before partaking of food and drink, than even before the study of the Law. For when the Torah had once been given by God the whole world became instinct with its grace. He who speaks of worldly matters and religious matters as if they were separate and distinct, is a heretic.

Upon the continual and uninterrupted study of the Law, Baalshem lays but little stress. He accepted the ordinary belief that the Law (under which term are included not only the Pentateuch, but the whole Old Testament and the major portion of the old Rabbinic literature) was a revelation of God. But, as the world itself is equally a divine revelation, the Torah becomes little more than a part of a larger whole. To understand it aright one needs to penetrate to the inward reality — to the infi-

nite light which is revealed in it. We should study the
Law not as we study a science for the sake of acquiring
knowledge (he who studies it so has in truth been concerning himself with its mere outward form), but we
should learn from it the true service of God. Thus the
study of the law is no end in itself. It is studied because,
as the word of God, God is more easily discerned and
absorbed in this revelation of Him than in any other.
The Torah is eternal, but its explanation is to be made by
the spiritual leaders of Judaism. It is to be interpreted
by them in accordance with the Attribute of the age.
For he regarded the world as governed in every age by a
different Attribute of God — one age by the Attribute of
Love, another by that of Power, a third again, by Beauty,
and so on — and the explanation of the Torah must be
brought into agreement with it. The object of the whole
Torah is that man should become a Torah himself. Every
man being a Torah in himself, said a disciple of Baalshem,
has got not only his Abraham and Moses, but also his
Balaam and Haman: he should try to expel the Balaam
and develop the Abraham within him. Every action of
man should be a pure manifestation of God.

The reason why we should do what the Law commands
is not to gain grace thereby in the eyes of God, but to
learn how to love God and to be united to Him. The
important thing is not how many separate injunctions are
obeyed, but how and in what spirit we obey them. The
object of fulfilling these various ordinances is to put oneself, as it were, on the same plane with God, and thus, in
the ordinary phrase of the religious mystic, to become one
with Him, or to be absorbed in Him. People should get
to know, says Baalshem, what the unity of God really

means. To attain a part of this indivisible unity is to attain the whole. The Torah and all its ordinances are from God. If I therefore fulfil but one commandment in and through the love of God, it is as though I have fulfilled them all.

I have now briefly to refer to the three virtues to which the Chassidim assigned the highest place of honour. Of these the first is called in Hebrew " Shiphluth," [15] and is best rendered by our word "Humility," but in Chassidic usage it includes the ideas of modesty, considerateness, and sympathy. The prominence given to these qualities is in sharp contrast to the faults of conceit, vanity, and self-satisfaction, against which Baalshem was never weary of protesting. He regarded these as the most seductive of all forms of sin. But a few minutes before his death he was heard to murmur, "O vanity, vanity! even in this hour of death thou darest to approach me with thy temptations: 'Bethink thee, Israel, what a grand funeral procession will be thine because thou hast been so wise and good.' O vanity, vanity! beshrew thee." "It should be indifferent to man," says the master, "whether he be praised or blamed, loved or hated, reputed to be the wisest of mankind or the greatest of fools. The test of the real service of God is that it leaves behind it the feeling of humility. If a man after prayer be conscious of the least pride or self-satisfaction, if he think, for instance, that he has earned a reward by the ardour of his spiritual exercises, then let him know that he has prayed not to God but to himself. And what is this but disguised idolatry? Before you can find God you must lose yourself." The Chassidim treated Shiphluth from two sides: a negative side in thinking humbly of oneself, a positive in thinking highly of one's neighbour, in other words the love for our fellow-man.

He who loves the father will also love his children. The true lover of God is also a lover of man. It is ignorance of one's own errors that makes one ready to see the errors of others. "There is no sphere in heaven where the soul remains a shorter time than in the sphere of merit, there is none where it abides longer than in the sphere of Love."

The second Cardinal Virtue is "Cheerfulness," in Hebrew "Simchah."[16] Baalshem insisted on cheerfulness of heart as a necessary attitude for the due service of God. Once believe that you are really the servant and the child of God and how can you fall again into a gloomy condition of mind? Nor should the inevitable sins which we all must commit disturb our glad serenity of soul. For is not repentance ready at hand by which we may climb back to God? Every penitent thought is a voice of God. Man should detect that voice in all the evidence of his senses, in every sight and sound of external nature. It is through his want of faith in the universality of God's presence that he is deaf to these subtle influences and can read only the lessons which are inscribed in books.

The reader will be prepared to learn that Baalshem, taking this cheerful view of things, was opposed to every kind of asceticism. Judaism, or rather Israelitism, it is true, was not originally much of an ascetic religion. But there can be little doubt that in the course of history there came in many ascetic doctrines and practices, quite enough at least to encourage such tender souls the bent of whose minds lay in this direction. To one of these, a former disciple, Baalshem wrote: "I hear that you think yourself compelled from religious motives to enter upon a course of fasts and penances. My soul is outraged at your determination. By the counsel of God I order you to abandon such dangerous practices, which are but the outcome of a disordered brain. Is it not written 'Thou shalt not hide thyself from thine own flesh?' Fast then no more than is prescribed. Follow my command and God shall be with you." On another occasion Baalshem was heard to observe that it is a machination of Satan to drive us into a condition of gloom and despondency in which the smallest error is regarded as a deadly sin. Satan's object is to keep us away from the true service of God, and God can only be truly served from a happy and confident disposition. Anxious scrupulosity in details is therefore to be avoided. It is the counsel of the Devil to persuade us that we never have done and shall never do our duty fully, and that moral progress is impossible. Such ideas beget melancholy and despair, which are of evil.

The third virtue is called in the Hebrew Chassidic literature "Hithlahabuth," [17] and is derived from a verb meaning "to kindle" or "set on fire." The substantive "Hithlahabuth," so far as I am aware, was first coined by Baalshem's followers. It is best rendered by our word "Enthusiasm." Every religious action, to be of any avail, must be done with enthusiasm. A mere mechanical and lifeless performance of an ordinance is valueless. A man is no step nearer the goal if he thinks, forsooth, that he has done his duty when he has gone through the whole round of laws in every section of the code. This essential enthusiasm is only begotten of Love. The service of fear, if not wholly useless, is yet necessarily accompanied by a certain repulsion and heaviness, which effectually

prevent the rush and ardour of enthusiasm. The inspiration of true service is its own end. There is no thought
of this world, and there is none of the world to come.
In the Talmud there is frequent reference to one Rabbi
Elisha ben Abuyah, an apostate from Judaism, who, when
urged to repent, replied that repentance was useless, and
that for this mournful belief he had direct divine authority.
For he had been told by a voice from heaven that even
though he repented he would be excluded from sharing
the happiness of the world to come. Of him it was said by
one of the Chassidim, " This man indeed missed a golden
opportunity. How purely could he have served God, knowing that for his service there could never be a reward ! "

From the conception of Enthusiasm springs the quality
of mobility, suggesting spiritual progress, and commonly
opposed by Baalshem and his followers to the dull religious stagnation of self-satisfied contemporaries. Man
should not imagine himself to have attained the level of
the righteous; let him rather regard himself as a penitent
who should make progress every day. Always to remain
on the same religious plane, merely repeating to-day the
religious routine of yesterday, is not true service. There
must be a daily advance in the knowledge and love of the
Divine Master. Mere freedom from active sin is not
sufficient; such negative virtue may be but another word
for the chance absence of temptation. What boots it
never to have committed a sin if sin lies concealed in the
heart? It is only the uninterrupted communion with
God which will raise and ennoble your thoughts and
designs, and cause the roots of sin to die. The patriarch
Abraham, without any command from God, fulfilled the
whole Torah, because he perceived that the Law was the

D

life of all created things.   In the Messianic age the law
will no longer seem to man as something ordained for him
from without; but the law will be within the hearts of
men ;   it will seem   natural   and   self-evident   to them,
because they will realise that God and life are manifested
through the law.

Baalshem, who dealt largely. in parable, has left the
following, which we may fitly add to   our   somewhat
inadequate presentation of his doctrine.

There was once a king who built himself a glorious
palace.   By means of magical illusion it seemed as if the
palace were full of devious corridors and mazes, preventing the approach to the royal presence.   But as there was
much gold and silver heaped up in the entrance halls,
most people were content to go no further, but take their
fill of treasure.   The king himself they did not notice.
At last the king's intimate had compassion upon them
and exclaimed to them, " All these walls and mazes which
you see before you do not in truth exist at all.   They are
mere illusions.   Push forward bravely, and you shall find
no obstacle."

We must not interpret the parable to mean that Baalshem denied the reality or even the importance of the
actual phenomenal world.   The very contrary is the truth.
The world is for him full of God, penetrated through and
through by the divine, and therefore as real as God himself.   It was quite in Baalshem's manner when one of his
disciples declared that only fools could speak of the
world as vanity or emptiness.   " It is in truth a glorious
world.   We must only learn how rightly to make use of
it.   Call nothing common or profane: by God's presence
all things are holy."

Above we have reviewed the essential doctrines of Baalshem and his immediate followers; we have now to see how they fared at the hands of the sect which he founded. This is a sad part of our task, for the subsequent history of Chassidism is almost entirely a record of decay. As formulated by its founder the new creed amounted to a genuine Reformation, pure and lofty in ideal. After his death unhappily it was rapidly corrupted and perverted. This was due almost exclusively to the dangerous and exaggerated development of a single point in his teaching. That point, the honour due to the divine in man, was relatively a minor article in the original creed. But the later Chassidism has given it a distorted and almost exclusive importance wholly out of proportion to the grander and more essential features of Baalshem's teaching, until the distinctive feature of the Chassidism of to-day is an almost idolatrous service of their living leaders. What little there is to say of the history of the sect after Baalshem's death would be unintelligible without some explanation of the origin and growth of this unfortunate perversion.

It has been explained that Baalshem laid but little stress upon the study of the Law or the observance of its precepts in themselves, but regarded them only as means to an end. The end is union with God. Man has to discover the presence of God in the Divine word and will. Now this mystical service of God, although perhaps sufficing to sensitive and enthusiastic natures, is scarcely plain or definite enough for ordinary men. Few can realise abstractions: and yet fewer can delight in them and find in their contemplation sufficient nurture for their religious needs. What then had Chassidism to offer to the ordinary majority who could not recognise God in all the plenitude of His disguise? The want of something tangible whereon to fix the minds of the people, which has confronted the teachers of so many creeds, was also encountered by the Chassidim, and they unfortunately found their way out of the difficulty by relying on and developing their doctrine of man's position in the Universe. Man's ideal is to be a law himself; himself a clear and full manifestation of God. Now, not only is he God's servant and child, but in highest development he becomes himself a part of God, albeit in human shape, so that he may become wholly one with his divine Father. But if man may reach this highest level of holiness, he is virtually a kind of God-man, whom his fellow-men of lower levels perceive by reason of his manhood, but his essential office consists in raising them up to God by reason of his Divinity.

The few chosen spirits who through the successful persistency with which they have sought God in all things have become, though yet on earth, absorbed in Him, are known in Chassidic literature by the name of the "Zaddikim." The Hebrew word Zaddik [18] means "just" or "righteous," and the term was probably chosen in conscious opposition to the title of Rabbinic heroes, "disciples of the wise." For the Zaddik is not so much the product of learning as of intuition: his final consummation is reached by a sudden and direct illumination from God. The Zaddik not only resembles Moses, but, in virtue of his long communion with the Divine, he is also the true child of God. He is, moreover, a vivifying power in creation, for he is the connecting bond between God and his creatures. He is the source of blessing and the fount of grace. Man must therefore learn to love the Zaddik, so that through the Zaddik he may win God's grace. He who does not believe in the Zaddik is an apostate from God. Here then we have the fatal exaggeration to which I have alluded, and here its logical consequence. The step to man-worship is short.

This peculiar doctrine of the Intermediary soon became the distinguishing feature of Chassidism. By a Chassid was understood not a man who held such and such opinions in theology and religion, but a believer in the Zaddik, and one who sought to attain salvation through the worship of the Zaddik. Every other doctrine of Chassidism was rapidly pushed into the background and overlooked. Even the grand and fundamental doctrine of Omnipresence in the Creation was veiled by the special presence in the Zaddik. Chassidism became mere Zaddikism, and its subsequent history is identical with the downward development of that cult.

Whether Baalshem named his successor is doubtful. But the lead after his death was assumed by his disciple Beer of Mizriez. This man's conversion to Chassidism was an important event for the new community; his piety and learning were beyond dispute, and, whereas during Baalshem's life Chassidism had found its chief adherents among the lower classes of society, Beer managed to gather round him many of the most learned among his contemporaries. It was to these new and ardent disciples of Beer that the expansion of Chassidism was chiefly due. They came together from many quarters, and after Beer's death separated and preached the new doctrine far and wide. Many even went forth during the lifetime of their master, and at his command, to found fresh branches of the new sect. Like Beer himself, they directed their ef-

forts mainly to winning over the educated sections of
the Jews. The elder men paid little heed to their word,
but the youths, just fresh from their casuistic studies,
which had sharpened their wits and starved their souls,
lent a ready ear and an eager heart to the new doctrine. The uneducated were by no means excluded; to
them Chassidism held out a deeper consolation and a
grander hope than the current Rabbinism of the age;
they therefore joined the young community in large numbers without any special effort being necessary to gain
them over.

In their methods of Prayer the Chassidim most conspic-
uously differed from the older communities. Laying as
they did supreme stress on the importance and efficacy of
prayer, they soon found it necessary to secede from the existing synagogues and erect separate buildings for themselves. The usual salaried Reader "with the beautiful
voice and empty head," who naturally regarded his function as a matter of business, was done away with and his
place taken either by the Zaddik himself or by some other
distinguished person in the community. The Chassidim
also effected many changes in the liturgy. Instead of the
German they adopted the Spanish ritual. They excised
many prayers which, lacking the authority of antiquity,
were cumbrous in form or objectionable in matter. They
inserted new prayers and hymns of their own. They paid
little regard to the prescribed hours at which public worship should be held. Prayer began when they had got
themselves into the proper devotional frame of mind.
Frequent ablutions, perusal of mystical writings, intro-
spective meditation were the means by which they sought
to gain the befitting mood. The prayers themselves were

accompanied by the usual phenomena of religious excitement. Some in the zeal of their devotion began to dance; others were rapt in a motionless ecstasy; some prayed aloud; others in solemn silence. They justified their abrogation of fixed hours for prayer by saying that you cannot order a child when to speak with its father: such restraint were fit only for slaves.

As a rule the larger number of the younger Chassidim were able to devote their whole time to religious exercises. It was the custom among the Jews in Eastern Europe for the young men to live at the expense of their own or their wives' parents, in order that they might give themselves up entirely to religious study. According to the old notions, this meant the study of the Talmud and its Commentaries; the Chassidim who cared little for the legal side of Jewish literature betook themselves to the literature of edification and mysticism. No small part of their time was taken up with endless conversations about the Zaddik, his piety, goodness, and self-sacrifice and the wonderful miracles which he had wrought. If a Zaddik was living in his own town, the youthful Chassid spent as many hours as he could in the Zaddik's company, in order to observe and study this embodied Torah as constantly as possible. Where no Zaddik was at hand, periodical pilgrimages were made to the town in which he lived, and endless were the tales which were afterwards repeated, to those who were obliged to stay at home, of the Zaddik's marvellous wisdom and extraordinary deeds. The last hours of the Sabbath day were looked upon as a special season of grace, and the Chassidim were therefore in the habit of collecting together in the waning of the Sabbath and celebrating the so-called " Supper of the Holy Queen."

The meal was accompanied by the usual conversations as well as by hymns and prayers.

The Chassidim were second to no other sect in their loyalty and affection for each other. No sacrifice for a brother Chassid was too great. They knew no difference of rich and poor, old and young, wise and ignorant; for they all, with one accord, worshipped one common ideal, the Zaddik, who in his exalted position was equally raised above them all. Before him all minor differences of rank disappeared. When a Chassid travelled, he had no scruple in asking for lodging or entertainment in the house of any Chassid who could afford to give them. If he was in money difficulties the purse of his host was at his disposal. If that was not sufficient, it was supplemented by a grant from the fund of the community. These gifts were not looked upon in the light of charity either by giver or receiver; they were made to the Zaddik, to whom all Chassidim alike were debtors. It sometimes even happened that a Zaddik said that the son of some rich merchant was to marry the daughter of a poor school-master, and both parties were equally delighted to fulfil the wish of their beloved chief.

It may easily be imagined that the innovations of the Chassidim provoked the wrath of the orthodox communities. But in their detestation of the Rabbis the Chassidim returned in full measure all the hatred they received. The Zaddik is the Moses of his age : the Rabbis its Korah and Abiram. Where the Chassidic party in any community gained the upper hand, the Rabbi was deposed and a Zaddik, if that was possible, elected in his place. The issue of these bitter attacks upon the old nobility of the Jewish race was a rigorous persecution. In many places the Chassidim were excommunicated, in others their leaders were publicly scourged and put into the stocks. Their books were burnt and their synagogues forcibly closed. But persecution produced only the usual result of increasing the popularity and the numbers of the sect. The devotion of the Chassidim to each other and to their common cause was increased a hundred-fold by suffering. In one case a distinguished Zaddik was accused of treason, before the Russian authorities, and was thrown into prison. In Russia, however, the power of money is considerable, and on payment of a large ransom not only was the beloved Zaddik released but as an obvious consequence his reputation greatly profited: the day of his release was celebrated as a yearly festival, while his sufferings were regarded by his followers as a sin-offering that atoned for the iniquities of his age. From this time the government maintained a purely neutral attitude towards the new sect, and ere long the persecution by the orthodox ceased.

The cessation of persecution may possibly be accounted for by the fact that Chassidism as a secession soon ceased to be formidable. There were early divisions within the sect. Even Beer's disciples began to quarrel over theological differences and to found separate communities. When once the course of corruption and spiritual decay had begun, it was the interest of the false Zaddikim to accentuate these differences. Each Zaddik sought to have a whole little sect to himself, from which to draw an undivided revenue. And each deluded little sect as it arose boasted of the exclusive possession of the true Zaddik.

It must not be supposed that these strictures apply to the whole class of Zaddikim. The greater number of Baalshem's leading disciples as well as Beer's were beyond question men of pure, unalloyed piety, who would have rejected with scorn any idea of making a trade of their sacred profession. Their motives and their zeal were alike ideal. Many gave up highly paid posts as Rabbis when they joined the new sect. Some emigrated to Palestine to lead a holy life on holy ground, others sought to become religious specialists, following out practically, although with some exaggeration, a favourite doctrine of the Founder, that he who observes but one commandment devotedly and lovingly, may reach the goal desired : the union with God. Thus one Zaddik made it his business never to tell the smallest falsehood, whatever the cost or the inconvenience of truth might be. It is related that the Russian Government, suspecting the Jews of his town of smuggling, consented to withdraw the charge if he declared his brethren innocent. Having no alternative but either to bring misfortune on his brethren or to tell an untruth, he prayed to God to save him from this dilemma by sending death upon him. And lo ! when the officials came to fetch him before the law court they found him dead. Another, thinking that the commandment in Exodus xxiii. 3, relating to the help that should be given to a neighbour or enemy when " his ass is lying under its burden," was practically unobserved, devoted himself to its fulfilment. He was continually to be seen in the streets, helping one man to load his waggon, and another to drag his cart out of the mire. A third made the service of the oppressed his religious speciality. It is said that one day his wife, having had a quarrel with her maid, was setting out to the magistrate of the town to obtain satisfaction. Noticing that her husband was about to accompany her, she asked him whither he was bound. He replied, "to the magistrate." His wife declared that it was below his dignity to take any part in a quarrel with a servant. She could deal with the matter herself. The Zaddik replied, "That may be, but I intend to represent your maid, who when accused by my wife will find no one willing to take her part." And then, bursting into a passion of tears, he quoted Job xxxi. 13: "If I did despise the cause of my man-servant or of my maid-servant, when they contended with me, what shall I do when God riseth up?"

Several Zaddikim were learned men and thinkers of no ordinary kind. The works of Solomon Ladier or of Mendel Witipsker, read with attention and without Western preconceptions, certainly give the impression of both originality and depth of thought. But most characteristic of all is the passionate yearning of authors such as these towards the Divine. The reader is astonished and moved by the intense sincerity and ardour of their longing after God. But, despite the adherence of these worthy men, the fate of Chassidism, as a regenerative force, was sealed from the day when Zaddikism replaced the original doctrines of the sect.

For, apart from the obvious theological considerations already suggested, there are two points of inherent weakness in the cult of the Zaddik which naturally doomed it to perversion and failure. The necessary qualifications for "Zaddikship" are wholly undefined. We hear a great deal about what a Zaddik actually is, but we hear very little about what he should be. The Zaddik has many virtues, but we are nowhere told what are his indispensable qualifications. Moreover, the Zaddik is a being who can be comprehended by the understanding as little as an angel, or as God Himself. He is realised by faith, not conceived by thought.   Hence there is no human test of a true Zaddik except the test of miracles; and every student of religious history knows the deceitful character of that test.

The second source of danger arose from the Chassidim holding it to be their sacred duty to provide for the Zaddik a life of comfort and ease.   The Zaddik must pursue his divine avocations undisturbed by grosser cares.   But what were the consequences?   The Chassidim believed they could win the grace and blessing of the Zaddik by the richness and variety of their gifts.   A Zaddik's career became a very profitable concern.   The result of both defects was that not only was the opportunity given for every scheming charlatan to become a Zaddik, but inducements were offered to make the deception lucrative.   Hence the anxiety of the false Zaddikim, already noticed, to found separate communities.

Among the Chassidim of to-day there is not one in ten thousand who has the faintest conception of those sublime ideas which inspired Baalshem and his immediate disciples.   It is still the interest of the wretched ringleaders of a widely spread delusion to crush and keep down every trace of reflection and thought so that they may play at will with the conscience and purses of their adherents.   The new scientific movement, inaugurated by such men as Krochmal, Zunz, and others who came under the influence of the German critical spirit, found in them its hottest and most fanatical opponents.   That the cult of the Zaddikim has not led to still more disastrous consequences is solely due to the fact that the Chassidim in general have remained faithful to the Law.   It is the Law, against the excessive study of which the original

Chassidim protested, that has put limits to the license of its modern false prophets.

Amid much that is bad, the Chassidim have preserved through the whole movement a warm heart, and an ardent, sincere faith. There is a certain openness of character and a ready friendliness about even the modern Chassidim which are very attractive. Religion is still to them a matter of life and death. Their faith is still real enough to satisfy the demands of a Luther, but it is diverted and wasted upon unworthy objects. If Chassidism is to be reformed, its worship must no longer be of man; it must be brought back again to the source of all Beauty, all Wisdom, and all Goodness; it must be restored to God.

II

NACHMAN KROCHMAL AND THE "PER-
PLEXITIES OF THE TIME"

In her good-natured panegyric of mediocrity which is known under the title of *Scenes of Clerical Life*, George Eliot remarked: "Let us hope that there is a saving ignorance."

Strange as this demand may sound, the wish of the great novelist to see her favoured mediocrities "saved," has been shared by the great majority of mankind. I know that I, at least, echo that desire with all my heart. And I am afraid that I am prompted by some rather self-ish reasons. It would be somewhat hard, when one is born with small abilities, but a great desire for being saved, to be deprived of the hope held out by the author of *Adam Bede*.

But there are some, I am afraid, who are not satisfied with this dictum of George Eliot. They show a strong tendency to make salvation a monopoly of ignorance. This is a little too selfish. With all due respect to every form of ignorance, sacred as well as profane, we ought, I think, to believe that there is also such a thing as a saving knowledge. Nay, we might go even farther. There may be certain epochs in history when there is hardly any other path to salvation than knowledge, and the deep search after truth.

We all know the words of the Psalmist, "The Lord preserveth the simple." But as there are periods in the life of the individual when naïveté has to give way to sagacity and reflection, so there are times in history at which Providence does not choose to leave men in simplicity. At such times doubts arise, as though of themselves; questions suddenly become open when they had been supposed solved for centuries; and the human mind is stirred by a sceptical breeze of which no man can tell whence it came. One may under those circumstances be indifferent, but one can be simple no more.

Even in such cases, however, man has no cause to despair. When our dearest beliefs are shaken by all kinds of doubts, Providence sends us also great thinkers, earnest lovers of truth, who devote their lives to enlightening our puzzled minds. Not that these men try to answer all the questions by which we feel perplexed. They endeavour to satisfy us, partly by showing that many of our difficulties are not difficulties at all, but merely arise from superficiality, and partly by proving that the great cause about which we feel so much anxiety does not exactly depend on the solution of the questions that are troubling us. They give to the things which are dearer to us than our life a fresh aspect, which enables us to remain attached to them with the same devotion and love as before. To speak again in the words of the Psalmist: "Thou sendest forth Thy Spirit, and they are created, and Thou renewest the face of the earth."

This spirit that renews the face of things is what I understand by "saving knowledge." As men of that saving knowledge we may regard Rabban Johanan ben Zaccai[1] and his disciples, who made it possible for Judaism to survive the destruction of the Temple, which some believed to involve the end of the religion. As such men we may look upon R. Saadiah Gaon and his followers, who worked at a time when Judaism was menaced in its inner life, namely in the tradition, by the attempts of the narrow-minded Caraites to convert it into a bookish religion.[2] Such men were Maimonides and his successors, who came to the aid of religion when it had got into dogmatic troubles by reason of its coming into contact with various philosophical systems. And in order to approach the subject of the present essay, I venture to say that a man of such saving knowledge was also Nachman Krochmal, who lived and laboured in the first half of the present century, when Judaism had been terribly shaken by the scepticism of Voltaire, and the platitudes of the so-called Mendelssohnian school.

Nachman Krochmal was born on the 17th of February in the year 1785. His father, Solomon Krochmal, was a merchant of Brody, a commercial frontier town in the north-east of Galicia in Austria. In his early years Solomon often used to visit Berlin for business purposes. He is said to have seen Mendelssohn there on one occasion, and to have learned greatly to revere the Jewish sage. And it is not unlikely that Nachman's subsequent admiration for Mendelssohn was partly due to his father's influence.

Solomon was a man of considerable wealth, and he, therefore, endeavoured to give his son the best possible education. But as a respectable member of a Polish community a hundred years ago, Solomon had to follow the

fashion adopted by his neighbours, and the best possible
education consisted in affording the child an opportunity
to study the Talmud and other Rabbinical works. All
other languages and their literatures were sealed books to
the child — a very absurd and regrettable fashion indeed.
But let us not be too hard on Polish Jews. I have been
told that there are countries on our globe where people
have been driven by the force of fashion into the opposite
extreme ; where, with few exceptions, they think that the
Talmud, as well as the whole Hebrew literature, must
needs be excluded from the programme of a gentleman's
education.

Happily, or the reverse, Krochmal's childhood did not
last long, for in the year 1798 we find that Nachman, a
boy of fourteen, was already married to a Miss Haberman
in Zolkiew. As a result of this foolish custom of marrying
at so very early an age, Nachman was hardly ever a boy ;
we have at once to deal with him as a man.

It was then customary in Poland, and perhaps is so still,
for the father of the bride to provide for the support of the
young couple for some years after their marriage. In
order to reduce the expense of this arrangement, the
bridegroom had to reside in the same house as his father-
in-law. Thus we see Krochmal removing from Brody to
Zolkiew, the native town of his wife. Here Krochmal
lived in the house of her father for many years, entirely
devoted to his studies; and he certainly needed all his
time for them. For he now began to expand the sphere
of his education, to embrace subjects quite new to him.
By his marriage Nachman seems to have gained a certain
amount of independence, and the first use he made of it
was to study the *Guide of the Perplexed*[3] of Maimonides,

E

the *Commentaries* of Ibn Ezra on the Bible,[4] and other
more or less philosophical works written in the Hebrew
language. His next step was to learn German; but, as
his biographers inform us, he was not able to follow this
course without undergoing many struggles, and overcoming
many obstacles.

It would lead us too far to give a full account of the
difficulties which the young scholar had to conquer while
pursuing his new studies. They will be sufficiently
characterised by the following extract from a Hebrew
letter of his disciple, Solomon Leb Rapoport, who,
writing in 1841 concerning his master and friend, remarks: "Consider this, ye inhabitants of Germany" —
and, I may add, ye inhabitants of England — "and you
will be astounded. It is easy for you to avoid being one-
sided, and to study different sciences, for you possess
many schools and teachers from every branch of learning.
It is not so in Poland and Russia even at present, much
less was it so forty years ago. There is no teacher, no
guide, no supporter, for the Jew who desires any sort of
improvement. The Jew who wishes to enter on a new
path of learning has to prepare the road for himself. And
when he has entered on it, his friend will come to him and
ask, ' Is it true that you have got scientific books in your
house? Mind you do not mention it to any one. There
are enough bigots in the town to persecute you and all
your family if they get scent of it.' " It was under these
conditions that Krochmal pursued his studies, which were
by no means few or easy, for he was not content with a
knowledge of only the lighter portions of German literature. He soon began to read the works of Lessing,
Mendelssohn, and more especially of Kant, who always

remained his favourite philosopher. In his later years he also became acquainted with the writings of Fichte, Schelling, and Hegel. But to the last he could not console himself for having missed the advantages of a systematic university education.

After having learned German, Krochmal proceeded to acquire a knowledge of Latin and French, and to read the best books written in those languages. To deepen his knowledge of Hebrew, he studied Arabic and Syraic, but we are unable to say how far he succeeded in mastering these languages. With these studies, which appear to have occupied our philosopher for an interval of ten years after his marriage, the first period of his life seems also to end. But the hard work of ten years did not pass over the delicate youth without undermining his health for ever. At the age of twenty-four, Krochmal fell sick of an illness which compelled him to interrupt his work. He was forced to go to Lemberg to consult the doctors of that town, and he had to remain there for a long time. And now began Krochmal's career as a teacher. For during his stay at Lemberg there gathered round him a band of young scholars whom Krochmal's fame had already reached. It is useless to enumerate the names of all these students. Among them figured Isaac Erter, Samson Bloch, A. Bodek, and many others. The most gifted of them was undoubtedly Rapoport, who afterwards became even more famous than his master Krochmal. It is not easy to define accurately the relation that subsisted between these two men. Graetz, in his history, calls Rapoport a disciple of Krochmal. Rapoport himself, in his memoir of Krochmal, describes the latter as a dear friend with whom he was wont to discuss literary topics.

Zunz does not mention Rapoport at all in his account of our author. It seems to me that this relation may be most aptly defined by the Talmudic term "Talmid-Chaber," [5] "disciple-colleague."

Indeed, Krochmal's whole method of teaching was rather that of a companion than of a professor. He gave no set lectures on particular subjects, but conveyed his instruction rather by means of suggestive conversations with his younger friends. His usual habit was to walk with his pupils in the neighbourhood of the town, and to try to influence their minds each in accordance with its bent. If any of his disciples showed an inclination for poetry, Krochmal sought to refine his taste by directing his attention to the best works in Hebrew and German literature. To another, whose fancy strayed into mysticism, he recommended the writings of Philo and Ibn Ezra, at the same time suggesting how the works of the latter should be interpreted. A third who, like Rapoport, was interested in historical researches, Krochmal instructed in the methods of critical inquiry.

There must have been some fascinating charm in Nachman's personality, which made him irresistible to all who came into contact with him. Rapoport has described his first interview with Krochmal. "It is more than thirty years since I first made his acquaintance, and beheld the glory of his presence. Though he was in weak health, still his soul was strong; and as soon as I conversed with him there came over me a spirit of judgment and knowledge. I felt almost transformed into another man." Elsewhere the same writer says : "Oh, how sweet to me were these walks with Krochmal — sweeter than all the pleasures of this world. I could never have enough of his wisdom; with his every word he conveyed a new lesson."

After a lengthy stay at Lemberg, Krochmal partially, though not entirely, recovered from his severe illness; he remained weak and pale for the rest of his days. His antagonists, the Chassidim, believed him to be possessed by a demon who could find no better dwelling-place than in the person of this arch-heretic. Had it been in their power they would probably have dragged him to some exorcist for the purpose of driving out his German, French, Latin, and other symptoms of demoniacal heresy. Happily the orthodox were powerless to do this, so Krochmal was left unmolested, and was allowed to resume his walks and studies. It may be here remarked that Krochmal in general avoided giving the Chassidim any cause for reasonable complaint. Rapoport asserts that his master was "deeply religious and a strict observer of the law. He was zealously anxious to perform every ordinance, Biblical or Rabbinical." The only liberty that Krochmal claimed for himself and his disciples was the right to study what they thought best and in the way they thought best. When this liberty was attacked, he showed a firmness and resolution which would hardly have been expected from this quiet and gentle man. To one of his pupils, who made concessions to the Chassidim and their Zaddikim worship, Krochmal wrote: "Be firm in this matter unless you wish to earn the contempt of every honest man. One who is afraid of these people, and debases himself before them bears a mean soul that was born to slavery. The man that wishes to rise above the mob, with its confused notions and corrupt morality, must be courageous as a lion in conquering the obstacles that beset his path. Consideration of what people will say, what bigots will whisper, what crafty enemies will scheme — questions such as these can have but one effect, — to darken the intellect and confuse the faculty of judgment."

So Krochmal continued his studies without interruption till 1814, when the death of his wife's mother brought his period of ease and comfort to an end. His father-in-law seems to have died some time before, and Krochmal was forced to seek his own living. He became a merchant, but it is to be regretted that he did not prove as successful a man of business as he was a man of letters. He found it a hard struggle to earn a living. But the severest trial which he had to undergo was the death of his wife in 1826. In a letter, dating from about this time, to a friend who had asked him for assistance in his philosophical inquiries, Krochmal wrote — " How can I help you now? I am already an old man; my head is gray, and my health is broken. In the last three years I have met with many misfortunes. My beloved wife died after a long illness. My daughter will soon leave me to get married, my elder son will depart to seek his livelihood, and I shall be left alone with only a child of ten years, the son of my old age. I will lift up mine eyes unto the hills: From whence shall my help come?"

Nachman was evidently in very low spirits at this time, but he was in too true a sense a philosopher to despair. He turned for comfort to his studies, and at this dark epoch of his life he first became acquainted with the Philosophy of Hegel, whose system he was wont to call the " Philosophy of Philosophies."

For the next ten years the works of Hegel and inquiries into Jewish history appear to have absorbed all the leisure that his mercantile occupation left him. We shall presently see what the result of these studies was. No fresh subjects were undertaken by Krochmal in the last years of his life; he had already acquired a fund of knowledge vast enough to engage all his thoughts. There are, however, some remaining points in his private circumstances which it may not be uninteresting to mention.

Krochmal, as has been already related, was not prosperous in his business. Things went from bad to worse, and he was compelled in 1836 to seek a situation. "There ought to be literary men poor," some writer has maintained, "to show whether they are genuine or not." This test Krochmal successfully passed through. Even as a young man Nachman's strength of character was admired by his contemporaries not less than his rare learning. In his subsequent distress, he gave evidence of the truth of this judgment. Despite his poverty, his friends could not prevail upon him to accept the post of Rabbi in any Jewish community. "I am unwilling," he wrote to a friend, "to be the cause of dissensions in any Jewish congregation. I should prefer to die of hunger rather than become a Rabbi under present circumstances." He expressed his views on this subject even more decidedly on a later occasion when the Berlin congregation offered him the post of Chief Rabbi in that town. In a letter, conveying his refusal of this honourable office, he says: "I never thought of becoming the Conscience-counsellor (*Gewissensrath*) of men. My line of studies was not directed to that end, nor would it accord with my disposition and sentiments. The only post that I should care to accept would be that of teacher in the Jewish Theological Seminary, which, as I was informed, you were thinking of establishing in

Berlin." The plan to found such an institution was not realised till forty years later, and in the interval Nachman had to look for his living in other regions than Jewish theology. Being in poor circumstances, and as his children and friends had left him, he felt very lonely at Zolkiew. "Nobody cares for me here," he writes, "and I am equally indifferent." His one desire was to obtain a situation at Brody, possibly as book-keeper with a salary of some thirty pounds a year, on condition that he would be expected to devote only half the day to his business duties, thus securing for himself leisure for philosophical studies.

His terms were accepted, and he obtained the humble post he sought. He remained in Brody for the next two years, 1836–8, but at the end of 1838 he fell so dangerously ill that he could no longer resist the pressing request of his daughter to live with her at Tarnopol. She had urged him to take this step even previous to his removal to Brody, but he had declined on the plea that he preferred to live by the labour of his hands. Now, however, he yielded to her wish, and betook himself to Tarnopol, where for two years longer he lived affectionately tended by his children and respected by all who knew him. In May 1840, Krochmal's illness began to develop fatal symptoms, and he died in the arms of his daughter on the 31st of July (the first of Ab), at the age of fifty-five. As Zunz happily remarked : "This great man was born on the 7th of Adar, the birthday of Moses (according to Jewish tradition), and died on the first of Ab, the anniversary of the death of Aaron, the High Priest."

I have tried in the foregoing remarks to give a short sketch of our Rabbi's life according to the accounts of Zunz, Rapoport, and Letteris. There is one other point to which I must allude, as it involves a consideration on which Letteris seems to lay much stress. This biographer appears to think that Krochmal was in his youth greatly influenced by the society in which he moved, consisting as it did of many learned and enlightened men. There is, too, the oft-quoted saying of Goethe : —

> Wer den Dichter will verstehen
> Muss in Dichters Lande gehen.

And I am probably expected to give some account of the state of society in which Nachman grew up. I regret that I must ask to be excused from doing so. I cannot consent to take the reader to Krochmal's land. And if I might venture to give him my humble advice, I should only say, " By all means stop at home." Goethe may be right about the poet, but his remark does not apply to the case of the scholar. It may be true, as some think, that every great man is the product of his time, but it certainly does not follow that he is the product of his country. Nor could I name any other country of which Krochmal was the product. Many a city no doubt boasted itself a town full of " *Chakhamim* and *Sopherim* " [6] as the Hebrew phrase is, or, as we would express it, " a seat of learning," full of scholars of the ancient and modern schools. But neither these ancient scholars nor the modern were of a kind to produce a real scholar and an enlightened thinker like Krochmal. There were many men who knew by heart the whole of the Halachic works of Maimonides, the Mishnah, and even the whole of the Babylonian Talmud. This is very imposing. But if you look a little closer, you will find that with a few exceptions — such as the school of R. Elijah Wilna — these men, generally speaking, hardly deserve the name of scholars at all. They were rather a sort of studying engines. The steam-engine passes over a continent, here through romantic scenery, there in the midst of arid deserts, by stream and mountain and valley, always with the same monotonous hum and shriek. So these scholars went through the Talmud with never changing feelings. They did not rejoice at the description which is given in tractate *Biccurim*[7] of the procession formed when the first-fruits were brought into the Holy Temple. They were not much saddened when reading in tractate *Taanith*[8] of the unhappy days so recurrent in Jewish history. They were not delighted by the wisdom of *Seder Nezikin*,[9] which deals with civil law; nor were they vexed of *Seder Taharoth*,[10] which treats of the laws of cleanliness and uncleanliness, that by their exaggeration gave cause to much dissension in the time of the Temple. The pre-Talmudic literature, such as the *Siphra, Siphré*, and *Mechilta*[11] — the only existing means of obtaining an insight into the Talmud — were altogether neglected. All that these readers cared for was to push on to the end, and the prayer recited at the close was of more importance to them than the treatise they had perused.

Not less melancholy was the spectacle presented by the so-called men of "Enlightenment" (*Aufklärung*). They belonged chiefly to the rationalistic school of Mendelssohn, but they equalled their master neither in knowledge nor in moral character. It was an enlightenment without foundation in real scholarship, and did not lead to an ideal life, though again I must add that there were exceptions. These men were rather what Germans would term *Schöngeister*, a set of dilettanti who cared to study as little as

possible, and to write as much as possible. They wrote
bad grammars, superficial commentaries on the Bible,
and terribly dull poems. Of this literature, with the
exception of Erter's *Watchman*,[12] there is scarcely a work
that one would care to read twice. Most of them
despised Rabbinism, but without understanding its noblest
forms as they are to be traced in the Talmud and later
Hebrew literature. They did not dislike Judaism, but
the only Judaism they affected was one "which does not
oppose itself to anything in particular"; or, as Heine
would have described it, "Eine reinliche Religion." In
one respect these little men were great: in mutual
admiration, which reached such a pitch that such titles
as "Great Luminary," "World-famed Sage," were considered altogether too insignificant and commonplace.

I will now pass to the writings of Krochmal. It must
be premised that Krochmal was not a voluminous author.
All his writings, including a few letters which were published in various Hebrew periodicals, would scarcely
occupy four hundred pages. Krochmal used to call himself "der ewige Student" (the perpetual pupil). He did
not read books, nor study philosophical systems, with the
object of writing books of his own on them. He read
and studied in order that he might become a better and a
wiser man. Besides, he did not think himself competent
to judge on grave subjects, nor did he consider his judgment, even if he formed one, worthy of publication. He
counselled his friends to be equally slow in publishing
their views to the world. "Be not," he wrote to a correspondent,— " be not hasty in forming your opinions before
you have studied the literature of the subject with care
and devotion. This is no easy matter, for no man can

obtain any real knowledge of the Torah and philosophy unless he is prepared to give himself up in single-hearted devotion to his studies." Severe though he was to his friends, he was still more severe to himself. Though he had been collecting materials on subjects of Jewish history and philosophy from his early youth, it was not until he had endured much persuasion and pressure from his friends that he began to write down his thoughts in a connected form. We thus possess only one work from the pen of this author; but that work is the *Guide of the Perplexed of the Time*,[13] a posthumous book published in 1851, eleven years after Krochmal's death. His work had been much interrupted by illness during the last years of his life, and as a necessary consequence many parts of his treatise finally remained in an unfinished state. Krochmal commissioned his children to hand over his papers to Zunz, who was to arrange and edit them as best he might. Zunz, who in his reverence for Krochmal went so far as to call him the man of God, gladly accepted the task, in which he was aided by Steinschneider. Unfortunately, the work was published in Lemberg, a place famous for spoiling books. Even the skill of these two great masters did not suffice to save Krochmal's work from the fate to which all the books printed in Lemberg seem inevitably doomed. Thus Krochmal's work is printed on bad paper, and with faint ink; it is full of misprints and the text is sometimes confused with the notes. A second edition appeared in Lemberg in 1863; but, it is scarcely necessary to add, the reprint is even worse than the original issue.

The work occupies some 350 pages, and is divided into seventeen chapters. The opening six treat of Religion in general. The author first indicates the opposite dan-

gers to which men are liable. On the one hand, men
are exposed to extravagant phantasy (*Schwärmerei*), superstition and ceremonialism (*Werkheiligkeit*). Some, on
the other hand, in their endeavour to avoid this danger,
fall into the opposite extreme, materialism, unbelief, and
moral degeneracy as a consequence of their neglect of
all law. He proceeds to say: Even in the ritual part
of religion, such as the regulations of the Sabbath, the
dietary laws and so forth, we find abstract definitions
necessary, and differences of opinions prevalent. In the
dogmatic aspects of religion, dealing as they do with the
grave subjects of metaphysics, the mystery of life and
death, the destiny of man, his relation to God, reward
and punishment, the inner meaning of the laws, — in
these spiritual matters, the difficulty of accurate definition must be far greater and the opportunities for difference of opinion more frequent and important. What
guide are we to follow, seeing that every error involves
the most dangerous consequences? Shall we abandon
altogether the effort of thinking on these grave subjects?
Such a course is impossible. Do not believe, says Krochmal, that there ever was a time when the religious man
was entirely satisfied by deeds of righteousness, as some
people maintain. On the contrary, every man, whether
an independent thinker or a simple believer, always feels
the weight of these questions upon him. Every man
desires to have some ideal basis for his actions which
must constitute his real life in its noblest moments.
Krochmal here quotes a famous passage from the Midrash.[14] The Torah, according to one of our ancient sages,
may be compared to two paths, the one burning with fire,
the other covered with snow. If a man enters on the

former path he will die by the heat; if he walks by the
latter path he will be frozen by the snow. What, then,
must he do? He must walk in the middle, or, as we
should say, he must choose the golden mean. But, as
Krochmal suggests, the middle way in historical and
philosophical doubts does not consist, as some idle heads
suppose, in a kind of compromise between two opposing
views. If one of two contending parties declares that
twice two make six, while his opponent asserts that twice
two make eight, a sort of compromise might be arrived
at by conceding that twice two make seven. But such
a compromise would be as false as either extreme; and
the seeker after the truth must revert to that mean
which is the heart of all things, independently of all
factions, placing himself above them.

Having dealt with the arguments relating to the existence of God as elaborated in the philosophical systems
of his time, Krochmal leads up to his treatment of the
History of Israel by a chapter on the ideal gifts bestowed upon the various ancient nations, which, possessed
by them through many centuries, were lost when their
nationality ceased. We next come, in Chapter VII., to
the ideal gifts of Israel. These are the religious gift
and the faculty and desire for seeking the ideal of all
ideals, namely, God. But Israel, whose mission it was
to propagate this ideal, was, even as other nations, subject to natural laws; and its history presents progress
and reaction, rise and decline. Krochmal devotes his
next three chapters to showing how, in the history of
Israel, as in other histories, may be detected a triple
process. These three stages are the budding, the period
of maturity, and the decay. As the history of Israel is

more a history of religion than of politics and battles, its rise and decline correspond more or less with Israel's attachment to God, and its falling away from Him. The decay would be associated with the adoption of either of the extremes, the dangerous effects of which have been already mentioned. But "through progress and backsliding, amid infectious contact with idolatry, amid survival of old growths of superstition, of the crude practices of the past; amid the solicitation of new aspects of life; in material prosperity and in material ruin," Israel was never wholly detached from God. In the worst times it had its judges or its prophets, its heroes or its sages, its Rabbis or its philosophers, who strove to bring Israel back to its mission, and who succeeded in their efforts to do so. Even in its decay traces of the Divine spirit made themselves felt, and revived the nation, which entered again on a triple course and repeated its three phases. The first of these three-fold epochs began, according to Krochmal's eighth chapter, with the times of the Patriarchs, and ended with the death of Gedaliah after the destruction of the first Temple. Next, in the following two chapters, Krochmal finds the second triple movement in the interval between the prophets of the exile in Babylon and the death of Bar-Cochba about 135 A.C. The author also hints at the existence of a third such epoch beginning with R. Judah the Patriarch, the compiler of the Mishnah (220 A.C.),[15] and ending with the expulsion of the Jews from Spain (1492). This idea is not further developed by Krochmal; but it would be interesting to ask, by the way, in which phase of the three-fold process — rise, maturity, or decay — are we at the present time?

The next five chapters may be regarded as an excursus on the preceding two. Krochmal discusses the Biblical books which belong to the period of the Exile and of the Second Temple, such as the Second Isaiah, certain Exilic and Maccabean psalms, Ecclesiastes, certain Apocryphal books, and the work of the Men of the Great Synagogue. They contain, again, researches on the various sects, such as the Assideans, Sadducees, Pharisees, Essenes, the Gnostics, the Cabbalists and their relation to the latter, and the Minim,[16] who are mentioned in the Talmud. In another part of this excursus Krochmal describes the systems of the Alexandrian Jewish philosophers, such as Philo and Aristobulus, and discusses their relation to certain theosophic ideas in various Midrash-collections. The author also attempts to prove the necessity of Tradition ; he shows its first traces in the Bible, and explains the term Sopherim (scribes); and he points out the meaning of the phrase " A law unto Moses from Mount Sinai," [17] and similar expressions. He gives a summary of the development of the Halachah in its different stages, the criteria by which the older Halachahs may be discriminated ; he seeks to arrive at the origin of the Mishnah, and deals with various cognate topics. In another discourse Krochmal endeavours to explain the term Agadah,[18] its origin and development ; the different kinds of Agadah and their relative value. Chapter XVI. contains the Prolegomena to a philosophy of the Jewish religion in accordance with the principles laid down by Hegel. In the seventeenth and last chapter the author gives a general introduction to the Philosophy of Ibn Ezra, and quotes illustrative extracts.

The space of an essay does not permit me to give

further details of Krochmal's book. I am conscious that
the preceding outline is deficient in quality as well as in
quantity. Yet, even from this meagre abstract, the reader
will gather that Krochmal reviews many of the great
problems which concern religion in general and Judaism
in particular. Zunz somewhere remarks that Krochmal
was inspired in his work by the study of Hegel, just as
Maimonides had been by the study of Aristotle. I give
this statement solely on the authority of Zunz, as I myself
have never made a study of the works of the German
philosopher, and am therefore unable to express an opinion on the question.

Now there is no doubt that Krochmal's book is not
without defects. The materials are not always well
arranged, there is at times a want of proportion in the
length at which the various points are treated, and the
author occasionally seems to wander from the subject
in hand. But we shall be better able to account for these
and similar technical faults, as well as to appreciate the
real value of the author's work, if we consider the following fact. Nachman Krochmal's object was to elaborate a philosophy of Jewish history, to trace the leading
ideas that ran through it, and the ultimate causes that led
to its various phases. But, unfortunately, at the time
when Krochmal began to write, there did not exist a
Jewish history at all. The labours of Zunz were conducted in an altogether different field. Not to mention
the names of the younger scholars then unborn, Graetz,
the author of the *History of the Jews*, and Weiss, who
wrote a history of the Tradition, were still studying at
college. Frankel's masterly essays on the Essenes and
the Septuagint, his well-known work, *Introduction to the*

F

Mishnah, and the results of Geiger's most interesting and suggestive researches on the older and later Halachah, and on the Pharisees and Sadducees, had yet to be written. Rapoport's great treatise, *Erech Millin*,[19] had not been published at that time, and Steinschneider was not yet working at his historical sketch of Jewish literature. It was not till six years after Krochmal's death (viz. in 1846) that Landauer's memorable studies on the Jewish mystics were given to the world. Even the bad books of Julius Fürst, such as his *History of the Canon*, and his still worse *History of Jewish Literature in Babylon*, were then un-written. Neither the most charlatanic *History of the Opinions and Teachings of All the Jewish Sects*, by Peter Beer, the universal provider, nor Jost's most honest but narrow-minded and superficial *History of the Jews*, was of much use to Krochmal. Jost's more scholarly works were not published till long afterwards. Krochmal was thus without the guidance of those authorities to which we are now accustomed to turn for information. Except-ing the aid that he derived from the writings of Azariah de Rossi,[20] Krochmal was therefore compelled to prose-cute all the necessary research for himself; he had to establish the facts of Jewish history as well as to philoso-phise upon them. Hence, in the very midst of his philo-sophical analysis, the author was bound to introduce digressions on historical subjects, in order to justify as well as to form the basis of that analysis. He had to survey the ground and to collect the materials, besides constructing the plan of the edifice and working at its erection. Nevertheless, it is precisely for these historical excursuses that Krochmal has deserved the gratitude of posterity. He it was who taught Jewish scholars how to submit the ancient Rabbinic records to the test of criticism and the way in which they might be utilised for the purpose of historical studies; he it was who enabled them to trace the genesis of the tradition, and to watch the inner germination of that vast organism. He even indicated to them how they might continue to connect their own lives with it, how they might derive nourishment from it, and in their turn further its growth. I may assert with the utmost confidence that there is scarcely a single page in Krochmal's book that did not afterwards give birth to some essay or monograph or even elaborate treatise, though their authors were not always very careful about mentioning the source of their inspiration. Thus Krochmal justly deserves the honourable title assigned to him by one of our greatest historians, who terms him the Father of Jewish Science.

So far, I have been speaking of the importance of Krochmal's treatise and of its significance in the region of Jewish Science. It is necessary, I think, to add a few words with regard to the general tendency of his whole work. I have already alluded to the characteristic modesty of Krochmal; I have pointed out how little he cared for publicity, how dearly he loved retirement. The question accordingly presents itself — What can have been the real and sufficient causes that prevailed upon him to yield to the solicitations of his friends and to write upon what the Talmud would term "matters standing on the heights of the world"?

The answer to this question may, I think, be found in the title of Krochmal's book, the *Guide of the Perplexed of the Time*. It is indeed a rather unusual coincidence for the title of a Hebrew book to have any connection with its subject matter. The same merit is possessed by the *Guide of the Perplexed* of Maimonides, the title of which undoubtedly suggested that of Krochmal's treatise. There is, however, one little addition in Krochmal's title that contains a most important lesson for us. I mean the words " of the Time." By these words Krochmal reminds us that, great as are the merits of the immortal work of Maimonides — and it would be difficult to exaggerate its value and importance — still it will no longer suffice for us. For, as Krochmal himself remarks, every time has its own perplexities, and therefore needs its own guide. In order to show that these words are no idle phrase, I shall endeavour to illustrate them by one example at least. In the *Guide of the Perplexed* of Maimonides, Part II., Chapter XXVI., occurs a passage which runs thus: "In the famous chapters known as the 'Chapters of R. Eliezer the Great,'[21] I find R. Eliezer the Great saying something more extraordinary than I have ever seen in the utterances of any believer in the Law of Moses. I refer to the following passage: 'Whence were the heavens created? He (God) took part of the light of His garment, He stretched it like a cloth, and thus the heavens were extending continually, as it is said (Ps. civ. 2): He covereth Himself with light as with a garment, He stretcheth the heavens like a curtain. Whence was the earth created? He took of the snow under the throne of glory, and threw it; according to the words (in Job xxxvii. 6), He said to the snow be thou earth.' These are the words given there (in the 'Chapters of R. Eliezer the Great'), and I, in my surprise, ask, What was the belief of this sage? Did he think it impossible

that something be produced from nothing? . . . If the
terms · 'the light of His garment' and the 'snow of
glory' mean something eternal (as matter) they *must*
be rejected. . . . In short, it is a passage that greatly
confuses the notions of all intelligent and religious persons. I am unable to explain it sufficiently."

So far Maimonides; and we are quite able to conceive
his perplexity in dealing with this passage. On one side,
Maimonides himself believed that Judaism is a dogmatic
religion, and that one of its dogmas is the principle of
Creatio ex nihilo. On the other side, he found R. Eliezer
— one of the greatest authorities of the early part of the
second century — apparently denying this dogma. The
perplexity was indeed a serious one for Maimonides, but
we find no difficulty whatever in extricating ourselves from
it. In the first place, there are many who cling to the
theory which holds that there are no dogmas in Judaism
at all, and to them Maimonides' difficulty would have no
relevance. Secondly, those who believe that there are
dogmas in Judaism may regard such expressions as those
quoted above from the "Chapters of R. Eliezer" in the
light of mere poetical metaphors, or may call them fairy
tales or legends, or include them in some other section of
literature, known under the name of folklore, which is an
excuse for every absurdity, the fortunate authors of which
are responsible neither to philosophy nor to religion, and
sometimes not even to common sense. But there is a
third consideration that affords the best solution of the
difficulty. The "Chapters of R. Eliezer," despite their
pompous title, are not the work of R. Eliezer at all.
Criticism has taught us to attach no importance to the
heading of a chapter or the title-page of a book. We are

now in a position to judge from the tone, style, and contents of the work, that the "Chapters of R. Eliezer" is a later compilation of the eighth century, and that its author could not have been R. Eliezer, the teacher of R. Akiba, in the second century. In this way, these particular difficulties of Maimonides solve themselves for us in a sufficiently easy way. But it is just these solutions that open up new difficulties and perplexities which did not exist for the generation of the great Spanish philosopher. Suppose that we accept the view that Judaism is not a dogmatic religion. But how are we to conceive a religion without dogmas, or, if you prefer the expression, without principles or bases of belief? Or is Judaism, as some platitudinarians think, a mere national institute with some useful dietary and sanitary •laws, but with nothing that makes for the sanctification of man, with no guidance to offer us in the great problems of our life, and in the greatest anxieties of the human soul? On the other hand, granted that we may consider certain things as mere legend, how are we to discriminate between these and the things that must be taken seriously? Does it depend on the nature of the subject, or on the position of the book in the canon of Hebrew literature? In the thirteenth century symbolical meanings were given to certain difficult passages in the Talmud; but the process was carried further, and the Biblical narratives were subjected by philosophers to a like treatment. R. Solomon ben Adereth and his colleagues (in the thirteenth century) settled the question by indiscriminately excommunicating all young men who should study philosophy; but this method is scarcely one to be commended for present use.

The third, or the philological solution of difficulties,

leads to fresh troubles. A hundred years ago men were in that happy state of mind in which they knew everything. They knew the exact author and date of every Psalm; they knew the author of each and every ancient Midrash; they knew the originator of every law and ordinance; they even knew the writer of the Zohar, and of other mystical books. There were certainly a few who did not know all these things, among them Ibn Ezra, Azariah de Rossi, and the two Delmedigos.[22] But they were merely a miserable historical blunder, men who had no right to be born when they were. But the philological method has swept away all this knowingness as by a deluge from heaven, and men find that they know nothing. True, there linger on a few who still know all these things, but it is they who are now the anachronism. These, and such as these, are the perplexities of our time, to the resolution of which the labours of Krochmal and of a noble band of scholars have been directed in this century.

Have these perplexities, we must ask, and these puzzles been solved by Krochmal and his coadjutors? We may with all certainty answer: They have only pointed out the way, it is for ourselves to proceed by it. It would be unreasonable to expect that difficulties which have been accumulating during the course of thousands of years should be solved by the men of one or two generations. Again, we live in a century in which excavations and discoveries in other fields have added at once to our knowledge and to our uncertainty. Each country, we might almost say, over and above the perplexities that trouble mankind in general, has its own special difficulties which are entirely unknown to those who dwell outside its frontiers. I am not disposed to discuss these difficulties in this place. Nor have I the ability to do so. But of two things I am perfectly certain : the first is, that for a solution of these difficulties which, in the language of Maimonides, "confuse the notions of all intelligent and religious persons," the only hope is in true knowledge and not in ignorance; and secondly, this knowledge can only be obtained by a combination of the utmost reverence for religion and the deepest devotion to truth. The poor old Rabbis who have been so foully decried by their calumniators as hedonists, and so foolishly praised by sorry apologists as materialistic optimists, strongly insisted that when a man woos the truth, his suit can only prosper if he is influenced by the purest and most single-hearted affection. "A man," says the Siphré, "must not say : 'I will study the Torah in order that I may attain the title of Rabbi or savant, or that I may become rich by it, or that I may be rewarded for it in the world to come.' He must study for love's sake." Such a knowledge, which is free from all taint of worldliness and of other-worldliness, a knowledge sought simply and solely for pure love of God, who is Truth, — such a knowledge is in the highest sense a saving knowledge, and Nachman Krochmal was in possession of it.

III

RABBI ELIJAH WILNA, GAON

THE three great stars of German literature are usually characterised by German scholars in the following way: Goethe they say represents the beautiful, Schiller the ideal, while Lessing represents truth. I think that we may apply the same characteristics to the three great luminaries, with which the Jewish middle ages ceased — for as Zunz somewhere remarked, the Jewish middle ages lasted till the beginning of the eighteenth century — and the modern age of Judaism opened. I am thinking of Mendelssohn in Germany, Israel Baalshem, the founder of the sect of the Chassidim in Podolia, and Elijah Wilna, or as he is more frequently called, the Gaon,[1] the Great One, in Lithuania.

As to Mendelssohn, enough, and perhaps more than enough, has already been written and spoken about his merits in awakening the sense for the beautiful and the harmonious which was almost entirely dormant among the Jews of his age. In regard to the second, namely, Israel Baalshem, I have only to refer the reader to the first essay in this volume. The subject of the present essay will be R. Elijah Wilna, who, among the Jews, as Lessing among the Germans, represented truth, both by his life and by his literary activity.

I say that the Gaon represented truth, but these words must be taken *cum grano salis*. For I do not mean at all to say that he was in possession of the whole truth, still less in *exclusive* possession of it. It is true as we shall learn in the course of this essay, that the Gaon was a genius of the first order. But there are matters of truth, the obtaining of which cannot be accomplished by genius alone. R. Elijah Wilna did not know any other language than Hebrew. Truths, therefore, which are only to be reached through the medium of other languages, remained a secret to him. Again, records of ancient times which are buried in the shelves of remote libraries or under the ruins of past civilisations are not always a matter of intuition. Even the most gifted of men have to wait patiently till these are brought to light by the aid of spade and shovel, or the pen of some obscure copyist. But R. Elijah lived at a time when excavation had as yet done very little for Semitic studies, and when a Jew scarcely got admittance into the great libraries of Europe. Thus much truth which we get now in a very easy way was beyond this seer's eye.

But even if all the libraries on earth had been at his disposal, even if he had read all the cuneiform writings which ornament the British Museum, and had deciphered all the Hieroglyphics which the Louvre possesses, even in that case we should not be justified in terming him a representative of the truth, without qualifying our words.

"Truth," said the old Rabbis, "is the Seal of the Holy One, praised be He." But Heaven has no Lord Chancellor. Neither men nor angels are trusted with the great Seal. They are only allowed to catch a glimpse of it, or rather to long after this glimpse. However, even the longing and effort for this glimpse will bring man into communion with God, and make his life divine. And the life of the Gaon was, as we shall see, one long effort and unceasing longing after the truth.

Again, if I say that the Gaon represented truth, you must not think that he lacked the two other qualities. A life entirely devoted to such a great cause as that of seeking the truth is, *ipso facto*, ideal and harmonious. It is only in his influence on Judaism — more particularly on the Jews in the North of Europe — that this feature in his life becomes more prominent than his other admirable qualities.

In what this truth consisted, how the Gaon arrived at it, and by what means he conveyed it to others, we shall see in the course of this essay.

R. Elijah was born at Wilna in the year 1720. His father, Solomon Wilna, is called by his biographers the great Rabbi Solomon, and is said to have been the descendant of R. Moses Rivkas, the author of a learned work, containing notes to the Code of the Law by R. Joseph Caro.[2]

Having quoted the biographers, I must point out that there are only two biographies of the Gaon: the one by Finn, in his book *Faithful City*,[3] on the celebrities of Wilna, the other by Nachman of Horodna, in his book *Ascension of Elijah*.[4] The former is a very honest account of the Gaon's life, but a little too short. The latter is too long, or rather too much intermixed with that sort of absurd legend, the authors of which are incapable of marking the line which separates the monster from the hero.

Even in the region of imagination we must not for a moment forget the good advice given to us by one of our

greatest scholars who had to deal with a kindred subject:
"He," says this scholar, "who banishes the thought of
higher and lower from his study, degrades it into a mere
means of gratifying his curiosity, and disqualifies it for the
lofty task which it is called upon to perform for modern
society." We shall thus cling to the higher and stop at
the hero.

Our hero was the first-born of five brothers. They
were all famous men in their little world. According to
the tradition in Wilna, Elijah was a lovely child, with
beautiful eyes, and goodly to look at, or as it is expressed
in another place, "as beautiful as an angel!" The tradition, or rather the legend, relates that as a child of six
years he was already the pupil of R. Moses Margalith, the
famous author of a commentary on the Talmud of Jerusalem. At the age of seven years he is said to have already
perplexed the Chief Rabbi of his native town by his controversial skill in Talmudical subjects. At the ·early age
of nine he was acquainted with the contents of the Bible,
the Mishnah, the Talmud and its ancient commentaries;
and even the Cabbalistic works of R. Isaac Loria were no
secret to the youthful scholar.[5] At the age of twelve years
he is said to have acquired the seven liberal arts, and to
have puzzled the scholars of Wilna by his astronomical
knowledge. At thirteen, when according to Jewish law he
attained his majority, he was already the accomplished or
"the great one" (Gaon); so far tradition. I am afraid that
tradition is here, against all experience, too exact in its
dates. But we may learn from it that the child Elijah
showed many signs of the future Gaon, and was therefore
considered as the prodigy of his age. Again it is likewise
pretty certain that no man could boast of having been the

master of Elijah. He was not the product of any school, nor was he biassed by the many prejudices of his time. He was allowed to walk his own way in his struggle after truth.

It is rather an unfortunate thing that history is so much made up of parallels and contrasts that the historian or even the biographer cannot possibly point out the greatness of some men without touching, however slightly, on the smallness of others. It is only natural that every strong shining object should push the minor lights of its surroundings into the background and darken them. Thus, when we are speaking of the superiority of the Gaon, we cannot escape hinting at least at the shortcomings of his contemporaries, as well as of his predecessors.

To indicate briefly in what this superiority consisted, I will premise here a few words from a *Responsum* by one of his great predecessors, the Gaon Rabbi Hai.[6] Consulted by a student as to the meaning of certain mystical passages in the tractate *Chagigah*,[7] Rabbi Hai, in warning his correspondent not to expect from him a long philosophical dissertation, writes as follows : " Know that it never was our business to palliate matters and explain them in a way of which the author never could have thought. This is fashionable with other people, but our method is to explain the words of this or that authority in accordance with his own meaning. We do not pledge ourselves that this meaning is 'right rule' in itself, for there *do* exist statements made by the old authorities that cannot be accepted as norm." Thus far the words of the Gaon of the tenth century, which speak volumes. The Gaon of the eighteenth century followed the same course. All his efforts were directed to this point; namely, to find out the true meaning of the Mishnah, the true meaning of the Gemara,[8] the true meaning of the Gaonim, the true meaning of the great codifiers, and the true meaning of the commentators on the ancient Rabbinical literature. Whether this meaning would be acceptable to us mattered very little to him. His only object was to understand the words of his predecessors, and this he obtained, as we shall soon see, by the best critical means. This was the method of the Gaon; that of other scholars (at least of the great majority) was dictated by entirely different considerations. They would not suffer the idea that the great man could be wrong at times. To them, all that he said was "right rule." Now suppose a great author like Maimonides had overlooked an important passage in the Talmud or any other statement by a great authority, the alternative remaining to them was either to explain away the passage of the Talmud or to give the words of Maimonides a strange meaning. This led originally to the famous method of the *Pilpul* (casuistry), a kind of spiritual gymnastic, which R. Liva of Prague in the sixteenth century, and many others condemned as most pernicious to Judaism and leading to the decay of the study of the Torah.

Now it is beyond doubt that the method of the two Gaonim is the only right one. But, in justice to the casuistic school, which includes many a great name, it is only right to remember that this impartiality towards acknowledged authorities as maintained by our hero is not at all such an easy matter as we imagine. We quote often with great satisfaction the famous saying, *Amicus Plato, amicus Socrates, sed magis amica veritas*, "Plato is our friend, so is Socrates, but Truth is, or rather ought to be, our greatest friend." This sounds very nicely, but let us only realise what difficulties it involves. To be a friend of Socrates or Plato means to know them, or in other words to have a thorough knowledge of the writings of the one and the recorded utterances of the other. But such a knowledge can with most men only be obtained by devoting one's *whole* life to the study of their works, so that there is not left much time for new friendships. And the few who are able to save a few years after long wanderings with these Greek philosophers, seldom see the necessity of new friendships. For what else did those long courtships of Plato or Aristotle mean except that those who conducted them thought that thereby they would wed Truth ?

This impartiality is the more difficult when these friends are invested with a kind of religious authority where humility and submission are most important factors. The history of Lanfranc, the predecessor of Anselm of Canterbury, gives a striking example of what this submission meant in the Middle Ages. One day, we are told, when he was still an ordinary monk, he was reading at the table and pronounced a word as it ought to be pronounced, but not as seemed right to the person presiding, who bade him say it differently ; " as if he had said *docēre*, with the middle syllable long, as is right, and the other had corrected it into *docĕre*, with the middle short, which is wrong ; for that Prior was not a scholar. But the wise man, knowing that he owed obedience rather to Christ than to Donatus, the grammarian, gave up his pronunciation, and said what he was wrongly told to say ; for to make a short syllable long, or a long one short, he knew to be no deadly sin, but not to obey one set over him in God's behalf was no light transgression." [9]

But this admiration — and here we turn again to the Gaon — must not prevent us from believing that Providence is not confined to such ungrammatical Priors, and that the men who are really working on behalf of God are those who teach us to pronounce rightly, and to think rightly, and to take matters as they are, not as we desire them to be on account of our friends.

As for the critical means to which I have alluded, the Gaon himself said somewhere that simplicity is the best criterion of truth, and this is the most characteristic feature of all his literary career. The Gaon studied Hebrew grammar in order to obtain a clear notion of the language in which the Scriptures are written. He tried to attain to the knowledge of the Bible by reading the Bible itself; and was not satisfied to become acquainted with its contents from the numerous quotations which are made from it in Rabbinical literature. Again, he studied mathematics, astronomy, and philosophy, as far as they could be found in Hebrew books. Certainly the Gaon did not study these subjects for their own sake, and they were considered by him only as a means to the end, or as the phrase goes, as the " hand-maidens " of Theology, the queen of all sciences. But it may be looked upon as a mark of great progress in an age when Queen Theology had become rather sulky, continually finding fault with her hand-maidens, and stigmatising every attention paid to them as conducive to disloyalty. To these accusations the Gaon answered that Queen Theology does not study her own interests. Knowledge of all arts and sciences, the Gaon maintained, is necessary for the real understanding of the Torah which embraces the whole of them. From his own writings it is evident that he himself was familiar with Euclid, and his *Ayil Meshulash* contains several original developments of Euclid. It was at his suggestion that a certain Baruch of Sclow translated Euclid into the Hebrew language.

Another way which led the Gaon to the discovery of many truths was his study of the pre-Talmudic literature, and of the Jerusalem Talmud. By some accident or other it came to pass that only the Babylonian Talmud was recognised as a guide *in the practices of religious life.* As the great teachers and their pupils cared more for satisfying the religious wants of their flocks than for theoretic researches, the consequence was that a most important part of the ancient Rabbinic literature was almost entirely neglected by them for many centuries. And it was certainly no exaggeration, when R. Elijah said that even the Gaonim and Maimonides, occupied as they were with the practical part of the law, did not pay sufficient attention to the Talmud of Jerusalem and the Tosephta.[10] The Gaon was no official head of any Jewish community, and was but little troubled by decisions of questions which concern daily life. He was thus in a position to leave for a little while the Babylonian Talmud and to become acquainted with the guides of the guide. I refer to Siphra, Siphré, Mechilta, Tosephta, the Seder Olam,[11] the Minor Tractates,[12] and above all the Talmud of Jerusalem, which, regarded from an historical and critical point of view, is even of more importance than its Babylonian twin-brother. But by this means there came a new light upon the whole of ancient Rabbinic literature. The words of the Torah, the Midrash

G

says, are poor in one place, but we shall find them rich in another place. The Gáon by his acquaintance with the *whole* of the Torah had no difficulty whatever in discovering the rich places. If there was a difficult passage in this or that Tractate, he showed, by giving a reference to some other place, that it was wanting in some words or lines. Obscure passages in the Mishnah he tried to elucidate by parallel passages in the Tosephta. The too complicated controversies of the Babylonian Talmud he tried to explain by comparing them with the more ancient and more simple Talmud of Jerusalem.

There is little to be told of the Gaon's private affairs. Even the date of his marriage with a certain Miss Anna of Kaidon is not mentioned by his biographers. But it may be taken for granted that, in accordance with the custom in Poland, he married at a very early age, say about eighteen years. It was also when a young man that he travelled for some years through Poland and Germany. It is rather difficult to say what his object may have been in making these travels — for the Gaon was not the man to travel for pleasure's sake. Perhaps it was to become acquainted with the great Rabbis of these countries. It is also possible, as others maintain, that the Gaon considered the many privations which a traveller had to endure a hundred and fifty years ago, as an atonement for his imaginary sins. Indeed we find in many ascetic books that travelling, or as they term it "receiving upon oneself to be banished into the exile," [18] is recommended as a very successful substitute for penance. At least it seems that the coachmen whom the Gaon employed on his journeys looked at it from this point of view. One of them went so far in adding to

the privations of the Gaon as to run away with his car-
riage when the Rabbi alighted from it in order to read
his prayers. But the reading of the Eighteen Benedictions [14] must not be interrupted excepting in the case of
danger; and the Gaon did not consider it very dangerous
to be left without money and without luggage.

These travels ended in the year 1745. The Gaon left
Wilna again at a later date with the purpose of going to
Palestine and settling there. But he found so many obstacles on his way that he was soon compelled to give up
his favourite plan and to return to his native town. It is
not known whether he left Wilna again.

The position which the Gaon occupied in Wilna was, as
already hinted, that of a private man. He could never be
prevailed upon to accept the post of Rabbi or any other
office in a Jewish community. I am unable to give the
reason for his declining all the offers made to him in this
direction. But it may be suggested here that it was in
the time of the Gaon that there arose a bitter struggle
between the Rabbi and the Jewish wardens of his native
town, which ended in the abolition of the office of Rabbi.
The history of the struggle is the more irritating, as it
arose from the pettiest reasons imaginable. People actually discovered that there was no light in the house of
the Rabbi after the middle of the night, which fact might
lead to the conclusion that he did not study later than
12 o'clock P.M. What an idle man! And this idleness
was the less pardonable in the eyes of the community, as
the Rabbi's wife was so unfortunate as not to have been
polite enough to some Mrs. Warden. Under such circumstances we must not wonder if the Gaon did not find it
very desirable to meddle with congregational affairs in an

official capacity. The relation of the Gaon to his contemporaries resembles rather the position in the olden times of a Tanna or Amora,[15] who neither enjoyed the title of Nasin or that of Ab Beth Din.[16] Like R. Akiba, or Mar Samuel, the Gaon became influential among his contemporaries only by his teaching and his exemplary life.

It must be said in praise of the Jews of Wilna that, notwithstanding their petty behaviour towards their ecclesiastical chief, they willingly submitted to the authority of the Gaon (who was devoid of all official authority). They revered him as a saint. To converse with the Gaon was considered as a happy event in the life of a Jew in Wilna, to be of any use to him as the greatest distinction a man could attain on earth. But what is remarkable is the readiness with which even scholars acknowledged the authority of the Gaon. Scholars are usually more slow in recognising greatness than simple mortals. Every new luminary does not only outshine their minor lights and thus hurt their personal vanity, but it threatens also sometimes to obscure certain traditions which they wish to keep prominently in view. But the literary genius of the Gaon was too great to be opposed with success, and his piety and devotion to religion far above suspicion. Thus the Gaon was very soon recognised by his contemporaries as their master and guide; not only in literary questions, but also in matters of belief and conduct.

It would lead me too far to name here all the Gaon's disciples. It seems as if all the great scholars in his country considered themselves to be more or less his pupils. The Gaon used to give in the Beth Hammidrash, which he founded, public lectures on various subjects, and the students who attended these lectures also claimed the honour of being called his pupils. I shall mention here only his greatest disciple, R. Chayim Walosin, who, after the Gaon, influenced his countrymen more than any other scholar of that time. This R. Chayim also did not occupy any official post among his brethren. He was a cloth manufacturer by profession, and was very prosperous in his business. But it did not prevent him from being devoted to Hebrew literature, and he enjoyed a wide-spread fame as a great scholar. But as soon as the fame of the Gaon reached him, he left cloth manufactory and scholarship behind, and went to Wilna to "learn Torah" from the mouth of the great master. It must be noticed that even the giving up of his claim to scholarship was no little sacrifice. All our learning, said some scholar in Wilna, disappeared as soon as we crossed the threshold of the Gaon's house. He made every disciple who came into close contact with him begin at the beginning. He taught them Hebrew grammar, Bible, Mishnah, and many other subjects, which were, as already mentioned, very often neglected by the Talmudists of that time. R. Chayim had also to go through all this course. Some would have considered such treatment a degradation. R. Chayim, however, became the more attached to his master for it.

In such a way the life of the Gaon was spent, studying by himself or teaching his pupils. It must be understood that to learn Torah meant for the Gaon more than mere brain work for the purpose of gaining knowledge. To him it was a kind of service to God. Contemporaries who watched him when he was studying the Torah observed that the effect wrought on the personality of the Gaon was the same as when he was praying. With every word his countenance flushed with joy; with every line he was gaining strength for proceeding further. Only by looking at matters from this point of view shall we be able to understand the devotion and the love of the Gaon for study.

There has been, no doubt, among the Russian Jews a strong tendency to exaggerate the intellectual qualities of the Gaon. But one can readily excuse such a tendency. He was gifted by nature with such a wonderful memory that, having read a book once, he was able to recite it by heart for the rest of his life. Not less admirable was his sure grasp. The most complicated controversies in the Talmud, into which other scholars would require whole days and weeks to find their way, the Gaon was able to read by a glance at the pages. Already as a boy he is said to have gone through in a single night the tractates *Zebachim* and *Menachoth*,[17] containing not less than two hundred and thirty pages, the contents of which are sometimes so difficult as to make even an aged scholar despair of understanding them. Again, he possessed so much common-sense that all the intellectual tricks of the casuistic schools did not exist for him. And nevertheless his biographers tell us that he was so much occupied by his studies, that he could not spare more than one hour and a half for sleep out of twenty-four hours. This is, no doubt, an exaggeration. But let us say five hours a day. He had not time to take his meals regularly. He used also, according to tradition, to repeat every chapter in the Bible, every passage in the Talmud, hundreds of times, even if they presented no difficulty at all. But it was, as already said, a matter of love for the Gaon ; of love, not of passing affection.

Nothing on earth could be more despicable to the Gaon than amateurs who dabble with ancient literature. To

understand a thing clearly made him happy. He is said
to have spent more than six months on a single Mishnah
in the tractate *Kilayim*,[18] and felt himself the happiest
man when he succeeded in grasping its real meaning.
Not to be able to go into the depth of a subject, to miss
the truth embedded in a single passage, caused him the
most bitter grief. A story told by his pupil, R. Chayim,
may illustrate this fact. One Friday, narrates R. Chayim,
the servant of the Gaon came to him with the message
that his master wanted to see him as soon as possible.
R. Chayim went instantly. When he came into the house,
he found the Gaon lying in bed with a bandage on his
head and looking very ill. The wife of the Gaon also
reported to him that it was more than three days since
her husband had taken any food, and that he had hardly
enjoyed any sleep all this time. All this misery was
caused by reason of not having been able to understand
some difficult passages in the Talmud of Jerusalem. The
Gaon now asked his disciples to resume with him their
researches. Heaven, he said, might have mercy upon
them and open their eyes, for it is written, "Two are
better than one": and lo! Heaven did have mercy on
them; they succeeded in getting the true meaning of
the passage. The Gaon recovered instantly, and master
and disciple had a very joyful Sabbath.

He is also reported to have said on one occasion, he
would not like to have an angel for his teacher who would
reveal to him all the mysteries of the Torah. Such a condition is only befitting the world to come, but in *this* world
only things which are acquired by hard labour and great
struggle are of any value. The German representative of
truth expressed the same thought in other words, which

are well worth repeating here : " Did the Almighty," says
Lessing, " holding in His right hand Truth and in His left
Search after Truth, deign to tender me the one I might
prefer, in all humility and without hesitation I should
select Search after Truth."

This absorption of all his being in the study of the
Torah may also, I think, account for the fact that his
biographers have so little to say about the family of the
Gaon. Of his wife, we know only that she died in the
year 1783. Not much fuller is our knowledge about his
children. The biographers speak of them as of the family
" which the Lord has blessed," referring to his two sons,
Rabbi Aryeh Leb and Rabbi Abraham, who were known
as great scholars and very pious men. The latter one is
best known by his edition of a collection of smaller Midrashim. Mention is also made of the Gaon's sons-in-law,
especially one Rabbi Moses of Pinsk. But this is all, and
we are told nothing either about their lives or their call-
ings. From his famous letter which he sent to his family
when on his way to Palestine, we see that he was rather
what one may call a severe father. He bids his wife punish his children most severely for swearing, scolding, and
speaking untruth. He also advises her to live as retired
a life as possible. Retirement he considers as a condition
sine qua non for a religious life. He even advises his
daughter to read her prayers at home, for in the synagogue she may get envious of the finer dresses of her
friends, which is a most terrible sin. The only tender
feature in this letter is perhaps where he implores his
wife to be kind to his mother on account of her being a
widow, and it were a great sin to cause her the least an-
noyance. From other passages we may gather that his

family had at times to suffer hunger and cold by the excessive occupation of their father with the study of the Torah and other religious works. In short, the Gaon was a one-sided, severe ascetic, and would never have deserved the title of a good father, a good husband, an amiable man or any other appellation derived from those ordinary "household decencies" which, as Macaulay informs us, half of the tombstones claim for those who lie behind them. But I am very much afraid that many a great man who has made his mark in history could never claim these household virtues as his own. I do not want to enter here into the question whether Judaism be an ascetic religion or not. But even those who think Judaism identical with what is called "making the best of this life," will not dispute the fact that Jewish literature contains within it enough ascetic elements to justify the conduct of our greatest men whose lives were one long-continued self-denial and privation. "The Torah," says the Talmud, "cannot be obtained unless a man is prepared to give his life for it," or as the Talmud puts it, in another place, "if it be thy desire not to die, cease to live before thou diest." This was the principle by which the Gaon's life was actuated. And as he did not spare himself, he could not spare others. We could not expect him to act differently. The Scriptures tell us: "Thou shalt love thy neighbour as thyself." But how is it with the man who never loved himself, who never gave a thought to himself, who never lived for himself, but only for what he considered to be his duty and his mission from God on earth? Such a man we cannot expect to spend his time on coaxing and caressing us. As to the charge of one-sidedness at which I have hinted, if the giving up of everything else for the purpose of devoting oneself to a scholarly and saintly life is one-sidedness, the Gaon must certainly bear this charge; but in a world where there are so many on the other side, we ought, I think, to be only too grateful to Providence for sending us from time to time great and strong one-sided men, who, by their counterbalancing influence, bring God's spoilt world to a certain equilibrium again. To appease my more tender readers, I should like only to say that there is no occasion at all for pitying Mrs. Gaon. It would be a miserable world indeed if a good digestion and stupidity were, as a certain author maintained, the only conditions of happiness. Saints are happy in their sufferings, and noble souls find their happiness in sacrificing themselves for these sufferers.

Another severe feature in the life of the Gaon showed itself in his dispute with the Chassidim. I regret not to be able to enter here even into a brief account of the history of this struggle. I shall only take leave to say that I am afraid each party was right, the Gaon as well as the Chassidim; the latter, in attacking the Rabbis of their time, who mostly belonged to the casuistic schools, and in their intellectual pursuits almost entirely neglected the emotional side of religion; but none the less was the Gaon right in opposing a system which, as I have shown above, involved the danger of leading to a worship of men.

Excepting this incident, the Gaon never meddled with public affairs. He lived in retirement, always occupied with his own education and that of his disciples and friends. It is most remarkable that, in spite of his hard work and the many privations he had to endure, he enjoyed good health almost all his life. He never consulted a doctor. It was not until the year 1791, in the seventieth year of his life, that he began to feel the decline of his health. But he was not much interrupted by the failure of his powers. As a means of recovery, he estéemed very highly the conversation of the preacher Jacob of Dubna, better .known as the Dubna Maggid,[19] whose parables and sallies of wit the Gaon used to enjoy very much. On the eve of the Day of Atonement in the year 1797, he fell very ill and gave his blessing to his children. He died on the third day of the Feast of Tabernacles, with the branch of the Lulab[20] in his hands. The Feast of Joy, relates a contemporary, was turned into days of mourning. In all the streets of Wilna were heard only lamenting and crying voices. The funeral orations delivered on this occasion in Wilna, as well as in other Jewish communities, would form a small library. His disciples wept for their master, the people of Wilna for the ornament of their native town, and the feeling of the Jews in general was that "the Ark of God was taken away."

After the foregoing sketch, the reader will hardly expect me to give an account of the Gaon's literary productions. The results of so long a life and such powers of mind devoted to one cause with such zeal and fervour, would furnish by themselves the subject of a whole series of essays. The tombstone set on his grave by his pious admirers bears the inscription, "The Gaon gave heed and sought and set in order" — that is to say, he wrote commentaries or notes on — "the Bible, the Mishnah, both Talmuds, the Siphré, Siphra, the Zohar, and many other works." Inscriptions on tombstones are proverbial for exaggeration, and we all know the saying, "as mendacious as an epitaph." But a glance at the catalogue of the

British Museum under the heading of Elijah Wilna, will show that this inscription makes a praiseworthy exception. We will find that this list might be lengthened by many other works of great importance for Jewish life and thought. His commentary to the Code of R. Joseph Caro, in which one will find that in many cases he knew the sources of the religious customs and usages, put together in this work, better than its compiler himself, would have been sufficient to place him at the head of Halachic scholarship, whilst his notes and textual emendations to the Tosephta and Seder Olam, to the restoration of which he contributed so much, would have sufficed to establish his fame as a critic of the first order. And this is the more astonishing when we consider that all this was done without manuscripts or any other aid, and by mere intuition. We cannot wonder that scholars who had the opportunity of visiting great libraries and saw how the emendations of the Gaon agreed sometimes with the readings given in the best manuscripts exclaimed very often: "Only by inspiration could he have found out these secrets." We have no need to go so far; we shall simply say with the Talmud, "The powers of the real sage surpass those of the prophet." Nay, even had we possessed only his *Gleanings*, which form a kind of *obiter dicta* on various topics of Jewish literature, the Gaon would have remained a model of clear thinking and real ingenuity for all future generations.

However, a real appreciation of the Gaon's greatness as a scholar would only be possible either by a thorough study of his works, to which I have alluded, or by giving many specimens of them. The short space I am limited to makes such an undertaking impossible. I shall therefore use what remains to me to say a few words on the salutary influence the Gaon had on his countrymen, the Russian Jews.

The Russian Jew is still a riddle to us. We know this strange being only from the Reports of the Board of Guardians or from bombastic phrases in public speeches; for he has always been the victim of platform orators,

> So over violent or over civil,
> That every man with them is God or Devil.

From all, however, that I can gather from the best Jewish writers in Russia, I can only judge that the Russian Jew, when transplanted to a foreign soil, where he is cut off from the past and uncertain of his future, is for the time at least in a position in which his true character cannot be truly estimated. His real life is to be sought in his own country. There, amidst his friends and kinsmen who are all animated by the same ideals, attached to the same traditions, and proud of the same religious and charitable institutions, everything is full of life and meaning to him. Thus, a certain Russian writer addresses his younger colleagues who find so much fault with the bygone world: " Go and see how rich we always were in excellent men. In every town and every village you would find scholars, saints, and philanthropists. Their merits could sustain worlds, and each of them was an ornament of Israel." And he proceeds to give dozens of names of such excellent men, who are not all indeed known to us, but with whom the Russian Jew connects many noble and pious reminiscences of real greatness and heroic self-denial, and of whom he is justly proud.

The focus, however, of all this spiritual life is the Yeshibah (Talmudical College) [21] in Walosin. I hope that a glance at its history and constitution will not be found uninteresting. The intellectual originator of this institution which bears the name *Yeshibah Ets Chayim* (Tree of Life College), [22] was the Gaon himself. Being convinced that the study of the Torah is the very life of Judaism, but that this study must be conducted in a scientific, not in a scholastic way, he bade his chief disciple, the R. Chayim already mentioned, to found a college in which Rabbinical literature should be taught according to his own true method. It would seem that, as long as the Gaon was alive, R. Chayim preferred to be a pupil rather than a teacher. When, however, the Gaon died, R. Chayim did not rest till he had carried out the command of his master, and in the year 1803 the College was opened in Walosin. The cloth manufacturer and disciple now became Rabbi and master. He began on a small scale, teaching at first only a few pupils. But even for the sustenance of a small number he had not sufficient means, and his pious wife sold her jewellery to help him in accomplishing his favourite plan. This is the best refutation of the French proverb *Avare comme une Rabbine.* The number, however, increased daily, and before he died (1828), he was fortunate enough to lecture to a hundred students. The number of students in the year 1888 amounted to 400, and the Russian Jews are thus right in asserting that they have the greatest Talmudical College in the world. It is evident that no private charity by a single man, however great, could suffice to maintain such large numbers. Thus R. Chayim was already compelled to appeal to the liberality of his Russian brethren. The name of R. Chayim, and the still greater name of his master, were recommendation enough, and besides private offerings, many communities promised large sums towards supporting the students in Walosin. From time to time also messengers are sent out by the committee to promote the interests of the Yeshibah. The writers to whom I owe these data tell us that these messengers travel to all parts of the world to collect offerings for Walosin: so that it is a standing joke with the students that the existence of the mythical river Sambatyon [23] may be questioned after all, otherwise it must long have been discovered by these messengers who explore the whole world in their journeys. But it would seem that this world is only a very small one. For the whole income of the Yeshibah has never exceeded the sum of about £1800. Of this a certain part is spent in providing the salaries of the teaching staff and proctors, and on the repairs of the building; whilst the rest is distributed amongst the students. Considering that no scholarship exceeds £13 — it is only the forty immortals of Walosin who receive such high stipends — considering again that the great majority of the students belong to the poorer classes and thus receive no remittance from their parents, we may be sure that the words of the Talmud: "This is the way to study the Torah; eat bread and salt, drink water by measure, sleep on the earth, and live a life of care," are carried out by them literally. But it would seem that the less they eat and the less they sleep, the more they work. Indeed the industry and the enthusiasm of these Bachurim (*alumni*) [24] in the study of the Torah is almost unsurpassable. The official hours alone extend from nine in the morning until ten in the evening, while many of the students volunteer to continue their studies till the middle of the night, or to begin the day at three in the morning.

As to the subject of these studies, it is confined, as may be imagined, to the exploration of the old Rabbinic literature in all its branches. But it would be a mistake to think that the modern spirit has left Walosin quite untouched. It would be impossible that among 400 thinking heads there should not be a few who are interested in mathematics, others again in philosophy or history, while yet others would conjugate the irregular verbs of some classical language when moving to and fro over their Talmud folios and pretending to *"learn."* Indeed, almost all the writers who demand that these subjects should be introduced as obligatory into the programme of Walosin, belonged themselves to this Yeshibah. And it is these writers who betray the secret how secular knowledge is now invading the precincts of Walosin, as well as of other Talmudical Colleges in spite of all obstacles and prohibitions. In conquering these difficulties seem to consist the pleasures of life of many Bachurim at Walosin. Look only at that undergraduate, how, after a heavy day's work he is standing there in the street reading Buckle's *History of Civilisation* in the moonlight! Poor man, he is not so romantic as to prefer the moonlight to a cheerful, warm room, with the more prosaic light of a candle, but he has got tired of knocking at the door, for his landlady, to whom he has neglected to pay rent for the last three terms, made up her mind to let him freeze to-night. But still more cruel to him is his fellow-sufferer, who is also wandering in the streets with an overloaded brain and empty stomach; he roughly shakes him out of his dreams by telling him that Buckle is long ago antiquated, and that he had better study the works of Herbert Spencer, who has spoken the last word on every vital subject in the world. Still these two starving and freezing representatives of English thought in Walosin form only an exception. The general favourites are the representatives of Jewish thought. That such books as the *Guide of the Perplexed*, by Maimonides, the Metaphysical Researches of Levi b. Gershom,[25] and other philosophical works of the Spanish school are read by the Walosin students it is needless to say. These books now form a part of the Rabbinic literature, and it would be almost unorthodox to suspect their readers. But is worth noticing that even the productions of the modern historico-critical school, such as the works of Zunz, Frankel, Graetz, Weiss, are very popular with the Bachurim, being much read and discussed by them.

Thus Walosin deserves rightly to be considered as the centre of Jewish thought in Russia, in which the spirit of the Gaon is still working.

I have very often, however, heard doubts expressed as to the continuance of this spirit when, as it is to be hoped, better times come for the Jews in Russia. Is it not to be feared that liberty and emancipation will render untenable ideas and notions which arose under entirely different circumstances? There is no need of entertaining such fears. Rabbi Jedaiah of Bedres[26] concludes his philosophical work *Examination of the World*, with the following words: "The conclusion of the whole matter is, go either to the right, my heart, or go to the left, but believe all that R. Moses ben Maimon (Maimonides) has believed, the last of the Gaonim by time, but the first in rank." About five hundred years have passed away since these lines were written. Time, as we have seen, has brought another

H

Gaon, and probably Time will favour us in future with still another. But times have also altered. The rebellious hearts of a liberal age are not likely to obey always the command, "believe all that the Gaon said." But the heart of man will in all ages retain idealism enough to love and revere the greatest of men and to follow what was best in them.

IV

NACHMANIDES[1]

R. CHAYIM VITAL, in his *Book of the Transmigrations of Souls*, gives the following bold characteristic of the two great teachers of Judaism, Maimonides and Nachmanides. Their souls both sprang forth from the head of Adam — it is a favourite idea of the Cabbalists to evolve the whole of ideal humanity from the archetype Adam — but the former, Maimonides, had his genius placed on the left curl of Adam, which is all judgment and severity, whilst that of the latter, Nachmanides, had its place on the right curl, which represents rather mercy and tenderness.

I start from these words in order to avoid disappointment. For Nachmanides was a great Talmudist, a great Bible student, a great philosopher, a great controversialist, and, perhaps, also a great physician; in one word, great in every respect, possessed of all the culture of his age. But, as I have already indicated by the passage quoted by way of introduction, it is not of Nachmanides in any of these excellent qualities that I wish to write here. For these aspects of his life and mind I must refer the reader to the works of Graetz, Weiss, Steinschneider, Perles, and others. I shall mostly confine myself to those features and peculiarities in his career and works which will illustrate Nachmanides the tender and compassionate, the

Nachmanides who represented Judaism from the side of emotion and feeling, as Maimonides did from the side of reason and logic.

R. Moses ben Nachman, or Bonastruc de Portas, as he was called by his fellow-countrymen, or Nachmanides, as he is commonly called now, was born in Gerona about the year 1195. Gerona is a little town in the province of Catalonia in Spain. But though in Spain, Gerona was not distinguished for its philosophers or poets like Granada, Barcelona, or Toledo. Situated as it was in the North of Spain, Gerona was under the influence of Franco-Jewish sympathies, and thus its boast lay in the great Talmudists that it produced. I shall only mention the name of R. Zerahiah Hallevi Gerundi — so-called after his native place — whose strictures on the Code of R. Isaac Alfasi, which he began as a youth of nineteen years, will always remain a marvel of critical insight and independent research. Nachmanides is supposed by some authors to have been a descendant of R. Isaac ben Reuben of Barcelona, whose hymns are still to be found in certain rituals. The evidence for this is insufficient, but we know that he was a cousin of R. Jonah Gerundi, not less famous for his Talmudic learning than for his saintliness and piety. Nachmanides thus belonged to the best Jewish families of Gerona. Various great men are mentioned as his teachers, but we have certainty only about two, namely R. Judah ben Yakar, the commentator of the prayers, and R. Meir ben Nathan of Trinquintaines. The mystic, R. Ezra (or Azriel), is indeed alleged to have been his instructor in the Cabbalah, and this is not impossible, as he also was an inhabitant of Gerona; but it is more probable that Nachmanides was initiated into the Cabbalah by the R. Judah just mentioned, who also belonged to the mystical school.

Whoever his masters were, they must have been well satisfied with their promising pupil, for he undertook, at the age of fifteen, to write supplements to the Code of R. Isaac Alfasi. Nor was it at a much later date that he began to compose his work, *The Wars of the Lord*, in which he defends this great codifier against the strictures of R. Zerahiah, to which we have referred above. I shall in the course of this essay have further occasion to speak of this latter work; for the present we will follow the career of its author.

Concerning the private life of Nachmanides very little has come down to us. We only know that he had a family of sons and daughters. He was not spared the greatest grief that can befall a father, for he lost a son; it was on the day of the New Year.[2] On the other hand, it must have been a great source of joy to him when he married his son Solomon to the daughter of R. Jonah, whom he revered as a saint and a man of God. As a token of the admiration in which he held his friend, the following incident may be mentioned. It seems that it was the custom in Spain to name the first child in a family after his paternal grandfather; but Nachmanides ceded his right in behalf of his friend, and thus his daughter-in-law's first son was named Jonah. Another son of Nachmanides whom we know of was Nachman, to whom his father addressed his letters from Palestine, and who also wrote Novellæ to the Talmud, still extant in MS. But the later posterity of Nachmanides is better known to fame. R. Levi ben Gershom was one of his descendants; so was also R. Simeon Duran;[3] whilst R. Jacob

Sasportas, in the eighteenth century,[4] derived his pedigree from Nachmanides in the eleventh generation.

As to his calling, he was occupied as Rabbi and teacher, first in Gerona and afterwards in Barcelona. But this meant as much as if we should say of a man that he is a philanthropist by profession, with the only difference that the treasures of which Nachmanides disposed were more of a spiritual kind. For his livelihood he probably depended upon his medical practice.

I need hardly say that the life of Nachmanides, "whose words were held in Catalonia in almost as high authority as the Scriptures," was not without its great public events. At least we know of two.

The one was about the year 1232, on the occasion of the great struggle about Maimonides' *Guide of the Perplexed*, and the first book of his great Compendium of the Law. The Maimonists looked upon these works almost as a new revelation, whilst the Anti-Maimonists condemned both as heretical, or at least conducive to heresy.[5] It would be profitless to reproduce the details of this sad affair. The motives may have been pure and good, but the actions were decidedly bad. People denounced each other, excommunicated each other, and did not (from either side) spare even the dead from the most bitter calumnies. Nachmanides stood between two fires. The French Rabbis, from whom most of the Anti-Maimonists were recruited, he held in very high esteem and considered himself as their pupil. Some of the leaders of this party were also his relatives. He, too, had, as we shall see later on, a theory of his own about God and the world little in agreement with that of Maimonides. It is worth noting that Nachmanides objected to calling Maimonides "our teacher Moses" (Rabbenu Mosheh),[6] thinking it improper to confer upon him the title by which the Rabbis honoured the Master of the Prophets. The very fact, however, that he had some theory of the Universe shows that he had a problem to solve, whilst the real French Rabbis were hardly troubled by difficulties of a metaphysical character. Indeed, Nachmanides pays them the rather doubtful compliment that Maimonides' work was not intended for them, who were barricaded by their faith and happy in their belief, wanting no protection against the works of Aristotle and Galen, by whose philosophy others might be led astray. In other words, their strength lay in an ignorance of Greek philosophy, to which the cultivated Jews of Spain would not aspire. Nachmanides was also a great admirer of Maimonides, whose virtues and great merits in the service of Judaism he describes in his letter to the French Rabbis. Thus, the only way left open to him was to play the part of the conciliator. The course of this struggle is fully described in every Jewish history. It is sufficient to say that, in spite of his great authority, Nachmanides was not successful in his effort to moderate the violence of either party, and that the controversy was at last settled through the harsh interference of outsiders who well-nigh crushed Maimonists and Anti-Maimonists alike.

The second public event in the life of Nachmanides was his Disputation, held in Barcelona, at the Court and in the presence of King Jayme I., of Aragon, in the year 1263. It was the usual story. A convert to Christianity, named Pablo Christiani, who burned with zealous anxiety to see his former co-religionists saved, after many vain attempts in this direction, applied to the King of Aragon to order Nachmanides to take part in a public disputation. Pablo maintained that he could prove the justice of the Messianic claims of Jesus from the Talmud and other Rabbinic writings. If he could only succeed in convincing the great Rabbi of Spain of the truth of his argument, the bulk of the Jews was sure to follow. By the way, it was the same Talmud which some twenty years previously was, at the instance of another Jewish convert, burned in Paris, for containing passages against Christianity. Nachmanides had to conform with the command of the king, and, on the 21st of July, 1263, was begun the controversy, which lasted for four or five days.

I do not think that there is in the whole domain of literature less profitable reading than that of the controversies between Jews and Christians. These public disputations occasionally forced the Jews themselves to review their position towards their own literature, and led them to draw clearer distinctions between what they regarded as religion and what as folklore. But beyond this, the polemics between Jews and Christians were barren of good results. If you have read one you have read enough for all time. The same casuistry and the same disregard of history turn up again and again. Nervousness and humility are always on the side of the Jews, who know that, whatever the result may be, the end will be persecution; arrogance is always on the side of their antagonists, who are supported by a band of Knights of the Holy Cross, prepared to prove the soundness of their cause at the point of their daggers.

Besides, was there enough common ground between Judaism and thirteenth century Christianity to have justified the hope of a mutual understanding? The Old

Testament was almost forgotten in the Church. The
First Person in the Trinity was leading a sort of shadowy
existence in art, which could only be the more repulsive
to a Jew on that account. The largest part of Church
worship was monopolised by devotion to the Virgin
Mother, prayers to the saints, and kneeling before their
relics. And a Jew may well be pardoned if he did not
entertain higher views of this form of worship than Luther and Knox did at a later period. It will thus not be
worth our while to dwell much on the matter of this
controversy, in which the essence of the real dispute is
scarcely touched. There are only two points in it which
are worth noticing. The first is that Nachmanides declared the Agadoth[7] in the Talmud to be only a series
of sermons (he uses this very word), expressing the individual opinions of the preacher, and thus possessing no
authoritative weight. The convert Pablo is quite aghast
at this statement, and accuses Nachmanides of heter-
odoxy.

Secondly, — and here I take leave to complete the
rather obscure passage in the controversy by a parallel
in his book, *The Date of Redemption*,[8] quoted by Azariah
de Rossi — that the question of the Messiah is not of that
dogmatic importance to the Jews that Christians imagine.
For even if Jews supposed their sins to be so great that
they forfeited all the promises made to them in the Scriptures, or that, on some hidden ground, it would please the
Almighty never to restore their national independence,
this would in no way alter the obligations of Jews towards
the Torah. Nor is the coming of the Messiah desired by
Jews as an end in itself. For it is not the goal of their
hopes that they shall be able again to eat of the fruit of

Palestine, or enjoy other pleasures there; not even the chance of the restoration of sacrifices and the worship of the Temple is the greatest of Jewish expectations (connected with the appearance of the Messiah). What makes them long for his coming is the hope that they will then witness, in the company of the prophets and priests, a greater spread of purity and holiness than is now possible. In other words, the possibility for them to live a holy life after the will of God will be greater than now. But, on the other hand, considering that such a godly life under a Christian government requires greater sacrifices than it would under a Jewish king; and, considering again that the merits and rewards of a good act increase with the obstacles that are in the way of executing it — considering this, a Jew might even prefer to live under the King of Aragon than under the Messiah, where he would perforce act in accordance with the precepts of the Torah.

Now there is in this statement much that has only to be looked upon as a compliment to the government of Spain. I am inclined to think that if the alternative laid before Nachmanides had been a really practical one, he would have decided in favour of the clement rule of the Messiah in preference to that of the most cruel king on earth. But the fact that he repeats this statement in another place, where there was no occasion to be over polite to the Government, tends to show, as we have said, that the belief in the Messiah was not the basis on which Nachmanides' religion was built up.

The result of the controversy is contested by the different parties; the Christian writers claim the victory for Pablo, whilst the Jewish documents maintain that the issue was with Nachmanides. In any case, "*Der Jude wird verbrannt.*" For in the next year (1264) all the books of the Jews in Aragon were confiscated and submitted to the censorship of a commission, of which the well-known author of the *Pugio Fidei*, Raymund Martini, was, perhaps, the most important member. The books were not burned this time, but had to suffer a severe mutilation; the anti-Christian passages, or such as were supposed to be so, were struck out or obliterated. Nachmanides' account of the controversy, which he probably published from a sense of duty towards those whom he represented, was declared to contain blasphemies against the dominant religion. The pamphlet was condemned to be burned publicly, whilst the author was, as it seems, punished with expulsion from his country. It is not reported where Nachmanides found a home during the next three years; probably he had to accept the hospitality of his friends, either in Castile or in the south of France; but we know that in the year 1267 he left Europe and emigrated to Palestine.

Nachmanides was, at this juncture of his life, already a man of about seventy. But it would seem as if the seven decades which he had spent in the Spanish Peninsula were only meant as a preparation for the three years which he was destined to live in the Holy Land, for it was during this stage of his life that the greatest part of his *Commentary on the Pentateuch* was written. In this work, as is agreed on all sides, his finest thoughts and noblest sentiments were put down.

Before proceeding to speak of his works, let us first cast a glance at his letters from Palestine, forming as they do a certain link between his former life and that

which was to occupy him exclusively for the rest of his
days. We have three letters, the first of which I shall
translate here *in extenso.*

The letter was written soon after his arrival at
Jerusalem in the year 1267. It was addressed to his
son Nachman, and runs as follows : —

> " The Lord shall bless thee, my son Nachman, and thou shalt
> see the good of Jerusalem. Yea, thou shalt see thy children's
> children (Ps. cxxviii.), and thy table shall be like that of our
> father Abraham ! [9] In Jerusalem, the Holy City, I write this
> letter. For, thanks and praise unto the rock of my salvation,
> I was thought worthy by God to arrive here safely on the 9th
> of the month of Elul, and I remained there till the day after the
> Day of Atonement. Now I intend going to Hebron, to the
> sepulchre of our ancestors, to prostrate myself, and there to dig
> my grave. But what am I to say to you with regard to the
> country ? Great is the solitude and great the wastes, and, to
> characterise it in short, the more sacred the places, the greater
> their desolation ! Jerusalem is more desolate than the rest
> of the country : Judæa more than Galilee. But even in this
> destruction it is a blessed land. It has about 2000 inhabitants,
> about 300 Christians live there who escaped the sword of the
> Sultan. There are no Jews. For since the arrival of the Tar-
> tars, some fled, others died by the sword. There are only two
> brothers, dyers by trade, who have to buy their ingredients
> from the government. There the Ten Men [10] meet, and on
> Sabbaths they hold service at their house. But we encouraged
> them, and we succeeded in finding a vacant house, built on pillars
> of marble with a beautiful arch. That we took for a synagogue.
> For the town is without a master, and whoever will take possession
> of the ruins can do so. We gave our offerings towards the repairs
> of the house. We have sent already to Shechem to fetch some
> scrolls of the Law from there which had been brought thither
> from Jerusalem at the invasion of the Tartars. Thus they will
> organise a synagogue and worship there. For continually people
> crowd to Jerusalem, men and women, from Damascus, Zobah

(Aleppo),[11] and from all parts of the country to see the Sanctuary and to mourn over it. He who thought us worthy to let us see Jerusalem in her desertion, he shall bless us to behold her again, built and restored, when the glory of the Lord will return unto her. But you, my son, and your brothers and the whole of our family, you all shall live to see the salvation of Jerusalem and the comfort of Zion. These are the words of your father who is yearning and forgetting, who is seeing and enjoying, Moses ben Nachman. Give also my peace to my pupil Moses, the son of Solomon, the nephew of your mother. I wish to tell him . . . that there, facing the holy temple, I have read his verses, weeping bitterly over them. May he who caused his name to rest in the Holy Temple increase your peace together with the peace of the whole community."

This letter may be illustrated by a few parallels taken from the appendix to Nachmanides' *Commentary to the Pentateuch*, which contains some rather incoherent notes which the author seems to have jotted down when he arrived in Jerusalem. After a lengthy account of the material as well as the spiritual glories of the holy city in the past, he proceeds to say : —

"A mournful sight I have perceived in thee (Jerusalem) ; only one Jew is here, a dyer, persecuted, oppressed and despised. At his house gather great and small when they can get the Ten Men. They are wretched folk, without occupation and trade, consisting of a few pilgrims and beggars, though the fruit of the land is still magnificent and the harvests rich. Indeed, it is still a blessed country, flowing with milk and honey. . . . Oh! I am the man who saw affliction. I am banished from my table, far removed from friend and kinsman, and too long is the distance to meet again. . . . I left my family, I forsook my house. There with my sons and daughters, and with the sweet and dear children whom I have brought up on my knees, I left also my soul. My heart and my eyes will dwell with them for ever. . . . But the loss of all this and of every other glory my eyes saw is compensated by having now the joy of being a day in thy courts (O Jerusalem), visiting the ruins of the Temple and crying over the ruined Sanctuary; where I am permitted to caress thy stones, to fondle thy dust, and to weep over thy ruins. I wept bitterly, but I found joy in my tears. I tore my garments, but I felt relieved by it."

Of some later date is his letter from Acra, which may be considered as a sort of ethical will, and which has been justly characterised as a eulogy of humility. Here is an extract from it: —

"Accustom yourself to speak gently to all men at all times, and thus you will avoid anger, which leads to so much sin. . . . Humility is the first of virtues; for if you think how lowly is man, how great is God, you will fear Him and avoid sinfulness. On the humble man rests the divine glory; the man that is haughty to others denies God. Look not boldly at one whom you address. . . . Regard every one as greater than thyself. . . . Remember always that you stand before God, both when you pray and when you converse with others. . . . Think before you speak. . . . Act as I have bidden you, and your words, and deeds, and thoughts, will be honest, and your prayers pure and acceptable before God."

The third letter is addressed to his son (R. Solomon?) who was staying (in the service of the king) in Castile. It is in its chief content a eulogy of chastity.[12] Probably Nachmanides had some dread of the dangerous allurements of the court, and he begs his son never to do anything of which he knows that his father would not approve, and to keep his father's image always before his eyes.

As to his works, we may divide them into two classes. The one would contain those of a strictly legalistic (Halachic), whilst the other those of a more homiletic-exegetical and devotional character (Agadic). As already indicated in the preliminary lines of this paper, I cannot dwell long

on the former cla ss of our author's writings. It consists
either of Glosses or Novellæ to the Talmud, in the style
and manner of the French Rabbis, or of Compendia of
certain parts of th e Law after the model set by R. Isaac
Alfasi or Maimoni des, or in defences of the "Earlier Authorities" against the strictures made on them by a later
generation. A few words must be said with regard to these
defences; for they reveal that deep respect for authority
which forms a spe cial feature of Nachmanides' writings.
His *Wars of the Lord*, in which he defends Alfasi against
R. Zerahiah of Gerona, was undertaken when he was very
young, whilst his defence of the author of the *Halachoth
Gedoloth* [13] against the attacks of Maimonides, which he
began at a much more mature age, shows the same deference "to the great ones of the past." Indeed, he says in
one place, "We bow before them (the earlier authorities),
and though their words are not quite evident to us we
submit to them"; or, as he expresses himself elsewhere,
"Only he who dips (deeply enough) in the wisdom of the
'ancient ones' will drink the pure (old) wine." But it
would be unjust to the genius of Nachmanides to represent him as a blind worshipper of authority. Humble and
generous in disposition, he certainly would bow before
every recognised authority, and he would also think it his
duty to take up the cudgels for him as long as there was
even the least chance of making an honourable defence.
But when this chance had gone, when Nachmanides was
fully convinced that his hero was in the wrong, he followed
no guide but truth. "Notwithstanding," he says in his
introduction to the defences of the *Halachoth Gedoloth*,
"my desire and delight to be the disciple of the Earlier
Authorities, to maintain their views and to assert them, I

do not consider myself a 'donkey carrying books.' I will explain their way and appreciate their value, but when their views are inconceivable to my thoughts, I will plead in all modesty, but shall judge according to the sight of my eyes. And when the meaning is clear I shall flatter none, for the Lord gives wisdom in all times and ages." But, on the other hand, there seems to have been a certain sort of literary agnosticism about Nachmanides which made it very difficult for him to find the "clear meaning." The passage in the *Wars of the Lord* to the effect "that there is in the art (of commenting) no such certain demonstration as in mathematics or astronomy," is well known and has often been quoted; but still more characteristic of this literary agnosticism is the first paragraph of the above-mentioned defences of the *Halachoth Gedoloth.* Whilst all his predecessors accepted, on the authority of R. Simlai,[14] the number (613) of the commandments as an uncontested fact, and based their compositions on it, Nachmanides questions the whole matter, and shows that the passages relating to this enumeration of laws are only of a homiletical nature, and thus of little consequence. Nay, he goes so far as to say, " Indeed the system how to number the commandments is a matter in which I suspect all of us (are mistaken) and the truth must be left to him who will solve all doubts." We should thus be inclined to think that this adherence to the words of the earlier Authorities was at least as much due to this critical scepticism as to his conservative tendencies.

The space left to me I shall devote to the second class of his writings, in which Nachmanides worked less after given types. These reveal to us more of his inner being, and offer us some insight into his theological system.

The great problem which seems to have presented itself to Nachmanides' mind was less how to reconcile religion with reason than how to reconcile man with religion. What is man? The usual answer is not flattering. He is an animal that owes its existence to the same instinct that produces even the lower creatures, and he is condemned, like them, to go to a place of worm and maggot. But, may not one ask, why should a creature so lowly born, and doomed to so hapless a future, be burdened with the awful responsibility of knowing that he is destined " to give reckoning and judgment before the King of kings, the Holy One, blessed be He " ? It is true that man is also endowed with a heavenly soul, but this only brings us back again to the antithesis of flesh and spirit which was the stumbling-block of many a theological system. Nor does it help us much towards the solution of the indicated difficulty ; for what relation can there be between this *materia impura* of body and the pure intellect of soul ? And again, must not the unfavourable condition in which the latter is placed through this uncongenial society heavily clog and suppress all aspiration for perfection ? It is " a house divided against itself," doomed to an everlasting contest, without hope for co-operation or even of harmony.

The works *The Sacred Letter* and *The Law of Man* may be considered as an attempt by Nachmanides, if not to remove, at least to relieve the harshness of this antithesis. The former, in which he blames Maimonides for following Aristotle in denouncing certain desires implanted in us by nature as ignominious and unworthy of man, may, perhaps, be characterised as a vindication of the flesh from a religious point of view. The contempt in

I

which "that Greek," as Nachmanides terms Aristotle, held the flesh is inconsistent with the theory of the religious man, who believes that everything (including the body, with all its functions) is created by God, whose work is perfect and good, without impure or inharmonious parts. It is only sin and neglect that disfigure God's creations. I cannot enter into any further details of this work, but I may be permitted to remark that there is a very strong similarity between the tendency of the *Sacred Letter* and certain leading ideas of Milton. Indeed, if the first two chapters of the former were a little condensed and put into English, they could not be better summarised than by the famous lines in the *Paradise Lost* : —

> Whatever hypocrites austerely talk
> Of purity, and place, and innocence,
> Defaming as impure what God declares
> Pure, and commands to some, leaves free to all,
> Our Maker bids increase ; who bids abstain
> But our destroyer, foe to God and man ?
> Hail, wedded love, mysterious law! . . .
> Far be it that I should write thee sin or blame
> Or think thee unbefitting holiest place,
> Perpetual fountain of domestic sweets.

The second of these two works, the *Law of Man*, may be regarded as a sanctification of grief, and particularly of the grief of griefs, death. The bulk of the book is legalistic, treating of mourning rites, burial customs, and similar topics ; but there is much in the preface which bears on our subject. For here again Nachmanides takes the opportunity of combating a chilling philosophy, which tries to arm us against suffering by stifling our emotions.

" My son," he says, " be not persuaded by certain propositions of the great philosophers who endeavour to
harden our hearts and to deaden our sensations by their
idle comfort, which consists in denying the past and de-
spairing of the future. One of them has even declared
that there is nothing in the world over the loss of which
it is worth crying, and the possession of which would
justify joy. This is an heretical view. Our perfect
Torah bids us to be joyful in the day of prosperity and
to shed tears in the day of misfortune. It in no way
forbids crying or demands of us to suppress our grief. On
the contrary, the Torah suggests to us that to mourn over
heavy losses is equivalent to a service of God, leading
us, as it does, to reflect on our end and ponder over our
destiny."

This destiny, as well as Reward and Punishment in
general, is treated in the concluding chapter of the *Law
of Man*, which is known under the title of *The Gate of
Reward*.[15] Nachmanides does not conceal from himself
the difficulties besetting inquiries of this description.
He knows well enough that in the last instance we must
appeal to that implicit faith in the inscrutable justice of
God with which the believer begins. Nevertheless he
thinks that only the " despisers of wisdom " would fail
to bring to this faith as full a conviction as possible, which
latter is only to be gained by speculation. I shall have
by and by occasion to refer to the results of this speculation. Here we must only notice the fact of Nachmanides
insisting on the *bodily* resurrection which will take place
after the coming of the Messiah, and will be followed by
the *Olam Habba* [16] (the life in the world to come) of which
the Rabbis spoke.

Irrational as this belief may look, it is only a consequence of his theory, which, as we have seen, assigns even
to the flesh an almost spiritual importance. Indeed, he
thinks that the soul may have such an influence on the
body as to transform the latter into so pure an essence
that it will become safe for eternity. For, as he hints in
another place, by the continual practising of a thing the
whole man, the body included, becomes so identified with
the thing that we call him after it, just as the Holy Singer
said : I am prayer,[17] so that —

> Oft converse with heavenly habitants
> Begins to cast a beam on the outward shape,
> The unpolluted temple of the mind,
> And turns it by degrees to the soul's essence,
> Till all be made immortal.

But if even the body holds such a high position as to
make all its instincts and functions, if properly regulated,
a service of God, and to destine it for a glorious future of
eternal bliss and rejoicing in God, we can easily imagine
what a high place the soul must occupy in the system of
Nachmanides. To be sure it is a much higher one than
that to which philosophy would fain admit her. A beautiful parable of the Persian poet Yellakadeen (quoted by
the late Mr. Lowell) narrates that " One knocked at the
beloved's door, and a voice asked from within, ' Who is
there ? ' and he answered, ' It is I.' Then the voice said,
' This house will not hold me and thee,' and the door was
not opened. Then went the lover into the desert and
fasted and prayed in solitude, and after a year he returned
and knocked again at the door, and again the voice asked
' Who is there ? ' and he said ' It is thyself '; and the door

was opened to him." This is also the difference between
the two schools — the mystical and the philosophical —
with regard to the soul. With the rationalist the soul is
indeed a superior abstract intelligence created by God, but,
like all His creations, has an existence of its own, and is
thus separated from God. With the mystic, however, the
soul is God, or a direct emanation from God. "For he
who breathes into another thing (Gen. ii. 7) gives unto it
something of his own breath (or soul)," and as it is said in
Job xxxii. 8, "And the soul of the Almighty giveth them
understanding." This emanation, or rather immanence —
for Nachmanides insists in another place that the Hebrew
term employed for it, *Aziluth*,[18] means a permanent
dwelling with the thing emanating — which became manifest with the creation of man, must not be confounded
with the moving soul (or the *Nephesh Chayah*),[19] which is
common to man with all creatures.

It may be remarked here that Nachmanides endows all
animals with a soul which is derived from the "Superior
Powers," and its presence is proved by certain marks of
intelligence which they show. By this fact he tries to
account for the law prohibiting cruelty to animals, "all
souls belonging to God." Their original disposition was,
it would seem, according to Nachmanides, peaceful and
harmless.

> About them frisking played
> All beasts of earth, since wild, and of all chace
> In wood or wilderness, forest or den.

It was only after man had sinned that war entered into
creation, but with the coming of the Messiah, when sin
will disappear, all the living beings will regain their

primæval gentleness, and be reinstituted in their first rights.

The special soul of man, however, or rather the "over-soul," was pre-existent to the creation of the world, treasured up as a wave in the sea or fountain of souls — dwelling in the eternal light and holiness of God. There, in God, the soul abides in its ideal existence before it enters into its material life through the medium of man ; though it must be noted that, according to Nachmanides' belief in the Transmigration of souls, it is not necessary to perceive in the soul of every new-born child, "a fresh message from heaven" coming directly from the fountain-head. Nachmanides finds this belief indicated in the commandment of levirate marriage, where the child born of the deceased brother's wife inherits not only the name of the brother of his actual father, but also his soul, and thus perpetuates his existence on earth. The fourth verse of Ecclesiastes ii. Nachmanides seems to interpret to mean that the very generation which passes away comes up again, by which he tries to explain the difficulty of God's visiting the iniquity of the fathers on their children ; the latter being the very fathers who committed the sins. However, whatever trials and changes the soul may have to pass through during its bodily existence, its origin is in God and thither it will return in the end, "just as the waters rise always to the same high level from which their source sprang forth."

It is for this man, with a body so superior, and a soul so sublime — more sublime than the angels — that the world was *created*. I emphasise the last word, for the belief in the creation of the world by God from nothing forms, according to Nachmanides, the first of the three fundamental dogmas of Judaism. The other two also refer to God's relation to the world and man. They are the belief in God's Providence and his *Yediah*.[20] Creation from nothing is for Nachmanides the keynote to his whole religion, since it is only by this fact, as he points out in many places, that God gains real dominion over nature. For, as he says, as soon as we admit the eternity of matter, we must (logically) deny God even "the power of enlarging the wing of a fly, or shortening the leg of an ant." But the whole Torah is nothing if not a record of God's mastery in and over the world, and of His miraculous deeds. One of the first proclamations of Abraham to his generation was that God is the Lord (or Master) of the world (Gen. xviii. 33). The injunction given to Abraham, and repeated afterwards to the whole of Israel (Gen. xvii. 2, and Deut. xviii. 13), to be perfect with God, Nachmanides numbers as one of the 613 commandments, and explains it to mean that man must have a whole belief in God without blemish or reservation, and acknowledge Him possessed of power over nature and the world, man and beast, devil and angel, power being attributable to Him alone. Indeed, when the angel said to Jacob, "Why dost thou ask after my name" (Gen. xxxii. 29), he meant to indicate by his question the impotence of the heavenly host, so that there is no use in knowing their name, the power and might belonging only to God.

We may venture even a step further, and maintain that in Nachmanides' system there is hardly room left for such a thing as nature or "the order of the world." There are only two categories of miracles by which the world is governed, or in which God's Providence is seen. The one is the category of the manifest miracles, as the ten plagues in Egypt, or the crossing of the Red Sea; the other is that of the hidden miracles, which we do not perceive as such, because of their frequency and continuity. "No man," he declares, "can share in the Torah of our Teacher, Moses (that is, can be considered a follower of the Jewish religion), unless he believes that all our affairs and events, whether they concern the masses or the individual, are all miracles (worked by the direct will of God), attributing nothing to nature or to the order of the world." Under this second order he classes all the promises the Torah makes to the righteous, and the punishments with which evil-doers are threatened. For, as he points out in many places, there is nothing in the nature of the commandments themselves that would make their fulfilment necessarily prolong the life of man, and cause the skies to pour down rain, or, on the other hand, would associate disobedience to them with famine and death. All these results can, therefore, only be accomplished in a supernatural way by the direct workings of God.

Thus miracles are raised to a place in the regular scheme of things, and the difficulty regarding the possibility of God's interferences with nature disappears by their very multiplication. But a still more important point is, that, by this unbroken chain of miracles, which unconditionally implies God's presence to perform them, Nachmanides arrives at a theory establishing a closer contact between the Deity and the world than that set forth by other thinkers. Thus, he insists that the term *Shechinah*, or *Cabod*[21] (Glory of God), must not be understood, with some Jewish philosophers, as something separate from God, or as *glory created* by God. "Were this the case," he proceeds to say, "we could not possibly say, 'Blessed be the glory of the Lord from his place,' since every mark of worship to anything *created* involves the sin of idolatry." Such terms as *Shechinah*, or *Cabod*, can therefore only mean the immediate divine presence. This proves, as may be noted in passing, how unphilosophical the idea of those writers is who maintain that the rigid monotheism of the Jews makes God so transcendental that He is banished from the world. As we see, it is just this assertion of His absolute Unity which not only suffers no substitute for God, but also removes every separation between Him and the world. Hence also Nachmanides insists that the prophecy even of the successors of Moses was a direct communion of God with the prophet, and not, as others maintained, furnished through the medium of an angel.

The third fundamental dogma, *Yediah*, includes, according to Nachmanides, not only the omniscience of God — as the term is usually translated — but also His recognition of mankind and His special concern in them. Thus, he explains the words in the Bible with regard to Abraham, "For I know him" (Gen. xviii. 19), to indicate the special attachment of God's Providence to the patriarch, which, on account of his righteousness, was to be uninterrupted for ever; whilst in other places we have to understand, under God's knowledge of a thing, his determination to deal with it compassionately, as, for instance, when Scripture says that God knew (Exod. ii. 25), it means that His relation to Israel emanated from His attribute of mercy and love. But just as God knows (which means loves) the world, He requires also to be recognised and known by it. "For this was the purpose of the whole creation, that man should recognise and know Him and give praise to His name," as

it is said, " Everything that is called by my name (meaning, chosen to promulgate God's name), for my glory have
I created it."

It is this fact which gives Israel their high prerogative,
for by receiving the Torah they were the first to know
God's name, to which they remained true in spite of all
adversities; and thus accomplished God's intention in
creating the world. It is, again, by this Torah that the
whole of Israel not only succeeded in being real prophets
(at the moment of the Revelation), but also became *Segu-
lah*,[22] which indicates the inseparable attachment between
God and His people, whilst the righteous who never dis-
obey His will become the seat of His throne.

The position of the rest of humanity is also determined
by their relation to the Torah. " It is," Nachmanides tells
us, " a main principle to know that all that man contrives
to possess of knowledge and wisdom is only the fruits of
the Torah or the fruits of its fruits. But for this knowledge there would be no difference between man and the
lower animated species. The existence of the civilised
nations of the world does not disprove this rule " both
Christians and Mahometans being also the heirs of the
Torah. For when the Romans gained strength over
Israel they made them translate the Torah which they
studied, and they even accommodated some of their laws
and institutions to those of the Bible." Those nations,
however, who live far away from the centre of the world
(the Holy Land) and never come into contact with Israel
are outside the pale of civilisation, and can hardly be
ranked together with the human species. " They are the
isles afar off, that have not heard my fame, neither have
seen my glory."

What Nachmanides meant by maintaining that all knowledge and wisdom were "the fruits of the Torah, or the fruits of these fruits," will be best seen from his *Commentary on the Pentateuch*. I have already made use of this Commentary in the preceding quotations, but, being the greatest of the works of Nachmanides, it calls for some special attention by itself. Its general purpose is edification, or as he says, "to appease the mind of the students (labouring under persecution and troubles) when they read the portion on Sabbaths and festivals, and to attract their heart by simple explanations and sweet words." The explanations occupy a considerable space. As Dr. Perles has shown in his able essay on this work of Nachmanides, our author neglected no resource of philology or archæology accessible in his age which could contribute to establish the "simple explanations" on a sound scientific basis. The prominent feature of this Commentary, however, is the "sweet words." Indeed, how sweet and soothing to his contemporaries must have been such words as we read at the end of the "Song of Moses" (Deut. xxxii.): "And behold there is nothing conditional in this Song. It is a charter testifying that we shall have to suffer heavily for our sins, but that, nevertheless, God will not destroy us, being reconciled to us (though we shall have no merits), and forgiving our sins for his name's sake alone. . . . And so our Rabbis said, Great is this song, embracing as it does both the past (of Israel) and the future, this world and the world to come. . . . And if this song were the composition of a mere astrologer we should be constrained to believe in it, considering that all its words were fulfilled. How much more have we to hope with all our hearts and to trust to the word of God, through the mouth of his prophet Moses, the faithful in all his house, like unto whom there was none, whether before him or after him." A part of these sweet words may also be seen in the numerous passages in which he attempts to account for various laws, and to detect their underlying principles.

For though "the Torah is the expression of God's simple and absolute will, which man has to follow without any consideration of reward," still this will is not arbitrary, and even that class of laws which are called *chukkim* [23] (which means, according to some Jewish commentators, motiveless decrees) have their good reasons, notwithstanding that they are unfathomable to us. "They are all meant for the good of man, either to keep aloof from us something hurtful, or to educate us in goodness, or to remove from us an evil belief and to make us know his name. This is what they (the Rabbis) meant by saying that commandments have a purifying purpose, namely, that man being purified and tried by them becomes as one without alloy of bad thoughts and unworthy qualities." Indeed, the soul of man is so sensitive to every impurity that it suffers a sort of infection even by an unintentional sin. Hence the injunction to bring a *Korban* (sacrifice) even in this case; the effect of the *Korban*, as its etymology (*Karab*) [24] indicates, is to bring man back to God, or rather to facilitate this approach. All this again is, as Nachmanides points out, only an affluence from God's mercy and love to mankind. God derives no benefit from it. "If he be righteous what can he give thee?" And even those laws and institutions which are intended to commemorate God's wonders and the creation of the world (for instance, the Passover festival and the Sabbath) are not meant for His glorification, or, as Heine maliciously expressed it : —

Der Weltkapellenmeister hier oben
Er selbst sogar hört gerne loben
Gleichfalls seine Werke. . . .

" For all the honour (we give to Him), and the praising of
His work are counted by Him less than nothing and as
vanity to Him." What He desires is that we may know
the truth, and be confirmed in it, for this makes us worthy
of finding in Him " our Protector and King."

The lessons which Nachmanides draws from the various
Biblical narratives also belong to these " sweet words."
They are mostly of a typical character. For, true as all
the stories in the Scriptures are, " the whole Torah is," as
he tells us (with allusion to Gen. v. 1.), "the book of the
generations of Adam," or, as we should say, a history of
humanity written in advance. Thus the account of the
six days of the creation is turned into a prophecy of the
most important events which would occur during the succeeding six thousand years, whilst the Sabbath is a fore-
cast of the millennium in the seventh thousand, which will
be the day of the Lord. Jacob and Esau are, as in the
old Rabbinic homilies generally, the prototypes of Israel
and Rome; and so is the battle of Moses and Joshua with
Amalek indicative of the war which Elijah and the
Messiah the son of Joseph will wage against Edom (the
prototype of Rome), before the Redeemer from the house
of David will appear.[25] Sometimes these stories convey
both a moral and a pre-justification of what was destined to
happen to Israel. So Nachmanides' remarks with reference to Sarah's treatment of Hagar (Gen. xvi. 6): " Our
mother Sarah sinned greatly by inflicting this pain on
Hagar, as did also Abraham, who allowed such a thing to
pass; but God saw her affliction and rewarded her by a

son (the ancestor of a wild race), who would inflict on the seed of Abraham and Sarah every sort of oppression." In this he alluded to the Islamic empires. Nor does he approve of Abraham's conduct on the occasion of his coming to Egypt, when he asked Sarah to pass as his sister (Gen. xii.). "Unintentionally," Nachmanides says, "Abraham, under the fear of being murdered, committed a great sin when he exposed his virtuous wife to such a temptation. For he ought to have trusted that God would save both him and his wife. . . . It is on account of this deed that his children had to suffer exile under the rule of Pharaoh. There, where the sin was committed, also the judgment took place." It is also worth noticing that, in opposition to Maimonides, he allows no apology for the attack of Simeon and Levi on the population of Shechem (Gen. xxxiv. 25). It is true that they were idolaters, immoral, and steeped in every abomination ; but Jacob and his sons were not commissioned with executing justice on them. The people of Shechem trusted their word, therefore they ought to have spared them. Hence Jacob's protest, and his curse against their wrath, which would have been quite unjustified had he looked on the action of his sons as a good work.

Besides these typical meanings, the matters of the Torah have also their symbolical importance, which places them almost above the sphere of human conception ; they are neither exactly what they seem to be nor entirely what their name implies, but a reflex from things unseen, which makes any human interference both preposterous and dangerous. Of "the things *called* Tree of Life and Tree of Knowledge," Nachmanides tells us that their mystery is very great, reaching into higher worlds. Otherwise, why should God, who is good and the dispenser of good, have prevented Adam from eating the fruit (of the latter), whilst in another place he says : " And if thou wilt be worthy, and understand the mystery of the word *Bereshith*[26] (with which the Torah begins), thou wilt see that in truth the Scripture, though apparently speaking of matters here below (on earth), is always pointing to things above (heaven); " for "every glory and every wonder, and every deep mystery, and all beautiful wisdom are hidden in the Torah, sealed up in her treasures."

It is very characteristic of the bent of Nachmanides' mind, that he is perhaps the first Jewish writer who mentions the apocryphal book *The Wisdom of Solomon*, which he knew from a Syriac version, and which he believed to be genuine. And when we read there (vii. 7–25), "Wherefore I prayed and understanding was given to me. I called upon God and the spirit of wisdom came upon me. . . . For God has given me unmistakable knowledge to know how the world was made, and the operations of the planets. The beginning, ending, and midst of the times, the alterations and the turnings of the sun, the changes of the seasons, the natures of the living creatures and the furies of the wild beasts, the force of the spirits and the reasonings of men, the diversities of plants and the virtues of the roots. All such things that are either secret or manifest, them I knew "— the wise king was, according to Nachmanides (who quotes the passages which I have just cited), speaking of the Torah, which is identical with this wisdom, a wisdom which existed before the creation, and by which God planned the world. Hence it bears the impression of all the universe, whilst on the other hand when it is said, "The king brought me into his chambers," those secret recesses of the Torah are meant in which all the great mysteries relating to Creation and to the Chariot (Ezekiel i.) are hidden.

We must content ourselves with these few sparks struck from the glowing fires of these inner compartments, which, imperfectly luminous as my treatment has left them, may yet shed some light on the personality of Nachmanides, which is the main object of this essay. But I do not propose to accompany the mystic into the " chambers of the king," lest we may soon get into a labyrinth of obscure terms and strange ways of thinking for which the Ariadne thread is still wanting. We might also be confronted by the Fifty Gates of Understanding, the Thirty-Two Paths of Wisdom, and the Two Hundred and Thirty-One Permutations or Ciphers of the Alphabet, the key to which I do not hold. It is also questionable whether it would always be worth while to seek for it. When one, for instance, sees such a heaping on of nouns (with some Cabbalists) as the Land of Life, the Land of Promise, the Lord of the World, the Foundation Stone, Zion, Mother, Daughter, Sister, the Congregation of Israel, the Twin Roes, the Bride, Blue, End, Oral Law, Sea, Wisdom, etc., meant to represent the same thing or attribute, and to pass one into another, one cannot possibly help feeling some suspicion that one stands before a conglomerate of words run riot, over which the writer had lost all control.

Indeed Nachmanides himself, in the preface to the above-mentioned Commentary, gives us the kind advice not to meditate, or rather brood, over the mystical hints which are scattered over this work, "speculation being (in such matters) folly, and reasoning over them fraught with danger." Indeed, the danger is obvious. I have, to give one or two instances, already alluded to the theory which accepts the Torah or the Wisdom as an agent in the creation of the world. But the mystic pushes further, and asks for the Primal Being to which this Wisdom owes its origin. The answer given is from the great Nothing, as it is written, And the Wisdom shall be found from Nothing.[27] What is intended by this, if it means anything, is probably to divest the first cause of every possible quality which by its very qualifying nature must be limiting and exclusive. Hence, God becomes the Unknowable. But suppose a metaphysical Hamlet, who, handling words indelicately, should impetuously exclaim, To be or not to be, that is the question? — into what abyss of utter negations would he drag all those who despair, by his terrible Nothing.

On the other hand, into what gross anthropomorphisms may we be drawn by roughly handling certain metaphors which some Cabbalists have employed in their struggling after an adequate expression of God's manifestations in His attribute of love, if we forget for a single moment that they are only figures of speech, but liable to get defiled by the slightest touch of an unchaste thought.

But the greater the dangers that beset the path of mysticism, the deeper the interest which we feel in the mystic. In connection with the above-mentioned warning, Nachmanides cites the words from the Scriptures, "But let not the priests and the people break through to come up unto the Lord, lest he break forth upon them" (Exod. xix. 24). Nevertheless, when we read in the Talmud the famous story of the four Rabbis[28] who went up into the *Pardes*, or Garden of Mystical Contemplation, we do not

K

withhold our sympathy, either from Ben Azzai, who shot
a glance and died, or from Ben Zoma, who shot a glance
and was struck (in his mind). Nay, we feel the greatest
admiration for these daring spirits, who, in their passionate attempt to "break through" the veil before the
Infinite, hazarded their lives, and even that which is
dearer than life, their minds, for a single glance. And
did R. Meir deny his sympathies even to Other One
or Elisha ben Abuyah, who "cut down the plants"?
He is said to have heard a voice from heaven, "Return,
oh backsliding children, except Other One," which prevented his repentance. Poor fallen Acher, he mistook
hell for heaven. But do not the struggle and despair
which led to this unfortunate confusion rather plead for
our commiseration?

Nachmanides, however, in his gentle way, did not mean
to storm heaven. Like R. Akiba, "he entered in peace,
and departed in peace." And it was by this peacefulness
of his nature that he gained an influence over posterity
which is equalled only by that of Maimonides. "If he
was not a profound thinker," like the author of the *Guide
of the Perplexed*, he had that which is next best — "he
felt profoundly." Some writers of a rather reactionary
character even went so far as to assign to him a higher
place than to Maimonides. This is unjust. What a
blank would there have been in Jewish thought but for
Maimonides' great work, on which the noblest thinkers of
Israel fed for centuries! As long as Job and Ecclesiastes hold their proper place in the Bible, and the Talmud
contains hundreds of passages suggesting difficulties relating to such problems as the creation of the world, God's
exact relation to it, the origin of evil, free will and pre-

destination, none will persuade me that philosophy does
not form an integral part of Jewish tradition, which, in its
historical developments, took the shape which Maimonides
and his successors gave to it. If Maimonides' *Guide*,
which he considered as an interpretation of the Bible and
of many strange sayings in the old Rabbinic homilies
in the Talmud, is Aristotelian in its tone, so is tradition
too; even the Talmud in many places betrays all sorts
of foreign influences, and none would think of declaring
it un-Jewish on this ground. I may also remark in passing that the certainty with which some writers deprecate
the aids which religion may receive from philosophy is
a little too hasty. For the question will always remain,
What religion? The religion of R. Moses of Tachau or
R. Joseph Jabez [29] would certainly have been greatly
endangered by the slightest touch of speculation, while
that of Bachya,[30] Maimonides, Jedaiah of Bedres, and
Delmedigo undoubtedly received from philosophy its
noblest support, and became intensified by the union.

But apart from that consideration, the sphere of the activity of these two leaders seems to have been so widely
different that it is hardly just to consider them as antagonists, or at least to emphasise the antagonism too much.
Maimonides wrote his chief work, the *Guide*, for the few
elect, who, like Ibn Tibbon [31] for instance, would traverse
whole continents if a single syllogism went wrong. And
if he could be of use to one wise man of this stamp,
Maimonides would do so at the risk of "saying things
unsuitable for ten thousand fools." But with Nachmanides, it would seem, it was these ten thousand who
formed the main object of his tender care. They are, as
we have seen, cultivated men, indeed "students," having

enjoyed a proper education; but the happy times of abstract thinking have gone, and being under a perpetual strain of persecutions and cares, they long for the Sabbath and Festivals, which would bring them both bodily and spiritual recreation. They find no fault with religion, a false syllogism does not jar on their ears; what they are afraid of is that, being engaged as they are, all the six days of work, in their domestic affairs, religion may be too good a thing for them. "To appease their minds," to edify them, to make life more sweet and death less terrible to them, and to show them that even their weaknesses, as far as they are conditioned by nature, are not irreconcilable with a holy life, was what Nachmanides strove after. Now and then he permits them a glance into the mystical world in which he himself loved to move, but he does not care to stifle their senses into an idle contemplation, and passes quickly to some more practical application. To be sure, the tabernacle is nothing but a complete map of the superlunar world; but nevertheless its rather minute description is meant to teach us "that God desires us to work."

This tendency toward being useful to the great majority of mankind may account for the want of consistency of which Nachmanides was so often accused. It is only the logician who can afford to be thoroughgoing in his theory, and even he would become most absurd and even dangerous but for the redeeming fact "that men are better than their principles." But with Nachmanides these "principles" would have proved even more fatal. Could he, for instance, have upset authority in the face of the ten thousand? They need to be guided rather than to guide. But he does not want them to follow either the Gaon or anybody else slavishly, "the gates of wisdom never having been shut," whilst on the other hand he hints to them that there is something divine in every man, which places him at least on the same high level with any authority. Take another instance — his wavering attitude between the Maimonists and the Anti-Maimonists, for which he was often censured. Apart from other reasons, to which I have pointed above, might he not have felt that, in spite of his personal admiration for Maimonides' genius, he had no right to put himself entirely on the side where there was little room for the ten thousand who were entrusted to his guidance, whilst the French Rabbis, with all their prejudices and intolerance, would never deny their sympathies to simple emotional folk?

This tender and absorbing care for the people in general may also account for the fact that we do not know of a single treatise by Nachmanides of a purely Cabbalistic character in the style of the *Book of Weight*, by Moses de Leon, or the *Orchard*, by R. Moses Cordovora, or the *Tree of Life* by R. Isaac Loria.[32] The story that attributes to him the discovery of the *Zohar* in a cave in Palestine, from whence he sent it to Catalonia, needs as little refutation as the other story connected with his conversion to the Cabbalah, which is even more silly and of such a nature as not to bear repetition. The *Lilac of Mysteries*[33] and other mystical works passed also for a long time under his name, but their claim to this honour has been entirely disproved by the bibliographers, and they rank now among the *pseudepigraphica*. It is true that R. Nissim, of Gerona, said of Nachmanides that he was too much addicted to the belief in the Cabbalah, and as a fellow-countryman he may have had some personal knowledge about the matter. But as far as his writings go, this belief finds expression only in incidental remarks and occasional citations from the Bahir,[34] which he never thrusts upon the reader. It was chiefly when philosophy called in question his deep sympathies with even lower humanity, and threatened to withdraw them from those ennobling influences under which he wanted to keep them, that he asserted his mystical theories.

Nachmanides' inconsistency has also proved beneficial in another respect. For mysticism has, by its over-emphasising of the divine in man, shown a strong tendency to remove God altogether and replace Him by the creature of His hands. Witness only the theological bubble of Shabbethai Tsebi — happily it burst quickly enough — which resulted in mere idolatry (in more polite language, Hero Worship) on the one side, and in the grossest antinomianism on the other. Nachmanides, however, with a happy inconsistency, combined with the belief of man's origin in God, a not less strong conviction of man's liability to sin, of the fact that he *does* sin — even the patriarchs were not free from it, as we have seen above — and that this sin *does* alienate man from God. This healthy control over man's extravagant idea of his own species was with Nachmanides also a fruit of the Torah, within the limits of which everything must move, the mystic and his aspirations included, whilst its fair admixture of 365 *Do not's* with 248 *Do's* preserved him from that "holy doing nothing" which so many mystics indulged in, and made his a most active life.

Much of this activity was displayed in Palestine, "the land to which the providence of God is especially attached," and which was, as with R. Judah Hallevi, always "his ideal home." There he not only completed his *Commentary on the Pentateuch*, but also erected synagogues, and engaged in organising communities, whose tone he tried to elevate both by his lectures and by his sermons. His career in Palestine was not a long one, for he lived there only about three years, and in 1270 he must already have been dead. A pretty legend narrates that when he emigrated to Palestine his pupils asked him to give them a sign enabling them to ascertain the day of his death. He answered them that on that day a rift in the shape of a lamp would be seen in the tombstone of his mother. After three years a pupil suddenly noticed this rift, when the mourning over the Rabbi began. Thus, stone, or anything else earthly, breaks finally, and the life of the master passes into light.

What life meant to him, how deeply he was convinced that there is no other life but that originating in God, how deeply stirred his soul was by the consciousness of sin, what agonies the thought of the alienation from God caused him, how he felt that there is nothing left to him but to throw himself upon the mercy of God, and how he rejoiced in the hope of a final reunion with Him — of all these sentiments we find the best expression in the following religious poem, with which this paper may conclude. Nachmanides composed it in Hebrew, and it is still preserved in some rituals as a hymn, recited on the ·Day of Atonement. It is here given in the English translation of Mrs. Henry Lucas.[35]

> Ere time began, ere age to age had thrilled,
> I waited in his storehouse, as he willed ;
> He gave me being, but, my years fulfilled,
>   I shall be summoned back before the King.

He called the hidden to the light of day,
To right and left, each side the fountain lay,
From out the stream and down the steps, the way
　　　That led me to the garden of the King.

Thou gavest me a light my path to guide,
To prove my heart's recesses still untried ;
And as I went, thy voice in warning cried :
　　　"Child ! fear thou him who is thy God and King !"

True weight and measure learned my heart from thee ;
If blessings follow, then what joy for me !
If nought but sin, all mine the shame must be,
　　　For that was not determined by the King.

I hasten, trembling, to confess the whole
Of my transgressions, ere I reach the goal
Where mine own words must witness 'gainst my soul,
　　　And who dares doubt the writing of the King?

Erring, I wandered in the wilderness,
In passion's grave nigh sinking powerless ;
Now deeply I repent, in sore distress,
　　　That I kept not the statutes of the King !

With worldly longings was my bosom fraught,
Earth's idle toys and follies all I sought ;
Ah! when he judges joys so dearly bought,
　　　How greatly shall I fear my Lord and King !

Now conscience-stricken, humbled to the dust,
Doubting himself, in thee alone his trust,
He shrinks in terror back, for God is just —
　　　How can a sinner hope to reach the King?

Oh, be thy mercy in the balance laid,
To hold thy servant's sins more lightly weighed,
When, his confession penitently made,
　　　He answers for his guilt before the King.

Thine is the love, O God, and thine the grace,
That folds the sinner in its mild embrace;
Thine the forgiveness, bridging o'er the space
    'Twixt man's works and the task set by the King.

Unheeding all my sins, I cling to thee;
I know that mercy shall thy footstool be:
Before I call, oh, do thou answer me,
    For nothing dare I claim of thee, my King!

O thou, who makest guilt to disappear,
My help, my hope, my rock, I will not fear;
Though thou the body hold in dungeon drear,
    The soul has found the palace of the King!

POSTSCRIPT

The third letter of Nachmanides to which I have alluded above, is embodied in the following will by R. Solomon, son of the martyr Isaac. Neither the date nor the country of the testator is known, but style and language make it probable that he was a Spanish Jew, and lived in the fourteenth century. I give here a translation from the whole document as it is to be found in the Manuscripts.

These are the regulations which I, Solomon, the son of the martyr, Rabbi Isaac, the son of R. Zadok, of blessed memory, draw up for myself. That as long as I am in good health, and free from accident, and think of it, I shall not eat before I have studied one page of the Talmud or of its commentaries. Should I transgress this rule intentionally, I must not drink wine on that day, or I shall pay half a *Zehub* [36] to charity. Again, that I shall every week read the Lesson twice in the Hebrew text, and once in the Aramaic version. Should I intentionally omit completing the Lesson as above, then I must pay two *Zehubs* to charity. Again, that I shall every Sabbath take three meals, consisting of bread or fruit. Should I omit to do so, I must give in charity half a *Zehub*.

Again, in order to subdue my appetites, and not to enjoy in this world more than is necessary for the maintenance of my body, I must not eat at one meal more than one course of meat, and not more than two courses altogether; nor must I drink more than two cups of wine at one meal, apart from the blessing-cup (over which grace is said), except on Sabbath, Festivals, Chanukah (the Maccabean Dedication Feast), New Moon, and at other religious meals (for instance, wedding-dinners and similar festive occasions). Again, I must not have any regular meal on the day preceding Sabbath or Festivals. I must not have during the day more than one course, so that I shall enter upon the holy day with a good appetite. Should I transgress this resolve intentionally I shall have to fast a day, or to pay two *Zehubs*. Again, that I shall not eat the fish called *burbot*,[37] if I think of it. Again, even on the above-mentioned days, I must not eat more than three courses at a meal, nor drink more than three cups of wine, exclusive of the blessing-cup. Again, . . . I must not swear by God, nor mention the name of Heaven without a purpose, nor curse any man in the name of God. Should I, God forbid, transgress it, I must not drink more than one cup of wine on that day exclusive of the blessing-cup. Should I, however, transgress this after dinner, I must abstain from wine the following day. Should I transgress it, I have to pay half a *Zehub*. Again, that I shall get up every night to praise God, to supplicate for His mercy, and to confess. On those nights when confession is not to be said (Sabbaths and Festivals), I shall say hymns and psalms. This I shall do when I am in my house, and in good health, free from any accident. Should I transgress it, I shall drink not more than one cup of wine the following day, except the blessing-cup. I again take upon myself to give in charity the following proportion of my expenditure — from each dress which I shall have made for myself or for one member of my family, costing more than ten *Zehubs*, I must pay one *Pashut* [38] for each ten *Zehubs*. Again, if I should buy an animal, or a slave, or a female slave, or ground, that I shall also pay at the same rate. And if I shall buy clothes for sale, called *fashas*, I shall pay two *Pashuts* for each garment. As often as I have occasion to say the benediction of thanksgivings for having escaped danger I shall pay a *Zehub*, except when I am travelling [also involving danger in those times!], in which case I shall have to pay a *Zehub* on my arrival, and two *Pashuts* daily during the journey. Again, from every kind of fish bought for me, costing more than a *Zehub*, I shall pay a *Pashut* for each *Zehub*. And also, if I shall be deemed worthy by God to marry my children, and to be present at their wedding, to cause them to give to the poor from the dowry brought to them by their wives, whether in money or in kind, at the rate of one per cent. If God will find me worthy of having sons, I must give in charity according to my means at the time.

I shall also, between New Year and the Day of Atonement in each year, calculate my profits during the past year and (after deducting expenses) give a tithe thereof to the poor. Should I be unable to make an accurate calculation, then I shall give approximately. This tithe I shall put aside, together with the other money for religious (charitable) purpose, to dispose of it as I shall deem best. I also propose to have the liberty of employing the money in any profitable speculation with a view to augmenting it. But in respect of all I have written above I shall not hold myself guilty if I transgress, if such transgression be the result of forgetfulness; but in order to guard against it, I shall read this through weekly.

I also command my children to take upon themselves as many of the above regulations as may be in their power to observe, and also to bind them (*i.e.* the regulations), from generation to generation, upon their children. And he who carries them out, and even adds to them, at pain of discomfort to himself, shall merit a special blessing. And this is the text of the will which I, the above-mentioned Solomon, draw up for my children, may God preserve them. That they shall pray thrice daily, and endeavour always to utter their prayers with devotion. Again, that this prayer shall be said in the *Beth Hammidrash*, or in the synagogue together with the congregation. Again, that they shall apply all their powers to maintain the synagogues and the houses of study, which our ancestors have built, as well as to continue the endowments established by my ancestors and myself. They must always endeavour to imitate them, so that goodness shall never cease from among them. Again, that they shall always have a chair on which a volume of the Talmud, or some other Talmudical work, shall lie; so that they shall always open a book when they come home. At least, they shall read in any book they like four lines before taking their meal. Again, that they shall every week read the Lesson twice in the Hebrew text, and once in the Aramaic version. Again, to take three meals on the Sabbath . . .

Again, that they shall be always modest, merciful, and charitable, for these are the qualities by which the children of Israel are known. Let also all their thoughts and meditations be always directed to the service of the Lord, and be as charitable and benevolent as possible, for this is all that remains to man of his labour. They shall also endeavour to regulate their diet according to the rules laid down by Rabbi Moses (b. Maimon, or Maimonides), so as to fulfil the words of Scripture: "The righteous eateth to the satisfying of his soul." And let them always be careful not to take the name of God in vain, to be honest in all business transactions, and let their yea be always yea. They shall always be under the obligation to train their children to the Study of the Torah, but one shall devote his life exclusively to the study thereof. And it shall be incumbent upon his brothers to support this one, and to invest his moneys, and to provide for him that he and his family may live respectably, so that he be not distracted by worldly cares from his studies. Let also the elder love the younger brothers as their own children, and the younger respect the elder as a parent. Thus they may always bear in mind that they are of a God-fearing family. Let them love and honour scholars, thus to merit the honour of having scholars for their sons and sons-in-law. This will they shall themselves read weekly, and shall also make it incumbent upon their children, from generation to generation, to read weekly, in order to fulfil what is written (Gen. xviii. 19), "For I know him that he will command his children," etc., and also the words of Isaiah (lix. 21), "And this is my covenant," etc. But as often as they shall read this will, they shall also read the two letters below written, which Rabbi Moses ben Nachman sent to his sons, with a view of being serviceable to them in many re-

spects. Should, heaven forbid, they be by any sad accident prevented from fulfilling the injunctions above laid down, they must
fine themselves by not drinking wine on that day, or by eating one
course less at the dinner, or by giving some fine in charity. . . .

And this is the letter which the above-mentioned Rabbi
sent from the Holy Land to Castile, when his son was
staying before the king (in his service): —

" . . . May God bless you and preserve you from sin and punishment. Behold, our master, King David, had a son, wise and
of an understanding heart, like unto whom there was never one
before or after. Nevertheless he said to him (1 Kings ii. 2) : 'And
keep the charge of the Lord thy God,' etc. He also said to him :
'And thou, my son, know the God of thy father' (1 Chron.
xxviii. 9). Now, my son, if thou wilt measure thyself with Solomon, thou wilt find thyself a worm — not a man, merely an insect ;
nevertheless, if thou wilt seek God, he will make thee great ; and if
thou wilt forsake him, thou wilt be turned out and forsaken. My
son, be careful that thou read the *Shema* [39] morning and evening,
as well as that thou say the daily prayers. Have always with thee
a Pentateuch written correctly, and read therein the Lesson for
each Sabbath. . . . 'Cast thy burden upon the Lord,' for the
thing which thou believest far from thee is often very near unto thee.
Know, again, that thou art not master over thy words, nor hast
power over thy hand ; but everything is in the hand of the Lord,
who formeth thy heart. . . . Be especially careful to keep aloof
from the women [of the court?]. Know that our God hates immorality, and Balaam could in no other way injure Israel than by
inciting them to unchastity. [Here come many quotations from
Malachi and Ezra.] . . . My son, remember me always, and let
the image of my countenance be never absent from before thine
eyes. Love not that which I hate. . . . Let the words of the
Psalmist be always upon thy lips, ' I am a stranger in the earth :
hide not thy commandments from me ' (Ps. cxix. 19) ; and God,
who is good and the dispenser of good, shall increase thy peace
and prolong thy life in peace and happiness, and promote thy honour
according to thy wish and the wish of thy father who begat thee,
Moses ben Nachman."

V

A JEWISH BOSWELL

THERE is a saying in the Talmud " Nothing exists of which there is not some indication in the Torah." These words are often quoted, and some modern authors have pressed them so far as to find even the discoveries of Columbus and the inventions of Watt and Stephenson indicated in the Law. This is certainly misapplied ingenuity. But it is hardly an exaggeration to maintain that there is no noble manifestation of real religion, no expression of real piety, reverence, and devotion, to which Jewish literature would not offer a fair parallel.

Thus it will hardly be astonishing to hear that Jewish literature has its Boswell to show, more than three centuries before the Scottish gentleman came to London to admire his Johnson, and more than four centuries before the Sage of Chelsea delivered his lectures on Hero Worship. And this Jewish Boswell was guided only by the motives suggested to him in the old Rabbinic literature. In this literature the reverence for the great man, and the absorption of one's whole self in him, went so far that one Rabbi declared that the whole world was only created to serve such a man as company.[1]

Again, the fact that, in the language of the Rabbis, the term for studying the Law and discussing it is " to

attend " or rather " to serve the disciples of the Wise "
may also have led people to the important truth that the
great man is not a lecturing machine, but a sort of living
Law himself. " When the man," said one Rabbi, " has
wholly devoted himself to the Torah, and thoroughly
identified himself with it, it becomes almost his own
Torah." Thus people have not only to listen to his
words but to observe his whole life, and to profit from
all his actions and movements.

This was what the Jewish Boswell sought to do. His
name was Rabbi Solomon, of St. Goar, a small town on
the Rhine, while the name of the master whom he served
was R. Jacob, the Levite, better known by his initials
Maharil, who filled the office of Chief Rabbi in Mayence
and Worms successively. The main activity of Maharil
falls in the first three decades of the fifteenth century.
Those were troublous times for a Rabbi. For the preceding century with its persecution and sufferings — one
has only to think of the Black Death and its terrible consequences for the Jews — led to the destruction of the
great Schools, the decay of the study of the Law, and
to the dissolution of many congregations. Those which
remained lost all touch with each other, so that almost
every larger Jewish community had its own *Minhag* or
ritual custom.[2]

It was Maharil who brought some order into this chaos,
and in the course of time his influence asserted itself
so strongly that the rules observed by him in the performing of religious ceremonies were accepted by the
great majority of the Jewish communities. Thus the personality of Maharil himself became a standing Minhag,
suppressing all the other Minhagim (customs).

But there must have been something very strong and very great about the personality of the man who could succeed in such an arduous task. For we must not forget that the Minhag or custom in its decay degenerates into a kind of religious fashion, the worst disease to which religion is liable, and the most difficult to cure. It is therefore an irreparable loss both for Jewish literature and for Jewish history, that the greatest part of Maharil's posthumous writings are no longer extant, so that our knowledge about him is very small. But the little we know of him we owe chiefly to the communicativeness of his servant, the Solomon of St. Goar whom I mentioned above.

Solomon not only gave us the "Customs" of his master, but also observed him closely in all his movements, and conscientiously wrote down all that he saw and heard, under the name of *Collectanea*. It seems that the bulk of these *Collectanea* was also lost. But in the fragments that we still possess we are informed, among other things, how Maharil addressed his wife, how he treated his pupils, how careful he was in the use of his books, and even how clean his linen was. Is this not out-Boswelling Boswell?

The most striking point of agreement between the Boswell of the fifteenth and him of the eighteenth century, is that they both use the same passage from the Talmud to excuse the interest in trifles which their labours of love betrayed. Thus Solomon prefaces his *Collectanea* with the following words: "It is written, His leaf shall not wither. These words were explained by our Sages to mean that even the idle talk of the disciples of the wise deserves a study. Upon this interpretation I have relied. In my love to R. Jacob the Levite, I collected everything about him. I did not refuse even small things, though many

derided me. Everything I wrote down, for such was the
desire of my heart."

Thus far Solomon. Now, if we turn to the introduction
to Boswell's *Life of Johnson*, we read the following sentence: "For this almost superstitious reverence, I have
found very old and venerable authority quoted by our
great modern prelate, Secker, in whose tenth sermon
there is the following passage: 'Rabbi Kimchi, a noted
Jewish commentator who lived about five hundred years
ago, explains that passage in the first Psalm, "His leaf
also shall not wither" from Rabbins yet older than himself, that even the idle talk, so he expressed it, of a good
man ought to be regarded.'"

Croker's note to this passage sounds rather strange.
This editor says: "Kimchi was a Spanish Rabbi, who
died in 1240. One wonders that Secker's good sense
should have condescended to quote this far-fetched and
futile interpretation of the simple and beautiful metaphor,
by which the Psalmist illustrates the prosperity of the
righteous man." Now Kimchi died at least five years
earlier than Croker states, but dates, we know from
Macaulay's essay on the subject, were not Croker's strong
point. But one can hardly forgive the editor of Boswell
this lack of sympathy. Had he known what strong
affinity there was between his most Christian author and
the humble Jew Solomon, he would have less resented
this condescension of Archbishop Secker.

As for the Jewish Boswell himself, we know very little
about him. The only place in which he speaks about his
own person is that in which he derives his pedigree from
R. Eleazar ben Samuel Hallevi (died 1357), and says that
he was generally called " Der gute (the good) R. Salman."

L

He well deserved this appellation. In his Will we find the following injunction to his children : " Be honest, and conscientious in your dealing with men, with Jews as well as Gentiles, be kind and obliging to them ; do not speak what is superfluous." And wisdom is surely rare enough to render inappropriate a charge of superfluousness against the work of those who in bygone times spent their energies in gathering the crumbs that fell from the tables of the wise.

VI

THE DOGMAS OF JUDAISM

THE object of this essay is to say about the dogmas of Judaism a word which I think ought not to be left unsaid.

In speaking of dogmas it must be understood that Judaism does not ascribe to them any saving power. The belief in a dogma or a doctrine without abiding by its real or supposed consequences (*e.g.* the belief in *creatio ex nihilo* without keeping the Sabbath) is of no value. And the question about certain doctrines is not whether they possess or do not possess the desired charm against certain diseases of the soul, but whether they ought to be considered as characteristics of Judaism or not.

It must again be premised that the subject, which occupied the thoughts of the greatest and noblest Jewish minds for so many centuries, has been neglected for a comparatively long time. And this for various reasons. First, there is Mendelssohn's assertion, or supposed assertion, in his *Jerusalem*, that Judaism has no dogmas — an assertion which has been accepted by the majority of modern Jewish theologians as the only dogma Judaism possesses. You can hear it pronounced in scores of Jewish pulpits ; you can read it written in scores of Jewish books. To admit the possibility that Mendelssohn was in error was hardly permissible, especially for those with whom he enjoys a certain infallibility. Nay, even the fact that he himself was not consistent in his theory, and on another occasion declared that Judaism *has* dogmas, only that they are purer and more in harmony with reason than those of other religions; or even the more important fact that he published a school-book for children, in which the so-called Thirteen Articles were embodied, only that instead of the formula "I believe," he substituted "I am convinced," — even such patent facts did not produce much effect upon many of our modern theologians.[1] They were either overlooked or explained away so as to make them harmonise with the great dogma of dogma-lessness. For it is one of the attributes of infallibility that the words of its happy possessor must always be reconcilable even when they appear to the eye of the unbeliever as gross contradictions.

Another cause of the neglect into which the subject has fallen is that our century is an *historical* one. It is not only books that have their fate, but also whole sciences and literatures. In past times it was religious speculation that formed the favourite study of scholars, in our time it is history with its critical foundation on a sound philology. Now as these two most important branches of Jewish science were so long neglected — were perhaps never cultivated in the true meaning of the word, and as Jewish literature is so vast and Jewish history so far-reaching and eventful, we cannot wonder that these studies have absorbed the time and the labour of the greatest and best Jewish writers in this century.

There is, besides, a certain tendency in historical studies that is hostile to mere theological speculation. The historian deals with realities, the theologian with abstractions. The latter likes to shape the universe after his system, and tells us how things *ought to be*, the former teaches us how they *are* or *have been*, and the explanation he gives for their being so and not otherwise includes in most cases also a kind of justification for their existence. There is also the *odium theologicum*, which has been the cause of so much misfortune that it is hated by the historian, whilst the superficial, rationalistic way in which the theologian manages to explain everything which does not suit his system is most repulsive to the critical spirit.

But it cannot be denied that this neglect has caused much confusion. Especially is this noticeable in England, which is essentially a theological country, and where people are but little prone to give up speculation about things which concern their most sacred interest and greatest happiness. Thus whilst we are exceedingly poor in all other branches of Jewish learning, we are comparatively rich in productions of a theological character. We have a superfluity of essays on such delicate subjects as eternal punishment, immortality of the soul, the day of judgment, etc., and many treatises on the definition of Judaism. But knowing little or nothing of the progress recently made in Jewish theology, of the many protests against all kinds of infallibility, whether canonised in this century or in olden times, we in England still maintain that Judaism has no dogmas as if nothing to the contrary had ever been said. We seek the foundation of Judaism in political economy, in hygiene, in everything except religion. Following the fashion of the day to esteem religion in proportion to its ability to adapt itself to every possible and impossible metaphysical and social system, we are anxious to squeeze out of Judaism the last drop of faith and hope, and strive to make it so flexible that we can turn it in every direction which it is our pleasure to follow. But alas! the flexibility has progressed so far as to classify Judaism among the invertebrate species, the lowest order of living things. It strongly resembles a certain Christian school which addresses itself to the world in general and claims to satisfy everybody alike. It claims to be socialism for the adherents of Karl Marx and Lassalle, worship of man for the followers of Comte and St. Simon; it carefully avoids the word " God" for the comfort of agnostics and sceptics, whilst on the other hand it pretends to hold sway over paradise, hell, and immortality for the edification of believers. In such illusions many of our theologians delight. For illusions they are; you cannot be everything if you want to be anything. Moreover, illusions in themselves are bad enough, but we are menaced with what is still worse. Judaism, divested of every higher religious motive, is in danger of falling into gross materialism. For what else is the meaning of such declarations as " Believe what you like, but conform to this or that mode of life "; what else does it mean but " We cannot expect you to believe that the things you are bidden to do are commanded by a higher authority; there is not such a thing as belief, but you ought to do them for conventionalism or for your own convenience."

But both these motives — the good opinion of our neighbours, as well as our bodily health — have nothing to do with our nobler and higher sentiments, and degrade Judaism to a matter of expediency or diplomacy. Indeed, things have advanced so far that well-meaning but ill-advised writers even think to render a service to Judaism by declaring it to be a kind of enlightened Hedonism, or rather a moderate Epicureanism.

I have no intention of here answering the question, What is Judaism? This question is not less perplexing than the problem, What is God's world? Judaism is also a great Infinite, composed of as many endless Units, the Jews. And these Unit-Jews have been, and are still, scattered through all the world, and have passed under an immensity of influences, good and bad. If so, how can we give an exact definition of the Infinite, called Judaism?

But if there is anything sure, it is that the highest motives which worked through the history of Judaism are the strong belief in God and the unshaken confidence that at last this God, the God of Israel, will be the God of the whole world; or, in other words, Faith and Hope are the two most prominent characteristics of Judaism.

In the following pages I shall try to give a short account of the manner in which these two principles of Judaism found expression, from the earliest times down to the age of Mendelssohn; that is, to present an outline of the history of Jewish Dogmas. First, a few observations on the position of the Bible and the Talmud in relation to our theme. Insufficient and poor as they may be in proportion to the importance of these two fundamental documents of Judaism, these remarks may nevertheless suggest a connecting link between the teachings of Jewish antiquity and those of Maimonides and his successors.

I begin with the Scriptures.

The Bible itself hardly contains a command bidding us *to believe*. We are hardly ordered, *e.g.*, to believe in the existence of God. I say hardly, but I do not altogether deny the existence of such a command. It is true that we do not find in the Scripture such words as: "You are commanded to believe in the existence of God." Nor is any punishment assigned as awaiting him who denies it. Notwithstanding these facts, many Jewish authorities — among them such important men as Maimonides, R. Judah Hallevi, Nachmanides — perceive, in the first words of the Ten Commandments, "I am the Lord thy God," the command to believe in His existence.[2]

Be this as it may, there cannot be the shadow of a doubt that the Bible, in which every command is dictated by God, and in which all its heroes are the servants, the friends, or the ambassadors of God, presumes such a belief in every one to whom those laws are dictated, and these heroes address themselves. Nay, I think that the word "belief" is not even adequate. In a world with so many visible facts and invisible causes, as life and death, growth and decay, light and darkness; in a world where the sun rises and sets; where the stars appear regularly; where heavy rains pour down from the sky, often accompanied by such grand phenomena as thunder and lightning; in a world full of such marvels, but into which no notion has entered of all our modern true or false explanations — who but God is behind all these things? "Have the gates," asks God, "have the gates of death been open to thee? or hast thou seen the doors of the shadow of death? . . . Where is the way where light dwelleth? and as for darkness, where is the place thereof? . . . Hath the rain a father? or who hath begotten the drops of dew? . . . Canst thou bind the sweet influences of Pleiades, or loose the bands of Orion? . . . Canst thou send lightnings, that they may go, and say unto thee, Here we are?" (Job xxxviii.). Of all these wonders, God was not merely the *prima causa;* they were the result of His direct action, without any intermediary causes. And it is as absurd to say that the ancient world believed in God, as for a future historian to assert of the nineteenth century that it believed in the effects of electricity. We *see* them, and so antiquity *saw* God. If there was any danger, it lay not in the denial of the existence of a God, but in having a wrong belief. Belief in as many gods as there are manifestations in nature, the investing of them with false attributes, the misunderstanding of God's relation to men, lead to immorality. Thus the greater part of the laws and teachings of the Bible are either directed against polytheism, with all its low ideas of God, or rather of gods; or they are directed towards regulating God's relation to men. Man is a servant of God, or His prophet, or even His friend. But this relationship man obtains only by his conduct. Nay, all man's actions are carefully regulated by God, and connected with His holiness. The 19th chapter of Leviticus, which is considered by the Rabbis as the portion of the Law in which the most important articles of the Torah are embodied, is headed, "Ye shall be holy, for I the Lord your own God am holy." And each law therein occurring, even those which concern our relations to each other, is *not* founded on utilitarian reasons, but is ordained because the opposite of it is an offence to the holiness of God, and profanes His creatures, whom He desired to be as holy as He is.[3]

Thus the whole structure of the Bible is built upon the visible fact of the existence of a God, and upon the belief in the relation of God to men, especially to Israel. In spite of all that has been said to the contrary, the Bible *does* lay stress upon belief, where belief is required. The unbelievers are rebuked again and again. "For all this they sinned still, and believed not for His wondrous work," complains Asaph (Ps. lxxviii. 32). And belief is praised in such exalted words as, "Thus saith the Lord, I remember thee, the kindness of thy youth, the love of thine espousals, when thou wentest after me in the wilderness, in a land that was not sown" (Jer. ii. 2). The Bible, especially the books of the prophets, consists, in great part, of promises for the future, which the Rabbis justly termed the "Consolations."[4] For our purpose, it is of no great consequence to examine what future the prophets had in view, whether an immediate future or one more remote, at the end of days. At any rate, they inculcated hope and confidence that God would bring to pass a better time. I think that even the most advanced Bible critic — provided he is not guided by some modern Aryan reasons — must perceive in such passages as, "The Lord shall reign for ever and ever," "The Lord shall rejoice in his works," and many others, a hope for more than the establishment of the "national Deity among his votaries in Palestine."

We have now to pass over an interval of many centuries, the length of which depends upon the views held as to the date of the close of the canon, and examine what the Rabbis, the representatives of the prophets, thought on this subject. Not that the views of the author of the *Wisdom of Solomon*, of Philo and Aristobulus, and many others of the Judæo-Alexandrian school would be uninteresting for us. But somehow their influence on Judaism was only a passing one, and their doctrines never became authoritative in the Synagogue. We must here confine ourselves to those who, even by the testimony of their bitterest enemies, occupied the seat of Moses.

The successors of the prophets had to deal with new circumstances, and accordingly their teachings were adapted to the wants of their times. As the result of manifold foreign influences, the visible fact of the existence of God as manifested in the Bible had been somewhat obscured. Prophecy ceased, and the Holy Spirit which inspired a few chosen ones took its place. Afterwards this influence was reduced to the hearing of a Voice from Heaven, which was audible to still fewer. On the other hand the Rabbis had this advantage that they were not called upon to fight against idolatry as their predecessors the prophets had been. The evil inclination to worship idols was, as the Talmud expresses it allegorically, killed by the Men of the Great Synagogue, or, as we should put it, it was suppressed by the sufferings of the captivity in Babylon. This change of circumstances is marked by the following fact: — Whilst the prophets mostly considered idolatry as the cause of all sin, the Rabbis show a strong tendency to ascribe sin to a defect in, or a want of, belief on the part of the sinner. They teach that Adam would not have sinned unless he had first denied the "Root of all" (or the main principle), namely, the belief in the Omnipresence of God. Of Cain they say that before murdering his brother he declared: "There is no judgment, there is no judge, there is no world to come, and there is no reward for the just, and no punishment for the wicked."[5]

In another place we read that the commission of a sin in secret is an impertinent attempt by the doer to oust God from the world. But if unbelief is considered as the root of all evil, we may expect that the reverse of it, a perfect faith, would be praised in the most exalted terms.   So we read : Faith is so great that the man who possesses it may hope to become a worthy vessel of the Holy Spirit, or, as we should express it, that he may hope to obtain by this power the highest degree of communion with his Maker.   The Patriarch Abraham, notwithstanding all his other virtues, only became "the possessor of both worlds" by the merit of his strong faith.   Nay, even the fulfilment of a single law when accompanied by true faith is, according to the Rabbis, sufficient to bring man nigh to God.   And the future redemption is also conditional on the degree of faith shown by Israel.[6]

It has often been asked what the Rabbis would have thought of a man who fulfils every commandment of the Torah, but does not believe that this Torah was given by God, or that there exists a God at all.   It is indeed very difficult to answer this question with any degree of certainty.   In the time of the Rabbis people were still too simple for such a diplomatic religion, and conformity in the modern sense was quite an unknown thing.   But from the foregoing remarks it would seem that the Rabbis could not conceive such a monstrosity as atheistic orthodoxy.   For, as we have seen, the Rabbis thought that unbelief must needs end in sin, for faith is the origin of all good.   Accordingly, in the case just supposed they would have either suspected the man's orthodoxy, or would have denied that his views were really what he professed them to be.

Still more important than the above cited Agadic passages is one which we are about to quote from the tractate Sanhedrin.   This tractate deals with the constitution, of the supreme law-court, the examination of the witnesses, the functions of the judges, and the different punishment to be inflicted on the transgressors of the law. After having enumerated various kinds of capital punishment, the Mishnah adds the following words: "These are (the men) who are excluded from the life to come: He who says there is no resurrection from death; he who says there is no Torah given from heaven, and the Epikurus."[7] This passage was considered by the Rabbis of the Middle Ages, as well as by modern scholars, the *locus classicus* for the dogma question. There are many passages in the Rabbinic literature which exclude man from the world to come for this or that sin. But these are more or less of an Agadic (legendary) character, and thus lend themselves to exaggeration and hyperbolic language. They cannot, therefore, be considered as serious legal dicta, or as the general opinion of the Rabbis.

The Mishnah in Sanhedrin, however, has, if only by its position in a legal tractate, a certain *Halachic* (obligatory) character. And the fact that so early an authority as R. Akiba made additions to it guarantees its high antiquity. The first two sentences of this Mishnah are clear enough. In modern language, and positively speaking, they would represent articles of belief in Resurrection and Revelation. Great difficulty is found in defining what was meant by the word *Epikurus*. The authorities of the Middle Ages, to whom I shall again have to refer, explain the Epikurus to be a man who denies the belief in reward and punishment; others identify him with one who denies the belief in Providence; while others again consider the Epikurus to be one who denies Tradition. But the paral-

lel passages in which it occurs incline one rather to think
that this word cannot be defined by one kind of heresy.
It implies rather a frivolous treatment of the words of
Scripture or of Tradition. In the case of the latter (Tradition) it is certainly not honest difference of opinion that
is condemned; for the Rabbis themselves differed very
often from each other, and even Mediæval authorities
did not feel any compunction about explaining Scripture
in variance with the Rabbinic interpretation, and sometimes they even went so far as to declare that the view
of this or that great authority was only to be considered
as an isolated opinion not deserving particular attention.
What they did blame was, as already said, scoffing and
impiety. We may thus safely assert that reverence for
the teachers of Israel formed the third essential principle
of Judaism.[8]

I have still to remark that there occur in the Talmud
such passages as "the Jew, even if he has sinned, is still a
Jew," or "He who denies idolatry is called a Jew." These
and similar passages have been used to prove that Judaism
was not a positive religion, but only involved the negation
of idolatry. But it has been overlooked that the statements
quoted have more a legal than a theological character.
The Jew belonged to his nationality even after having
committed the greatest sin, just as the Englishman does
not cease to be an Englishman — in regard to treason and
the like — by having committed a heinous crime. But he
has certainly acted in a very un-English way, and having
outraged the feelings of the whole nation will have to suffer for his misconduct. The Rabbis in a similar manner
did not maintain that he who gave up the belief in Revelation and Resurrection, and treated irreverently the teach-

ers of Israel, severed his connection with the Jewish nation, but that, for his crime, he was going to suffer the heaviest punishment. He was to be excluded from the world to come.

Still, important as is the passage quoted from Sanhedrin, it would be erroneous to think that it exhausted the creed of the Rabbis. The liturgy and innumerable passages in the Midrashim show that they ardently clung to the belief in the advent of the Messiah. All their hope was turned to the future redemption and the final establishment of the Kingdom of Heaven on earth. Judaism, stripped of this belief, would have been for them devoid of meaning. The belief in reward and punishment is also repeated again and again in the old Rabbinic literature. A more emphatic declaration of the belief in Providence than is conveyed by the following passages is hardly conceivable. "Everything is foreseen, and free will is given. And the world is judged by grace." Or, "the born are to die, and the dead to revive, and the living to be judged. For to know and to notify, and that it may be known that He (God) is the Framer and He the Creator, and He the Discerner, and He the Judge, and He the Witness," etc.[9]

But it must not be forgotten that it was not the habit of the Rabbis to lay down, either for conduct or for doctrine, rules which were commonly known. When they urged the three points stated above there must have been some historical reason for it. Probably these principles were controverted by some heretics. Indeed, the whole tone of the passage cited from Sanhedrin is a protest against certain unbelievers who are threatened with punishment. Other beliefs, not less essential, but less disputed, remain unmentioned, because there was no necessity to assert them.

It was not till a much later time, when the Jews came into closer contact with new philosophical schools, and also new creeds which were more liable than heathenism was to be confused with Judaism, that this necessity was felt. And thus we are led at once to the period when the Jews became acquainted with the teachings of the Mohammedan schools. The Caraites came very early into contact with non-Jewish systems. And so we find that they were also the first to formulate Jewish dogmas in a fixed number, and in a systematic order. It is also possible that their separation from the Tradition, and their early division into little sects among themselves, compelled them to take this step, in order to avoid further sectarianism.

The number of their dogmas amounts to ten. According to Judah Hadasi (1150), who would appear to have derived them from his predecessors, their dogmas include the following articles: — 1. *Creatio ex nihilo;* 2. The existence of a Creator, God; 3. This God is an absolute unity as well as incorporeal; 4. Moses and the other prophets were sent by God; 5. God has given to us the Torah, which is true and complete in every respect, not wanting the addition of the so-called Oral Law; 6. The Torah must be studied by every Jew in the original (Hebrew) language; 7. The Holy Temple was a place elected by God for His manifestation; 8. Resurrection of the dead; 9. Punishment and reward after death; 10. The Coming of the Messiah, the son of David.

How far the predecessors of Hadasi were influenced by a certain Joseph Albashir (about 950), of whom there exists a manuscript work, "Rudiments of Faith," I am unable to say. The little we know of him reveals more of his intimacy with Arabic thoughts than of his importance for his sect in particular and for Judaism in general. After Hadasi I shall mention here Elijah Bashazi, a Caraite writer of the end of the fifteenth century. This author, who was much influenced by Maimonides, omits the second and the seventh articles. In order to make up the ten he numbers the belief in the eternity of God as an article, and divides the fourth article into two. In the fifth article Bashazi does not emphasise so strongly the completeness of the Torah as Hadasi, and omits the portion which is directed against Tradition. It is interesting to see the distinction which Bashazi draws between the Pentateuch and the Prophets. While he thinks that the five books of Moses can never be altered, he regards the words of the Prophets as only relating to their contemporaries, and thus subject to changes. As I do not want to anticipate Maimonides' system, I must refrain from giving here the articles laid down by Solomon Troki in the beginning of the eighteenth century. For the articles of Maimonides are copied by this writer with a few slight alterations so as to dress them in a Caraite garb.

I must dismiss the Caraites with these few remarks, my object being chiefly to discuss the dogmas of the Synagogue from which they had separated themselves. Besides, as in everything Caraitic, there is no further development of the question. As Bashazi laid them down, they are still taught by the Caraites of to-day. I return to the Rabbanites.[10]

As is well known, Maimonides (1130–1205), was the first Rabbanite who formulated the dogmas of the Synagogue. But there are indications of earlier attempts. R. Saadiah

M

Gaon's (892–942) work, *Creeds and Opinions*, shows such traces. He says in his preface, " My heart sickens to see that the belief of my co-religionists is impure and that their theological views are confused." The subjects he treats in this book, such as creation, unity of God, resurrection of the dead, the future redemption of Israel, reward and punishment, and other kindred theological subjects might thus, perhaps, be considered as the essentials of the creed that the Gaon desired to present in a pure and rational form. R. Hannaneel, of Kairowan,[11] in the first half of the eleventh century, says in one of his commentaries that to deserve eternal life one must believe in *four* things : in God, in the prophets, in a future world where the just will be rewarded, and in the advent of the Redeemer. From R. Judah Hallevi's *Cusari*, written in the beginning of the twelfth century, we might argue that the belief in the election of Israel by God was the cardinal dogma of the author.[12] Abraham Ibn Daud, a contemporary of Maimonides, in his book *The High Belief*,[13] speaks of *rudiments*, among which, besides such metaphysical principles as unity, rational conception of God's attributes, etc., the belief in the immutability of the Law, etc., is included. Still, all these works are intended to furnish evidence from philosophy or history for the truth of religion rather than to give a definition of this truth. The latter task was undertaken by Maimonides.

I refer to the thirteen articles embodied in his first work, *The Commentary to the Mishnah.* They are appended to the Mishnah in Sanhedrin, with which I dealt above. But though they do not form an independent treatise, Maimonides' remarks must not be considered as merely incidental.

That Maimonides was quite conscious of the importance of this exposition can be gathered from the concluding words addressed to the reader : " Know these (words) and repeat them many times, and think them over in the proper way. God knows that thou wouldst be deceiving thyself if thou thinkest thou hast understood them by having read them once or even ten times. Be not, therefore, hasty in perusing them. I have not composed them without deep study and earnest reflection."

The result of this deep study was that the following Thirteen Articles constitute the creed of Judaism. They are : —

1. The belief in the existence of a Creator; 2. The belief in His Unity; 3. The belief in His Incorporeality; 4. The belief in His Eternity; 5. The belief that all worship and adoration are due to Him alone; 6. The belief in Prophecy; 7. The belief that Moses was the greatest of all Prophets, both before and after him ; 8. The belief that the Torah was revealed to Moses on Mount Sinai; 9. The belief in the Immutability of this revealed Torah ; 10. The belief that God knows the actions of men; 11. The belief in Reward and Punishment; 12. The belief in the coming of the Messiah; 13. The belief in the Resurrection of the dead.

The impulse given by the great philosopher and still greater Jew was eagerly followed by succeeding generations, and Judaism thus came into possession of a dogmatic literature such as it never knew before Maimonides. Maimonides is the centre of this literature, and I shall accordingly speak in the remainder of this essay of Maimonists and Anti-Maimonists. These terms really apply to the great controversy that raged round Maimonides' *Guide of the Perplexed*, but I shall, chiefly for brevity's sake, employ them in these pages in a restricted sense to refer to the dispute concerning the Thirteen Articles.

Among the Maimonists we may probably include the great majority of Jews, who accepted the Thirteen Articles without further question. Maimonides must indeed have filled up a great gap in Jewish theology, a gap, moreover, the existence of which was very generally perceived. A century had hardly elapsed before the Thirteen Articles had become a theme for the poets of the Synagogue. And almost every country where Jews lived can show a poem or a prayer founded on these Articles. R. Jacob Molin (1420) of Germany speaks of metrical and rhymed songs in the German language, the burden of which was the Thirteen Articles, and which were read by the common people with great devotion. The numerous commentaries and homilies written on the same topic would form a small library in themselves.[14] But on the other hand it must not be denied that the Anti-Maimonists, that is to say those Jewish writers who did not agree with the creed formulated by Maimonides, or agreed only in part with him, form also a very strong and respectable minority. They deserve our attention the more as it is their works which brought life into the subject and deepened it. It is not by a perpetual Amen to every utterance of a great authority that truth or literature gains anything.

The Anti-Maimonists can be divided into two classes. The one class categorically denies that Judaism has dogmas. I shall have occasion to touch on this view when I come to speak of Abarbanel. Here I pass at once to the second class of Anti-Maimonists. This consists of those who agree with Maimonides as to the existence of dogmas in Judiasm, but who differ from him as to what these dogmas are, or who give a different enumeration of them.

As the first of these Anti-Maimonists we may regard Nachmanides, who, in his famous *Sermon in the Presence of the King*, speaks of three fundamental principles: Creation (that is, non-eternity of matter), Omniscience of God, and Providence. Next comes R. Abba Mari ben Moses, of Montpellier. He wrote at the beginning of the fourteenth century, and is famous in Jewish history for his zeal against the study of philosophy. We possess a small pamphlet by him dealing with our subject, and it forms a kind of prologue to his collection of controversial letters against the rationalists of his time.[15] He lays down three articles as the fundamental teachings of Religion: 1. Metaphysical: The existence of God, including His Unity and Incorporeality; 2. Mosaic: *Creatio ex nihilo* by God — a consequence of this principle is the belief that God is capable of altering the laws of nature at His pleasure; 3. Ethical: Special Providence — *i.e.* God knows all our actions in all their details. Abba Mari does not mention Maimonides' Thirteen Articles. But it would be false to conclude that he rejected the belief in the coming of the Messiah, or any other article of Maimonides. The whole tone and tendency of this pamphlet is polemical, and it is therefore probable that he only urged those points which were either doubted or explained in an unorthodox way by the sceptics of his time.

Another scholar, of Provence, who wrote but twenty years later than Abba Mari — R. David ben Samuel d'Estella (1320) — speaks of the seven pillars of religion. They are: Revelation, Providence, Reward and Punishment, the Coming of the Messiah, Resurrection of the Dead, *Creatio ex nihilo*, and Free Will.[16]

Of authors living in other countries, I have to mention here R. Shemariah, of Crete, who flourished at about the same time as R. David d'Estella, and is known from his efforts to reconcile the Caraites with the Rabbanites. This author wrote a book for the purpose of furnishing Jewish students with evidence for what he considered the five fundamental teachings of Judaism, viz.: 1. The Existence of God; 2. The Incorporeality of God; 3. His Absolute Unity; 4. That God created heaven and earth; 5. That God created the world after His will 5106 years ago — 5106 (1346 A.C.), being the year in which Shemariah wrote these words.[17]

In Portugal, at about the same time, we find R. David ben Yom-Tob Bilia adding to the articles of Maimonides thirteen of his own, which he calls the "Fundamentals of the Thinking Man." Five of these articles relate to the functions of the human soul, that, according to him, emanated from God, and to the way in which this divine soul receives its punishment and reward. The other eight articles are as follows: 1. The belief in the existence of spiritual beings — angels; 2. *Creatio ex nihilo;* 3. The belief in the existence of another world, and that this other world is only a spiritual one; 4. The Torah is above philosophy; 5. The Torah has an outward (literal) meaning and an inward (allegorical) meaning; 6. The text of the Torah is not subject to any emendation; 7. The reward of a good action is the good work itself, and the doer must not expect any other reward; 8. It is only by the "commands relating to the heart," for instance, the belief in one eternal God, the loving and fearing Him, and not through good actions, that man attains the highest degree of perfection.[18] Perhaps it would be suitable to mention here another contemporaneous writer, who also enumerates twenty-six articles. The name of this writer is unknown, and his articles are only gathered from quotations by later authors. It would seem from these quotations that the articles of this unknown author consisted mostly of statements emphasising the belief in the attributes of God: as, His Eternity, His Wisdom and Omnipotence, and the like.[19]

More important for our subject are the productions of the fifteenth century, especially those of Spanish authors. The fifteen articles of R. Lipman Muhlhausen, in the preface to his well-known *Book of Victory*[20] (1410), differ but slightly from those of Maimonides. In accordance with the anti-Christian tendency of his polemical book, he lays more stress on the two articles of Unity and Incorporeality, and makes of them four. We can therefore dismiss him with this short remark, and pass at once to the Spanish Rabbis.

The first of these is R. Chasdai Ibn Crescas, who composed his famous treatise, *The Light of God*, about 1405. Chasdai's book is well known for its attacks on Aristotle, and also for its influence on Spinoza. But Chasdai deals also with Maimonides' Thirteen Articles, to which he was very strongly opposed. Already in his preface he attacks Maimonides for speaking, in his *Book of the Commandments*, of the belief in the existence of God as an "affirmative precept." Chasdai thinks it absurd; for every commandment must be dictated by some authority, but on whose authority can we dictate the acceptance of this authority? His general objection to the Thirteen Articles is that Maimonides confounded dogmas or *fundamental beliefs* of Judaism, without which Judaism is inconceivable, with beliefs or *doctrines* which Judaism inculcates, but the denial of which, though involving a strong heresy, does not make Judaism impossible. He maintains that if Maimonides meant only to count fundamental teachings, there are not more than seven; but that if he intended also to include doctrines, he ought to have enumerated sixteen. As beliefs of the first class — namely, fundamental beliefs — he considers the following articles: 1. God's knowledge of our actions; 2. Providence; 3. God's omnipotence — even to act against the laws of nature; 4. Prophecy; 5. Free will; 6. The aim of the Torah is to make man long after the closest communion with God. The belief in the existence of God, Chasdai thinks, is an axiom with which every religion must begin, and he is therefore uncertain whether to include it as a dogma or not. As to the doctrines which every Jew is bound to believe, but without which Judaism is not impossible, Chasdai divides them into two sections: (*a*) 1. *Creatio ex nihilo;* 2. Immortality of the soul; 3. Reward and Punishment; 4. Resurrection of the dead; 5. Immutability of the Torah; 6. Superiority of the prophecy of Moses; 7. That the High Priest received from God the instructions sought for, when he put his questions through the medium of the Urim and Thummim; 8. The coming of the Messiah. (*b*) Doctrines which are expressed by certain religious ceremonies, and on belief in which these ceremonies are conditioned: 1. The belief in the efficacy of prayer — as well as in the power of the benediction of the priests to convey to us the blessing of God; 2. God is merciful to the penitent; 3. Certain days in the year — for instance, the Day of Atonement — are especially qualified to bring us near to God, if we keep them in the way we are commanded. That Chasdai is a little arbitrary in the choice of his "doctrines," I need hardly say. Indeed, Chasdai's importance for the dogma-question consists more in his critical suggestions than in his positive results. He was, as we have seen, the first to make the distinction between fundamental teachings which form the basis of Judaism, and those other simple Jewish doctrines without which Judaism is not impossible. Very daring is his remark, when proving that Reward and Punishment, Immortality of the soul, and Resurrection of the dead must not be considered as the basis of Judaism, since the highest ideal of religion is to serve God without any hope of reward. Even more daring are his words concerning the Immutability of the Law. He says: "Some have argued that, since God is perfection, so must also His law be perfect, and thus unsusceptible of improvement." But he does not think this argument conclusive, though the fact in itself (the Immutability of the Law) is true. For one might answer that this perfection of the Torah could only be in accordance with the intelligence of those for whom it was meant; but as soon as the recipients of the Torah have advanced to a higher state of perfection, the Torah must also be altered to suit their advanced intelligence. A pupil of Chasdai illustrates the words of his master by a medical parallel. The physician has to adapt his medicaments to the various stages through which his patient has to pass. That he changes his prescription does not, however, imply that his medical knowledge is imperfect, or that his earlier remedies were ignorantly chosen; the varying condition of the invalid was the cause of the variation in the doctor's treatment. Similarly, were not the Immutability of the Torah a "doctrine," one might maintain that the perfection of the Torah would not be inconsistent with the assumption that it was susceptible of modification, in accordance with our changing and progressive circumstances. But all these arguments are purely of a theoretic character; for, practically, every Jew, according to Chasdai, has to accept all these beliefs, whether he terms them fundamental teachings or only Jewish doctrines.[21]

Some years later, though he finished his work in the same year as Chasdai, R. Simeon Duran (1366–1444,) a younger contemporary of the former, made his researches on dogmas. His studies on this subject form a kind of introduction to his commentary on Job, which he finished in the year 1405. Duran is not so strongly opposed to the Thirteen Articles as Chasdai, or as another "thinker of our people," who thought them an arbitrary imitation of the thirteen attributes of God. Duran tries to justify Maimonides; but nevertheless he agrees with "earlier authorities," who formulated the Jewish creed in Three Articles — The Existence of God, Revelation, and Reward and Punishment — under which Duran thinks the Thirteen Articles of Maimonides may be easily classed. Most interesting are his remarks concerning the validity of dogmas. He tells us that only those are to be considered as heretics who abide by their own opinions, though they know that they are contradictory to the views of the Torah. Those who accept the fundamental teachings of Judaism, but are led by their deep studies and earnest reflection to differ in details from the opinions current among their co-religionists, and explain certain passages in the Scripture in their own way, must by no means be considered as heretics. We must, therefore, Duran proceeds to say, not blame such men as Maimonides, who gave an allegorical interpretation to certain passages in the Bible about miracles, or R. Levi ben Gershom, who followed certain un-Jewish views in relation to the belief in *Creatio ex nihilo.* Only the views are condemnable, not those who cherish them. God forbid, says Duran, that such a thing should happen in Israel as to condemn honest inquirers on account of their differing opinions. It would be interesting to know of how many divines as tolerant as this persecuted Jew the fifteenth century can boast.[22]

We can now pass to a more popular but less original writer on our theme. I refer to R. Joseph Albo, the author of the *Roots,*[23] who was the pupil of Chasdai, a younger contemporary of Duran, and wrote at a much later period than these authors. Graetz has justly denied him much originality. The chief merit of Albo consists in popularising other people's thoughts, though he does not always take care to mention their names. And the student who is a little familiar with the contents of the *Roots* will easily find that Albo has taken his best ideas either from Chasdai or from Duran. As it is of little consequence to us whether an article of faith is called "stem," or "root," or "branch," there is scarcely anything fresh left to quote in the name of Albo. The late Dr. Löw, of Szegedin, was indeed right, when he answered an adversary who challenged him — "Who would dare to declare me a heretic as long as I confess the Three Articles laid down by Albo?" with the words "Albo himself." For, after all the subtle distinctions Albo makes between different classes of dogmas, he declares that every one who denies even the immutability of the Law or the coming of the Messiah, which are, according to him, articles of minor importance, is a heretic who will be excluded from the world to come. But there is one point in his book which is worth noticing. It was suggested to him by Maimonides, indeed; still Albo has the merit of having emphasised it as it deserves. Among the articles which he calls "branches" Albo counts the belief that the perfection of man, which leads to eternal life, can be obtained by the fulfilling of *one* commandment. But this command must, as Maimonides points out, be done without any worldly regard, and only for the love of God. When one considers how many platitudes are repeated year by year by certain theologians on the subject of Jewish legalism, we cannot lay enough stress on this article of Albo, and we ought to make it better known than it has hitherto been.[24]

Though I cannot enter here into the enumeration of the Maimonists, I must not leave unmentioned the name of R. Nissim ben Moses of Marseilles, the first great Maimonist, who flourished about the end of the thirteenth century, and was considered as one of the most enlightened thinkers of his age.[25] Another great Maimonist deserving special attention is R. Abraham ben Shem-Tob Bibago, who may perhaps be regarded as the most prominent among those who undertook to defend Maimonides against the attacks of Chasdai and others. Bibago wrote *The Path of Belief*[26] in the second half of the fifteenth century, and was, as Dr. Steinschneider aptly describes him, a *Denkgläubiger*. But, above all, he was a believing Jew. When he was once asked, at the table of King

John II., of Aragon, by a Christian scholar, " Are you the Jewish philosopher?" he answered, " I am a Jew who believes in the Law given to us by our teacher Moses, though I have studied philosophy." Bibago was such a devoted admirer of Maimonides that he could not tolerate any opposition to him. He speaks in one passage of the prudent people of his time who, in desiring to be looked upon as orthodox by the great mob, calumniated the Teacher (Maimonides), and depreciated his merits. Bibago's book is very interesting, especially in its controversial parts ; but in respect to dogmas he is, as already said, a Maimonist, and does not contribute any new point on our subject.

To return to the Anti-Maimonists of the second half of the fifteenth century. As such may be considered R. Isaac Aramah, who speaks of three foundations of religion : *Creatio ex nihilo*, Revelation (?), and the belief in a world to come.[27] Next to be mentioned is R. Joseph Jabez, who also accepts only three articles : *Creatio ex nihilo*, Individual Providence, and the Unity of God.[28] Under these three heads he tries to classify the Thirteen Articles of Maimonides.

The last Spanish writer on our subject is R. Isaac Abarbanel. His treatise on the subject is known under the title *Top of Amanah*,[29] and was finished in the year 1495. The greatest part of this treatise forms a defence of Maimonides, many points in which are taken from Bibago. But, in spite of this fact, Abarbanel must not be considered a Maimonist. It is only a feeling of piety towards Maimonides, or perhaps rather a fondness for argument, that made him defend Maimonides against Chasdai and others. His own view is that it is a mistake to formulate dogmas of Judaism, since every word in the Torah has to be considered as a dogma for itself. It was only, says Abarbanel, by following the example of non-Jewish scholars that Maimonides and others were induced to lay down dogmas. The non-Jewish philosophers are in the habit of accepting in every science certain indisputable axioms from which they deduce the propositions which are less evident. The Jewish philosophers in a similar way sought for first principles in religion from which the whole of the Torah ought to be considered as a deduction. But, thinks Abarbanel, the Torah as a revealed code is under no necessity of deducing things from each other, for all the commands came from the same divine authority, and, therefore, all are alike evident, and have the same certainty. On this and similar grounds Abarbanel refused to accept dogmatic articles for Judaism, and he thus became the head of the school that forms a class by itself among the Anti-Maimonists to which many of the greatest Cabbalists also belong. But it is idle talk to cite this school in aid of the modern theory that Judaism has no dogmas. As we have seen, it was rather an *embarras de richesse* that prevented Abarbanel from accepting the Thirteen Articles of Maimonides. To him and to the Cabbalists the Torah consists of at least 613 Articles.

Abarbanel wrote his book with which we have just dealt, at Naples. And it is Italy to which, after the expulsion of the Jews from Spain, we have to look chiefly for religious speculation. But the philosophers of Italy are still less independent of Maimonides than their predecessors in Spain. Thus we find that R. David Messer Leon, R. David Vital, and others were Maimonists.

Even the otherwise refined and original thinker, R. Elijah Delmedigo (who died about the end of the fifteenth century) becomes almost impolite when he speaks of the adversaries of Maimonides in respect to dogmas. "It was only," he says, "the would-be philosopher that dared to question the articles of Maimonides. Our people have always the bad habit of thinking themselves competent to attack the greatest authorities as soon as they have got some knowledge of the subject. Genuine thinkers, however, attach very little importance to their objections.[30]

Indeed, it seems as if the energetic protests of Delmedigo scared away the Anti-Maimonists for more than a century. Even in the following seventeenth century we have to notice only two Anti-Maimonists. The one is R. Tobijah, the Priest (1652), who was of Polish descent, studied in Italy, and lived as a medical man in France. He seems to refuse to accept the belief in the Immutability of the Torah, and in the coming of the Messiah, as fundamental teachings of Judaism.[31] The other, at the end of the seventeenth century (1695), is R. Abraham Chayim Viterbo, of Italy. He accepts only six articles: 1. Existence of God; 2. Unity; 3. Incorporeality; 4. That God was revealed to Moses on Mount Sinai, and that the prophecy of Moses is true; 5. Revelation (including the historical parts of the Torah); 6. Reward and Punishment. As to the other articles of Maimonides, Viterbo, in opposition to other half-hearted Anti-Maimonists, declares that the man who denies them is *not* to be considered as a heretic; though he ought to believe them.[32]

I have now arrived at the limit I set to myself at the beginning of this essay. For, between the times of

Viterbo and those of Mendelssohn, there is hardly to be found any serious opposition to Maimonides worth noticing here. Still I must mention the name of R. Saul Berlin (died 1794); there is much in his opinions on dogmas which will help us the better to understand the Thirteen Articles of Maimonides. As the reader has seen, I have refrained so far from reproducing here the apologies which were made by many Maimonists in behalf of the Thirteen Articles. For, after all their elaborate pleas, none of them was able to clear Maimonides of the charge of having confounded dogmas or fundamental teachings with doctrines. It is also true that the Fifth Article — that prayer and worship must only be offered to God — cannot be considered even as a doctrine, but as a simple precept. And there are other difficulties which all the distinctions of the Maimonists will never be able to solve. The only possible justification is, I think, that suggested by a remark of R. Saul. This author, who was himself — like his friend and older contemporary Mendelssohn — a strong Anti-Maimonist, among other remarks, maintains that dogmas must never be laid down but with regard to the necessities of the time.[33]

Now R. Saul certainly did not doubt that Judaism is based on eternal truths which can in no way be shaken by new modes of thinking or changed circumstances. What he meant was that there are in every age certain beliefs which ought to be asserted more emphatically than others, without regard to their theological or rather logical importance. It is by this maxim that we shall be able to explain the articles of Maimonides. He asserted them, because they were necessary for his time.

We know, for instance, from a letter of his son and from other contemporaries, that it was just at his time that the belief in the incorporeality of God was, in the opinion of Maimonides, a little relaxed. Maimonides, who thought such low notions of the Deity dangerous to Judaism, therefore laid down an article against them. He tells us in his *Guide* that it was far from him to condemn any one who was not able to demonstrate the Incorporeality of God, but he stigmatised as a heretic one who refused to believe it. This position might be paralleled by that of a modern astronomer who, while considering it unreasonable to expect a mathematical demonstration of the movements of the earth from an ordinary unscientific man, would yet regard the person who refused to believe in such movements as an ignorant faddist.

Again, Maimonides undoubtedly knew that there may be found in the Talmud — that bottomless sea with its innumerable undercurrents — passages that are not quite in harmony with his articles; for instance, the well-known dictum of R. Hillel, who said, there is no Messiah for Israel — a passage which has already been quoted *ad nauseam* by every opponent of Maimonides from the earliest times down to the year of grace 1896. Maimonides was well aware of the existence of this and similar passages. But, being deeply convinced of the necessity of the belief in a future redemption of *Israel* — in opposition to other creeds which claim this redemption exclusively for their own adherents — Maimonides simply ignored the saying of R. Hillel, as an isolated opinion which contradicts all the consciousness and traditions of the Jew as expressed in thousands of other passages, and

N

especially in the liturgy. Most interesting is Maimonides' view about such isolated opinions in a letter to the wise men of Marseilles. He deals there with the question of free will and other theological subjects. After having stated his own view he goes on to say : " I know that it is possible to find in the Talmud or in the Midrash this or that saying in contradiction to the views you have heard from me. But you must not be troubled by them. One must not refuse to accept a doctrine, the truth of which has been proved, on account of its being in opposition to some isolated opinion held by this or that great authority. Is it not possible that he overlooked some important considerations when he uttered this strange opinion ? It is also possible that his words must not be taken literally, and have to be explained in an allegorical way. We can also think that his words were only to be applied with regard to certain circumstances of his time, but never intended as permanent truths. . . . No man must surrender his private judgment. The eyes are not directed backwards but forwards." In another place Maimonides calls the suppression of one's own opinions — for the reason of their being irreconcilable with the isolated views of some great authority — a moral suicide.

By such motives Maimonides was guided when he left certain views hazarded in the Rabbinic literature unheeded, and followed what we may perhaps call the religious instinct, trusting to his own conscience. We may again be certain that Maimonides was clear-headed enough to see that the words of the Torah : " And there arose no prophet since in Israel like unto Moses " (Deut. xxxiv. 10), were as little intended to imply a doctrine as the passage relating to the king Josiah, " And like unto him was there no king before him that turned to the Lord with all his heart . . . neither after him arose there any like him " (2 Kings xxiii. 25). And none would think of declaring the man a heretic who should believe another king to be as pious as Josiah. But living among followers of the "imitating creeds" (as he calls Christianity and Mohammedism), who claimed that their religion had superseded the law of Moses, Maimonides, consciously or unconsciously, felt himself compelled to assert the superiority of the prophecy of Moses. And so we may guess that every article of Maimonides which seems to offer difficulties to us contains an assertion of some relaxed belief, or a protest against the pretensions of other creeds, though we are not always able to discover the exact necessity for them. On the other hand, Maimonides did not assert the belief in free will, for which he argued so earnestly in his *Guide*. The common "man," with his simple unspeculative mind, for whom these Thirteen Articles were intended, "never dreamed that the will was not free," and there was no necessity of impressing on his mind things which he had never doubted.[34]

So much about Maimonides. As to the Anti-Maimonists, it could hardly escape the reader that in some of the quoted systems the difference from the view of Maimonides is only a logical one, not a theological. Of some authors again, especially those of the thirteenth and fourteenth centuries, it is not at all certain whether they intended to oppose Maimonides. Others again, as for instance R. Abba Mari, R. Lipman, and R. Joseph Jabez, acted on the same principle as Maimonides, urging only those teachings of Judaism which they thought endangered. One could now, indeed, animated by the praiseworthy exam-

ple given to us by Maimonides, also propose some articles of faith which are suggested to us by the necessities
of our own time. One might, for instance, insert the
article, "I believe that Judaism is, in the first instance,
a divine religion, *not* a mere complex of racial peculiarities and tribal customs." One might again propose
an article to the effect that Judaism is a proselytising
religion, having the mission to bring about God's kingdom on earth, and to include in that kingdom all mankind. One might also submit for consideration whether
it would not be advisable to urge a little more the principle that religion means chiefly a *Weltanschauung* and
worship of God by means of holiness both in thought
and in action. One would even not object to accept the
article laid down by R. Saul, that we have to look upon
ourselves as sinners. Morbid as such a belief may be, it
would, if properly impressed on our mind, have perhaps
the wholesome effect of cooling down a little our self-
importance and our mutual admiration that makes all
progress among us almost impossible.

But it was not my purpose to ventilate here the question
whether Maimonides' articles are sufficient for us, or
whether we ought not to add new ones to them. Nor do
I attempt to decide what system we ought to prefer for
recitation in the Synagogue — that of Maimonides or that
of Chasdai, or of any other writer. I do not think that
such a recital is of much use. My object in this sketch
has been rather to make the reader *think* about Judaism,
by proving that it regulates not only our actions, but also
our thoughts. We usually urge that in Judaism religion
means life ; but we forget that a life without guiding
principles and thoughts is a life not worth living. At

least it was so considered by the greatest Jewish thinkers, and hence their efforts to formulate the creed of Judaism, so that men should not only be able to do the right thing, but also to think the right thing. Whether they succeeded in their attempts towards formulating the creed of Judaism or not will always remain a question. This concerns the logician more than the theologian. But surely Maimonides and his successors *did* succeed in having a religion depending directly on God, with the most ideal and lofty aspirations for the future; whilst the Judaism of a great part of our modern theologians reminds one very much of the words with which the author of *Marius the Epicurean* characterises the Roman religion in the days of her decline: a religion which had been always something to be done rather than something to be thought, or believed, or loved.

Political economy, hygiene, statistics, are very fine things. But no sane man would for them make those sacrifices which Judaism requires from us. It is only for God's sake, to fulfil His commands and to accomplish His purpose, that religion becomes worth living and dying for. And this can only be possible with a religion which possesses dogmas.

It is true that every great religion is "a concentration of many ideas and ideals," which make this religion able to adapt itself to various modes of thinking and living. But there must always be a point round which all these ideas concentrate themselves. This centre is Dogma.

VII

THE HISTORY OF JEWISH TRADITION

THERE is an anecdote about a famous theologian to the effect that he used to tell his pupils, " Should I ever grow old and weak — which usually drives people to embrace the safer side — and alter my opinions, then pray do not believe me." The concluding volume of Weiss's *History of Jewish Tradition*[1] shows that there was no need for our author to warn his pupils against the dangers accompanying old age. For though Weiss had, when he began to write this last volume, already exceeded his three-score and ten, and, as we read in the preface, had some misgivings as to whether he should continue his work, there is no trace in it of any abatement of the great powers of the author. It is marked by the same freshness in diction, the same marvellous scholarship, the same display of astonishing critical powers, and the same impartial and straightforward way of judging persons and things, for which the preceding volumes were so much distinguished and admired.

This book, which is recognised as a standard work abroad, is, I fear, owing to the fact of its being written in the Hebrew language, not sufficiently known in this country. Weiss does not want *our* recognition; we are rather in need of his instruction. Some general view of his estimate of Jewish Tradition may, therefore, be of service to the student. It is, indeed, the only work of its kind. Zunz has confined himself to the history of the Agadah. Graetz gave most of his attention to the political side of Jewish history. But comparatively little has been done for the Halachah, though Frankel, Geiger, Herzfeld, and others have treated some single points in various monographs. Thus it was left for Weiss to write the *History of Tradition*, which includes both the Agadah and the Halachah. The treatment of this latter must have proved, in consequence of the intricate and intractable nature of its materials, by far the more difficult portion of his task.

In speaking of the *History* of Tradition, a term which suggests the fluctuating character of a thing, its origin, development, progress, and retrogression, we have already indicated that Weiss does not consider even the Halachah as having come down from heaven, ready-made, and definitely fixed for all time. To define it more clearly, Tradition is, apart from the few ordinances and certain usages for which there is no precedent in the Bible, the history of interpretation of the Scriptures, which was constantly liable to variation, not on grounds of philology, but through the subjective notions of successive generations regarding religion and the method and scope of its application.

Weiss's standpoint with reference to the Pentateuch is the conservative one, maintaining both its unity and its Mosaic authorship. Those passages and accounts in the Bible in which the modern critic discerns traces of different traditional sources, are for Weiss only indicative of the various stages of interpretation through which the

Pentateuch had to pass. The earliest stage was a very crude one, as may be seen from the case of Jephthah's vow, for which only a misinterpretation of certain passages in the Pentateuch (Gen. xxii. 2; Num. xxv. 4) could be made responsible. Nor was Jephthah, who felt himself bound to carry out his vow, acquainted with the provision for dissolving vows[2] that was sufficiently familiar to later ages. When, on the other hand, Jeremiah declared sacrifices to be altogether superfluous, and said that God did not command Israel, when he brought them from the land of Egypt, concerning burnt offerings or sacrifices (vii. 22), he was not in contradiction with Leviticus, but interpreted the laws contained in this book as a concession to popular custom, though not desirable on their own account. This concession, whenever it was of a harmless nature, the prophets carried so far as to permit altars outside the Tabernacle or Temple, though this was against the plain sense of Deuteronomy. Elijah even bewailed their destruction (1 Kings xix. 10). He and other prophets probably interpreted the law in question as directed against the construction and maintenance of several chief sanctuaries, but not against sacrificing in different places on minor occasions. This is evidently a free interpretation, or rather application, of the Law. Occasionally the conception as to when and how a law should be applied took a completely negative form. In this manner is to be explained the action of Solomon in suspending the Fast of the Day of Atonement before the festival he was going to celebrate in honour of the consecration of the Temple (1 Kings viii. 65), the king being convinced that on this unique occasion the latter was of more religious importance than the former. Weiss

thinks that the later custom of holding public dances in
the vineyards on the 10th of Tishri might have had its
origin in this solemn, but also joyful, festival. Ezekiel,
again, though alluding more frequently than any other
prophet to the laws in the Pentateuch, is exceedingly
bold in his interpretation of them, as, for instance, when
he says that *priests* shall not eat anything that is dead
or torn (xliv. 31), which shows that he took the verses
in Exod. xxii. 30, and Deut. xiv. 20, to have been meant
only as a good advice to the laymen to refrain from eating these unclean things, but not as having for them the
force of a real commandment.

Starting from this proposition, that there existed always
some sort of interpretation running side by side with the
recognised Scriptures, which from the very looseness of
its connection with the letter of the Scripture could claim
to be considered a thing independent in itself, and might
therefore be regarded as the *Oral Law*, in contradistinc-
tion to the *Written Law*, the author passes to the age of
the Second Temple, the period to which the rest of the
first volume is devoted. In these pages Weiss reviews the
activity of Ezra and Nehemiah, the ordinances of the Men
of the Great Synagogue, the institutions of the Scribes, the
Lives of the so-called Pairs,[3] the characteristics of the
three sects, the Sadducees, Pharisees, and Essenes, and
the differences between the schools of Shammai and Hillel.
To each of these subjects Weiss gives his fullest attention,
and his discussions of them would form perfect monographs in themselves. To reproduce all the interesting
matter would mean to translate the whole of this portion
of his work into English. I shall only draw attention to
one or two points.

First, this liberal interpretation was active during the whole period referred to. Otherwise no authority could have abolished the *lex talionis*, or have permitted war on Sabbath, or made the condition that no crime should be punished without a preceding warning (which was chiefly owing to the aversion of the Rabbis to the infliction of capital punishment), or have sanctioned the sacrificing of the Passover when the 14th of Nisan fell on Sabbath. Indeed Shemaiah and Abtalyon, in whose name Hillel communicated this last law, were called the Great Interpreters.[4]

Secondly, as to the so-called *laws given to Moses on Sinai*.[5] Much has been said about these. The distinction claimed for them by some scholars, viz. that they were never contested, is not tenable, considering that there prevailed much difference of opinion about some of them. Nor is the theory that they were ancient religious usages, dating from time immemorial, entirely satisfactory. For though the fact may be true in itself, this could not have justified the Rabbis in calling them all Sinaitic laws, especially when they were aware that not a few of them were contested by certain of their colleagues, a thing that would have been quite impossible if they had a genuine claim to Mosaic authority. But if we understand Weiss rightly these laws are only to be considered as a specimen of the whole of the Oral Law, which was believed to emanate, both in its institutional and in its expository part, from the same authority. The conviction was firmly held that everything wise and good, be it ethical or ceremonial in its character, whose effect would be to strengthen the cause of religion, was at least potentially contained in the Torah, and that it only required an earnest religious mind to find it there. Hence the famous adage that "everything which any student will teach at any future time was already communicated to Moses on Mount Sinai"; or the injunction that any acceptable truth, even if discovered by an insignificant man in Israel, should be considered as having the authority of a great sage or prophet, or even of Moses himself. The principle was that the words of the Torah are "fruitful and multiply."

It will probably be said that the laws of clean and unclean, and such like, have proved rather too prolific; but if we read Weiss carefully, we shall be reminded that it was by the same process of propagation that the Rabbis developed from Deut. xxii. 8, a whole code of sanitary and police-laws which could even now be studied with profit; from the few scanty civil laws in Exod. xxi., a whole *corpus juris*, which might well excite the interest and the admiration of any lawyer; and from the words "And thou shalt teach them diligently unto thy children," a complete school-system on the one hand, and on the other the *résumé* of a liturgy that appears to have sufficed for the spiritual needs of more than fifty generations of Israelites.

Before we pass to the age of the Tannaim,[6] the subject of Weiss's second volume, we must take account of two important events which have greatly influenced the further development of Tradition. I refer to the destruction of the Temple and the rise of Christianity. With the former event Judaism ceased to be a political commonwealth, and if "the nation was already in the times of Ezra converted into a church," — an assertion, by the way, which has not the least basis in fact, — it became the more so after it had lost the last remains of its independence. But it was a church without priests, or, since such a thing, as far as history teaches us, has never existed, let us rather call it a Synagogue.

From this fact diverse results flowed. A Synagogue can exist not only without priests, but also without sacrifices, for which prayer and charity were a sufficient substitute. With the progress of time also many agricultural laws, as well as others relating to sacerdotal purity, gradually became obsolete, though they lingered on for some generations, and, as a venerable reminiscence of a glorious time, entered largely into Jewish literature. This disappearance of so many laws and the weakening of the national element, however, required, if Judaism was to continue to exist, the strengthening of religion from another side. The first thing needed was the creation of a new religious centre which would not only replace the Temple to a certain degree, but also bring about a greater solidarity of views, such as would render impossible the ancient differences that divided the schools of Hillel and Shammai. The creator of this centre was R. Johanan ben Zaccai, who founded the school of Jamnia, and invested it with the same authority and importance as the Sanhedrin had enjoyed during Temple times. The consciousness that they were standing before a new starting-point in history, with a large religious inheritance from the past, actuated them not only to collect the old traditional laws and to take stock of their religious institutions, but also to give them more definite shape and greater stability. As many of these traditions were by no means undisputed, the best thing was to bring them under one or other heading of the Scriptures. This desire gave the impulse to the famous hermeneutic schools of R. Akiba and R. Ishmael.

The next cause that contributed to give a more determinate expression to the Law was the rise of Christianity. This is not the place to give an account of the views which the Rabbis entertained of Christianity. Suffice it to say they could not see in the destruction of the Law its fulfilment. They also thought that under certain conditions it is not only the letter that killeth, but also the spirit, or rather that the spirit may sometimes be clothed in a letter, which, in its turn, will slay more victims than the letter against which the loudest denunciations have been levelled. Spirit without letter, let theologians say what they will, is a mere phantasm. However, the new sect made claims to the gift of prophecy, which, as they thought, placed them above the Law. It would seem that this was a time of special excitement. The student of the Talmud finds that such marvels as predicting the future, reviving the dead, casting out demons, crossing rivers dry-shod, curing the sick by a touch or prayer, were the order of the day, and performed by scores of Rabbis. Voices from heaven were often heard, and strange visions were frequently beheld. Napoleon I. is said to have forbidden the holy coat of Treves to work miracles. The Jewish legislature, however, had no means of preventing these supernatural workings; but when the Rabbis saw their dangerous consequences, they insisted that miracles should have no influence on the interpretation and development of the Law. Hence the saying with regard to Lev. xxvii. 34, that no prophet is authorised to add a new law. And when R. Eliezer b. Hyrkanos (about 120 A.C.) thought to prove the justice of his case by the intervention of miracles, the majority answered that the fact of this or that variation, effected at his bidding, in the established order of nature, proved nothing for the soundness of his argument. Nay, they even ignored the *Bath-Kol*[7] (the celestial voice), which declared itself in favour of R. Eliezer, maintaining that the Torah having once been given to mankind, it is only the opinion of the majority that should decide on its interpretation and application. Very characteristic is the legend connected with this fact. When one of the Rabbis afterwards met Elijah and asked him what they thought in heaven of the audacity of his colleagues, the prophet answered, " God rejoiced and said, my children have conquered me."

Into such discredit did miracles fall at that period, whilst the opinion of the interpreting body, or the Sanhedrin, became more powerful than ever. These were merely dogmatical consequences. But new laws were enacted and old ones revived, with the object of resisting Christian influences over the Jews. To expand the Oral Law, and give it a firm basis in the Scriptures, were considered the best means of preserving Judaism intact. " Moses desired," an old legend narrates, " that the Mishnah also (that is Tradition) should be written down; " but foreseeing the time when the nations of the world would translate the Torah into Greek, and would assert their title to rank as the Children of God, the Lord refused to permit tradition to be recorded otherwise than by word of mouth. The claim of the Gentiles might then be refuted by asking them whether they were also in possession of "the Mystery." The Rabbis therefore concentrated their attention upon "the Mystery," and this contributed largely towards making the expository methods of R. Akiba and R. Ishmael, to which I have above referred, the main object of their study in the schools.

It would, however, be a mistake to think that the Sanhedrin now spent their powers in "enforcing retrograde measures and creating a strange exegesis." I especially advise the student to read carefully that admirable chapter (VII., of Vol. II.) in which Weiss classifies all the Ordinances, "Fences," Decrees, and Institutions, dating both from this and from earlier ages, under ten headings, and also shows their underlying principles. The main object was to preserve the Jewish religion by strengthening the principle of Jewish nationality, and to preserve the nationality by the aid of religion. But sometimes the Rabbis also considered it necessary to preserve religion against itself, so to speak, or, as they expressed it, "When there is time to work for the Lord, they make void thy Torah." This authorised the *Beth Din*[8] to act in certain cases against the letter of the Torah. "The welfare of the World" was another great consideration. By "World" they understood both the religious and the secular world. From a regard to the former resulted such "Fences" and Ordinances as were directed against "the transgressors," as well as the general injunction to "keep aloof from what is morally unseemly, and from whatever bears any likeness thereto." In the interests of the latter — the welfare of the secular world — they enacted such laws as either tended to elevate the position of women, or to promote the peace and welfare of members of their own community, or to improve the relations between Jews and their Gentile neighbours. They also held the great principle that nothing is so injurious to the cause of religion as increasing the number of sinners by needless severity. Hence the introduction of many laws "for the benefit of penitents," and the maxim not to issue any decree which may prove too heavy a burden to the majority of the community. The relaxation of certain traditional laws was also permitted when they involved a serious loss of property, or the sacrifice of a man's dignity. Some old decrees were even permitted to fall into oblivion when public opinion was too strong against them, the Rabbis holding that it was often better for Israelites to be unconscious sinners than wilful transgressors. The *Minhag*, or religious custom, also played an important part, it being assumed that it must have been first introduced by some eminent authority ; but, if there was reason to believe that the custom owed its origin to some fancy of the populace, and that it had a pernicious effect on the multitude, no compunction was felt in abolishing it.

Very important it is to note that the Oral Law had not at this period assumed a character of such rigidity that all its ordinances, etc., had to be looked upon as irremovable for all times. With those who think otherwise, a favourite quotation is the administratory measure laid dawn in Tractate *Evidences*,[9] I. 5, where we read that no *Beth Din* has the right of annulling the dicta of another *Beth Din*, unless it is stronger in numbers (having a larger majority) and greater in wisdom than its fellow tribunal. Confess with becoming modesty that the world is always going downhill, decreasing both in numbers and in wisdom, and the result follows that any decision by the earlier Rabbis is fixed law for all eternity. Weiss refutes such an idea not only as inconsistent with the nature of Tradition, but also as contradictory to the facts. He proves by numerous instances that the Rabbis did abolish ordinances and decrees introduced by preceding authorities, and that the whole conception is based on a misunderstanding. For the rule in question, as Weiss clearly points out, originally only meant that a *Beth Din* has no right to undo the decrees of another *contemporary Beth Din*, unless it was justified in doing so by the weight of its greater authority. This was necessary if a central authority was to exist at all. Weiss is indeed of opinion that the whole passage is a later interpolation from the age of R. Simeon b. Gamaliel II., when certain Rabbis tried to emancipate themselves from the authority of the Patriarch. But it was not meant that the decision of a *Beth Din* should have perpetual binding power for all posterity. This was left to the discretion of the legislature of each generation, who had to examine whether the original cause for maintaining such decision still existed.

The rest of this volume is for the greater part taken up with complete monographs of the Patriarchs and the heads of the schools of that age, whilst the concluding chapters give us the history of the literature, the Midrash, Mechilta, Siphra, Siphré, Mishnah, etc., which contain both the Halachic and the Agadic sayings emanating from these authorities.

With regard to these Patriarchs, I should like only to remark that Weiss defends them against the charge made by Schorr and others, who accuse them of having assumed too much authority on account of their noble descent, and who describe their opponents as the true friends of the people. Weiss is no lover of such specious phrases. The qualifications required for the leadership of the people were a right instinct for the necessities of their time, a fair amount of secular knowledge, and, what is of chief importance, an unbounded love and devotion to those over whose interests they were called to watch. These distinctions, as Weiss proves, the descendants of Hillel possessed in the

o

highest degree.   It is true that occasionally, as for instance in the famous controversy of R. Gamaliel II. with R. Joshua b. Hananiah, or that of R. Simeon b. Gamaliel II. with R. Nathan and R. Meir, they made their authority too heavily felt; [10] but this was again another necessity of those troubled times, when only real unity could save Israel.

However, Weiss is no partisan, and the love he lavishes on his favourite heroes does not exhaust his resources of sympathy and appreciation for members of the other schools.   Weiss is no apologist either, and does not make the slightest attempt towards explaining away even the defects of R. Akiba in his somewhat arbitrary method of interpretation, which our author thinks much inferior to the expository rules of R. Ishmael; but this does not prevent him from admiring his excellences.

Altogether it would seem that Weiss thinks R. Akiba more happy in his quality as a great saint than in that of a great exegete.   What is most admirable is the instinct with which Weiss understands how to emphasise the right thing in its right place.   As an indication of the literary honesty and marvellous industry of our author, I would draw attention to the fact that the sketch of R. Akiba and his school alone is based on more than two thousand quotations scattered over the whole area of the Rabbinic literature; but he points in a special note to a sentence attributed to R. Akiba, which presents the whole man and his generation in a single stroke.   I refer to that passage in Tractate *Joys*,[11] in which R. Akiba speaks of the four types of sufferers.   He draws the comparison of a king chastising his children; the first son maintains stubborn silence, the second simply rebels, the third suppli-

cates for mercy, and the fourth (the best of sons) says:
"Father, proceed with thy chastisement, as David said,
Wash me thoroughly from mine iniquity and cleanse me
from my sin" (Ps. li. 4). This absolute submission to
the will of God, which perceives in suffering only an expression of His fatherly love and mercy, was the ideal of
R. Akiba.

The great literary production of this period was the
Mishnah, which, through the high authority of its compiler, R. Judah the Patriarch, his saintliness and popularity, soon superseded all the collections of a similar
kind, and became the official text-book of the Oral Law.
But a text requires interpretation, whilst other collections
also demanded some attention. This brings us to the two
Talmuds, namely, the Talmud of Jerusalem and the Talmud of Babylon, the origin and history of which form
the subject of Weiss's third volume.

Here again the first chapters are more of a preliminary
character, giving the student some insight into the labyrinth of the Talmud. The two chapters entitled "The
instruments employed in erecting the great Edifice," and
the "Workmanship displayed by the Builders," give evidence of almost unrivalled familiarity with the Rabbinical
literature, and of critical powers of the rarest kind. Now
these instruments were by no means new, for, as Weiss
shows, the Amoraim employed in interpreting the Mishnah the same explanatory rules that are known to us
from the School of R. Ishmael as "the Thirteen Rules
by which the Torah is explained," though they appear
in the Talmud under other names, and are in reality only
a species of Midrash. Besides this there comes another
element into play. It was the exaggerated awe of all

earlier authorities that endeavoured to reconcile the most contradictory statements by means of a subtle dialectic for which the schools in Babylon were especially famous. There were certainly many opponents of this system, and from the monographs which Weiss gives on the various heads of the western and eastern schools we see that not all followed this method, and some among them even condemned it in the strongest words. However, it cannot be denied that there is a strong scholastic feature in the Talmud, which is very far from what we should look for in a trustworthy exegesis. Thus we must not always expect to find in the Talmud the true meaning of the sayings of their predecessors, and it is certain that a more scientific method in many cases has led to results the very opposite of those at which the later Rabbis have arrived. This fact was already recognised in the sixteenth century, though only in part, by R. Yom-Tob Heller and others. Only he insisted that in this matter a line must be drawn between theory and practice. But Weiss gives irrefragable proofs that even this line was often overstepped by the greatest authorities, though they remained always within the limits of Tradition. Indeed, as Weiss points out, not every saying to be found in the Talmud is to be looked upon as representing Tradition; for there is much in it which only gives the individual opinion or is merely an interpolation of later hands; nor does the Talmud contain the *whole* of Tradition, this latter proceeding and advancing with the time, and corresponding to its conditions and notions. As we read Weiss, the conviction is borne in upon us that there was a Talmud before, and another after *The Talmud.*

Much space in this volume is given to the Agadah and

the so-called "Teachers of the Agadah." Weiss makes
no attempt at apology for that which seems to us strange,
or even repugnant in this part of the Rabbinic literature.
The greatest fault to be found with those who wrote down
such passages as appear objectionable to us is, perhaps,
that they did not observe the wise rule of Johnson, who
said to Boswell on a certain occasion, "Let us get serious,
for there comes a fool." And the fools unfortunately
did come in the shape of certain Jewish commentators
and Christian controversialists, who took as serious things
which were only the expression of a momentary impulse,
or represented the opinion of some isolated individual, or
were meant simply as a piece of humorous by-play, calculated to enliven the interest of a languid audience. But
on the other hand, as Weiss proves, the Agadah contains
also many elements of real edification and eternal truths
as well as abundant material for building up the edifice
of dogmatic Judaism. Talmudical quotations of such a
nature are scattered by thousands over Weiss's work, particularly in those chapters in which he describes the lives
of the greatest Rabbinical heroes. But the author lays the
student under special obligations by putting together in
the concluding pages of this volume some of these sentences, and classifying them under various headings. I give
here a few extracts. For the references to authorities I
must direct the reader to the original : —

"The unity of God is the keystone of dogmatic Judaism.
The Rabbis give Israel the credit of having proclaimed to
the world the unity of God. They also say that Israel
took an oath never to change Him for another God. This
only God is eternal, incorporeal, and immutable. And
though the prophets saw Him in different aspects, He

warned them that they must not infer from the visions vouchsafed to them that there are different Gods. 'I am the first,' He tells them, which implies that he had no father, and the words, 'There is no God besides me,' mean that he has no son.   Now, this God, the God of Israel, is holy in every thinkable way of holiness.   He is merciful and gracious, as it is said, 'And I will be gracious to whom I will be gracious,' even though he who is the recipient of God's grace has no merit of his own.   'And I will show mercy to whom I will show mercy,' that is, even to those who do not deserve it.   His attributes are righteousness, loving-kindness, and truth.   God speaks words of eternal truth, even as He himself is the eternal life.   All that the Merciful One does is only for good, and even in the time of His anger He remembers His graciousness, and often suppresses His attribute of judgment before His attribute of mercy.   But with the righteous God is more severe than with the rest of the world, and when His hand falls in chastening on His saints His name becomes awful, revered, and exalted.   This God of Israel, again, extends His providence over all mankind, and especially over Israel. By His eye everything is foreseen, yet freedom of choice is given, and the world is judged by grace, yet all according to the works wrought.   Hence, know what is above thee, a seeing eye and a hearing ear, and that all thy deeds are written in a book.

" They [the Rabbis] believed that God created the world out of nothing, without toil and without weariness.   This world was created by the combination of His two attributes, mercy and justice.   He rejoices in His creation, and if the Maker praises it, who dares to blame it?   And if He exults in it, who shall find a blemish in it?   Nay, it is a glorious and a beautiful world. It is created for man, and its other denizens were all meant but to serve him. Though all mankind are formed after the type of Adam, no one is like his fellow-man (each one having an individuality of his own). Thus he is able to say, 'For my sake, also, was the world created'; and with this thought his responsibilities increase. But the greatest love shown to man is that he was created in the image of God. Man is a being possessed of free will, and, though everything is given on pledge, whosoever wishes to borrow may come and borrow. Everything is in the gift of Heaven except the fear of God. In man's heart abide both the evil inclination and the good inclination; and the words of Scripture, 'Thou shalt not bow down before a strange god,' point to the strange god who is within man himself, who entices him to sin in this world, and gives evidence against him in the next. But the Holy One — blessed be He! — said, 'I have created the evil inclination, but I have also created its antidote, the Torah.' And when man is occupied with the Torah and in works of charity, he becomes the master of the evil inclination; otherwise, he is its slave. When man reflects the image of God, he is the lord of creation, and is feared by all creatures; but this image is defaced by sin, and then he has no power over the universe, and is in fear of all things.

"Another principle of Judaism is the belief in reward and punishment. 'I am the Lord, your God,' means, 'it is I who am prepared to recompense you for your good actions, and to bring retribution upon you for your evil deeds.' God does not allow to pass unrewarded even the merit of a kind and considerate word. By the same measure which man metes out, it shall be meted out to

him.   Because thou drownedst others, they have drowned
thee, and at the last they who drowned thee shall themselves be drowned.   Though it is not in our power to
explain either the prosperity of the wicked or the affliction
of the righteous, nevertheless know before whom thou
toilest, and who thy employer is, who will pay thee the
reward of thy labour.   Here at thy door is a poor man
standing, and at his right hand standeth God.   If thou
grantest his request, be certain of thy reward; but if
thou refusest, think of him who is by the side of the
poor, and will avenge it on thee.   'God seeketh the
persecuted' to defend him, even though it be the wicked
who is persecuted by the righteous.   The soul of man
is immortal, the souls of the righteous being treasured
up under the throne of God.   Know that everything is
according to the reckoning, and let not thy imagination
give thee hope that the grave will be a place of refuge
for thee, for perforce thou wast formed, and perforce thou
wast born, and thou livest perforce, and perforce thou wilt
die, and perforce thou wilt in the future have to give
account and reckoning before the Supreme King of kings,
the Holy One, blessed be He.

"The advent of the Messiah is another article of the
belief of the Rabbis.   But if a man tell thee that he
knows when the redemption of Israel will take place,
believe him not, for this is one of the unrevealed secrets
of the Almighty.   The mission of Elijah is to bring peace
into the world, while the Messiah, in whose days Israel
will regain his national independence, will lead the whole
world in repentance to God.   On this, it is believed, will
follow the resurrection of the dead.

"Another main principle in the belief of the Rabbis

is the election of Israel, which imposes on them special duties, and gives them a peculiar mission. Beloved are Israel, for they are called the children of God, and His firstborn. 'They shall endure for ever' through the merit of their fathers. There is an especial covenant established between God and the tribes of Israel. God is their father, and He said to them, My children, even as I have no contact with the profanity of the world, so also withdraw yourselves from it. And as I am holy, be ye also holy. Nay, sanctify thyself by refraining even from that which is not forbidden thee. There is no holiness without chastity.

"The main duty of Israel is to sanctify the name of God, for the Torah was only given that His great name might be glorified. Better is it that a single letter of the law be cast out than that the name of Heaven be profaned. And this also is the mission of Israel in this world : to sanctify the name of God, as it is written, 'This people have I formed for myself, that they may show forth my praise.' Or, 'And thou shalt love the Lord thy God,' which means, Thou shalt make God beloved by all creatures, even as Abraham did. Israel is the light of the world ; as it is said, 'And nations shall walk by thy light.' But he who profanes the name of Heaven in secret will suffer the penalty thereof in public ; and this whether the Heavenly Name be profaned in ignorance or in wilfulness.

"Another duty towards God is to love Him and to fear Him. God's only representative on earth is the God-fearing man. Woe unto those who are occupied in the study of the Torah, but who have no fear of God. But a still higher duty it is to perform the commandments of God from love. For greater is he who submits to the will of God from love than he who does so from fear.

"Now, how shall man love God? This is answered in the words of Scripture, 'And these words shall be upon thy heart.' For by them thou wilt recognise Him whose word called the world into existence, and follow His divine attributes.

"God is righteous; be ye also righteous, O Israel. By righteousness the Rabbis understand love of truth, hatred of lying and backbiting. The seal of the Holy One, blessed be He, is Truth, of which the actions of man should also bear the impress. Hence, let thy yea be yea, and thy nay, nay. He who is honest in money transactions, unto him this is reckoned as if he had fulfilled the whole of the Torah. Greater is he who earns his livelihood by the labour of his hands than even the God-fearing man; whilst the righteous judge is, as it were, the companion of God in the government of the world. For upon three things the world stands: upon truth, upon judgment, upon peace; as it is said, 'Judge ye the truth and the judgment of peace in your gates.' But he who breaks his word, his sin is as great as if he worshipped idols; and God, who punished the people of the time of the Flood, will also punish him who does not stand by his word. Such a one belongs to one of the four classes who are not admitted into the presence of the Shechinah; these are the scoffers, the hypocrites (who bring the wrath of God into the world), the liars, and the slanderers. The sin of the slanderer is like that of one who would deny the root (the root of all religion, *i.e.* the existence of God). The greatest of liars, however, is he who perjures himself, which also involves the sin of profanation of the name of God. The hypocrite, who insinuates himself into people's good opinions, who wears his phylacteries and is en-

wrapped in his gown with the fringes, and secretly com-
mits sins, equally transgresses the command, 'Thou shalt
not take the name of the Lord thy God in vain.'

"God is gracious and merciful; therefore man also
should be gracious and merciful. Hence, 'Thou shalt
love thy neighbour as thyself,' which is a main principle
in the Torah. What is unpleasant to thyself, do not unto
thy neighbour. This is the whole Torah, to which the
rest is only to be considered as a commentary. And this
love is also extended to the stranger, for as it is said with
regard to Israel, 'And thou shalt love thy neighbour as
thyself,' so is it also said, 'And thou shalt love him (the
stranger) as thyself.' And thus said God to Israel, 'My
beloved children, Am I in want of anything that I should
request it of you? But what I ask of you is that you
should love, honour, and respect one another.' Therefore,
love mankind, and bring them near to the Torah. Let
the honour of thy friend be as dear to thee as thine own.
Condemn not thy fellow-man until thou art come into his
place, and judge all men in the scale of merit. Say not
'I will love scholars, but hate their disciples;' or even,·
'I will love the disciples, but hate the ignorant,' but love
all, for he who hates his neighbour is as bad as a mur-
derer. Indeed, during the age of the second Temple,
men studied the Torah and the commandments, and performed works of charity, but they hated each other, a sin
that outweighs all other sins, and for which the holy
Temple was destroyed. Be careful not to withdraw thy
mercy from any man, for he who does so rebels against
the kingdom of God on earth. Walk in the ways of God,
who is merciful even to the wicked, and as He is gracious
alike to those who know Him, and to those who know

Him not, so be thou. Indeed, charity is one of the three pillars on which the world is based. It is more precious than all other virtues. The man who gives charity in secret is greater even than Moses our teacher. An act of charity and love it is to pray for our fellow-man, and to admonish him. 'Thou shalt in any wise rebuke thy neighbour, and not suffer sin upon him' (Lev. xix. 18), means it is thy duty to admonish him a hundred times if need be, even if he be thy superior; for Jerusalem was only destroyed for the sin of its people in not admonishing one another. The man whose protest would be of any weight, and who does not exercise his authority (when any wrong is about to be committed), is held responsible for the whole world.

"Peacefulness and humility are also the fruit of love. Be of the disciples of Aaron, loving peace, and pursuing peace. Let every man be cautious in the fear of God; let him ever give the soft answer that turneth away wrath; let him promote peace, not only among his own relatives and acquaintances, but also among the Gentiles. For (the labour of) all the prophets was to plant peace in the world. Be exceeding lowly of spirit, since the hope of man is but the worm. Be humble as Hillel, for he who is humble causes the Divine presence to dwell with man. But the proud man makes God say, 'I and he cannot dwell in the same place.' He who runs after glory, glory flees from him, and he who flees from glory, glory shall pursue him. Be of those who are despised rather than of those who despise; of the persecuted rather than of the persecutors; be of those who bear their reproach in silence and answer not.

"Another distinctive mark of Judaism is faith in God,

and perfect confidence in Him. Which is the right course
for a man to choose for himself? Let him have a strong
faith in God, as it is said, 'Mine eye shall be upon the
faithful (meaning those possessing faith in God) of the
land.' And so also Habakkuk based the whole Torah on
the principle of faith, as it is said, 'And the just shall live
by his faith' (ii. 4). He who but fulfils a single commandment in absolute faith in God deserves that the Holy
Spirit should rest on him. Blessed is the man who fears
God in private, and trusts in Him with all his heart, for
such fear and trust arms him against every misfortune.
He who puts his trust in the Holy One, blessed be He,
God becomes his shield and protection in this world
and in the next. He who has bread in his basket for
to-day, and says, 'What shall I have to eat to-morrow?'
is a man of little faith. One consequence of real faith is
always to believe in the justice of God's judgments. It is
the duty of man to thank God when he is visited with
misfortune as he does in the time of prosperity. Therefore, blessed is the man who, when visited by suffering,
questions not God's justice. But what shall he do? Let
him examine his conduct and repent.

"For repentance is the greatest prerogative of man.
Better is one hour of repentance and good deeds in this
world than the whole life of the world to come. The aim
of all wisdom is repentance and good deeds. The place
where the truly penitent shall stand is higher than that of
the righteous. Repentance finds its special expression in
prayer; and when it is said in Scripture, 'Serve God with
all thy heart,' by this is meant, serve Him by prayer, which
is even greater than worship by means of sacrifices.
Never is a prayer entirely unanswered by God. There-

fore, even though the sword be on a man's neck, let him
not cease to supplicate God's mercy.   But regard not thy
prayer as a fixed mechanical task, but as an appeal for
mercy and grace before the All-Present; as it is said,
'For He is gracious and full of mercy, slow to anger,
abounding in loving-kindness, and repenteth him of the
evil.'"

The last two volumes of Weiss's work deal with the
history of Tradition during the Middle Ages, that is, from
the conclusion of the Talmud to the compilation of the
Code of the Law by R. Joseph Caro.   I have already indicated that with Weiss Tradition did not terminate with
the conclusion of the Talmud.   It only means that a
certain undefinable kind of literature, mostly held in dia-
logue form and containing many elements of Tradition,
was at last brought to an end.   The authorities who did
this editorial work were the so-called *Rabbanan Saburai* [12]
and the *Gaonim*, whose lives and literary activity are fully
described by Weiss.   But, while thus engaged in preserving their inheritance from the past, they were also enrich-
ing Tradition by new contributions, both the Saburai and
the Gaonim having not only added to and diminished from
the Talmud, but having also introduced avowedly new
ordinances and decrees, and created new institutions.

Now, it cannot be denied that a few of these ordinances
and decrees had a reforming tendency (see the second and
twentieth chapters of vol. iv.); in general, however, they
took a more conservative turn than was the case in the
previous ages.   This must be ascribed to the event of the
great schism within the Rabbinical camp itself.   I refer
to the rise of Caraism, which took place during the first
half of the eighth century.

There is probably no work in which the Halachic or legalistic side of this sect is better described than in this volume of Weiss. I regret that I am unable to enter into its details. But I cannot refrain from pointing to one of the main principles of the Caraites. This was "Search the Scriptures." Now this does not look very dissimilar from the principle held by the Rabbis. For what else is the Talmud, but a thorough searching through the Bible for whatever was suggestive by time and circumstances? The light which the Caraites applied to the searching of the Scriptures was the same which illumined the paths of the Rabbis' investigations. They employed most of the expository rules of the Tannaite schools. The fact is that they were only determined to find something different from what the Rabbis found in the Scriptures. They wanted to have gloomy Sabbaths and Festivals, and discovered authority for it in the Bible; they wanted to retain most of the dietary laws which had their root only in Tradition, but insisted on petty differences which they thought might be inferred from the Scriptures, and they created a new "order of inheritance," and varied the forbidden degrees in marriage, in all which the only merit was that they were in contradiction to the interpretation of the Rabbis. They also refused to accept the Liturgy of Rabbinical Judaism, but never succeeded in producing more than a patch-work from verses of the Bible, which, thus recast, they called a prayer-book. There were undoubtedly among their leaders many serious and sincere men, but they give us the impression of prigs, as for instance, Moses Darai, when he reproaches the Rabbinical Jews for having an "easy religion," or Israel Hammaarabi, when he recommended his book on the laws regarding the slaughtering

of animals, as having the special advantage that his decisions were always on the more stringent side. Those
who made a pilgrimage to the Holy Land were by the
Caraites canonised as "mourners." The Rabbanite R.
Judah Hallevi also visited the ruins of Jerusalem, but he
did something more than "mourn and sigh and cry," he
became a God-intoxicated singer, and wrote the "Zion-
Elegy." The novel terminology which they use in their ex-
egetical and theological works, was only invented to spite
the Rabbanites, and marks its authors as pedants. On
the other hand, it is not to be denied that their opponents
did not employ the best means to conciliate them. The
Middle Ages knew no other remedy against schism than
excommunication, and the Gaonim were the children of
their time. Nor were the arguments which the latter
brought forward in defence of Tradition always calculated
to convince the Caraites of their error. When R. Saadiah,
in his apology for the institution of the Second Day of
the Festival,[13] went the length of assigning to it a Sinaitic
origin, he could only succeed in making the Caraites more
suspicious of the claims of Tradition than before. In a
later generation one of his own party, R. Hai Gaon, had
to declare his predecessor's words a "controversial exaggeration." The zeal which some of the Gaonim showed
in their defence of such works as the *Chambers* and the
Measure of the Stature [14] was a not less unfortunate thing,
for it involved the Rabbanites in unnecessary responsibilities for a new class of literature of doubtful origin,
which in succeeding centuries was disowned by the best
minds in Judaism.

The Gaonic period, to which we also owe the rise of the
Massorah and the introduction of points in the text of the

Bible — of which Weiss treats fully in the twenty-third and twenty-fourth chapters of vol. iv. — comes to an end with the death of R. Hai. The famous schools of Sura and Pumbeditha, over which these two Gaonim presided, fell into decay, and Babylon ceased to be the centre of Judaism. To be more exact, we should say that Judaism had no longer any real centre. Instead of dwelling in one place for centuries, we now have to be perpetually on our journey, accompanying our authors through all the inhabited parts of the world — France, Italy, Spain, Germany, with an occasional trip to Africa and Russia. There we shall meet with the new schools, each of which, though interpreting the same Torah, occupied with the study of the same Talmud, and even conforming more or less to the same mode of life, has an individuality and character of its own, reflecting the thought and habits of the country which it represents. Thus "geographical Judaism" becomes a factor in history which no scholar can afford to neglect. It is true that Judaism never remained entirely unbiassed by foreign ideas, and our author points in many a place to Persian, Greek, and Roman influences on Tradition; still, these influences seem to have undergone such a thorough "Judaization" that it is only the practised eye of the scholar that is able to see through the transformation. But it requires no great skill to discriminate between the work produced by a Spanish and that of a French Rabbi. Though both would write in Hebrew, they betray themselves very soon by the style, diction, and train of thought peculiar to each country. The Spaniard is always logical, clear, and systematising, whilst the French Rabbi has very little sense of order, is always writing occasional notes, has a great tendency to be

P

obscure, but is mostly profound and critical. Hence the fact that whilst Spain produced the greatest codifiers of the law, we owe to France and Germany the best commentaries on the Talmud. What these codes and commentaries meant for Judaism the student will find in Weiss's book, and still more fully in his admirable essays on Rashi (Solomon b. Isaac), Maimonides, and R. Jacob Tam (published in his periodical, *Beth Talmud*, and also separately). It is enough for us here only to notice the fact of the breadth of Tradition, which could include within its folds men of such different types as the sceptics, Maimonides, Solomon b. Gabirol, and Abn Ezra on one side, and the simple "non-questioning" Rabbenu Gershom, Rashi, and Jacob Tam on the other.

The last three centuries, which occupy our author's attention in the fifth volume, are not remarkable for their progress. The world lives on the past. The rationalists write treatises on Maimonides' philosophical works, whilst the German Talmudists add commentary to commentary. It is, indeed, the reign of authority, "modified by accidents." Such an accident was the struggle between the Maimonists and Anti-Maimonists, or the rise of the Cabbalah, or the frequent controversies with Christians, all of which tended to direct the minds of people into new channels of thought. But though this period is less original in its work, it is not on that account less sympathetic. One cannot read those beautiful descriptions which Weiss gives of R. Meir of Rothenburg and his school, or of R. Asher and his descendants, without feeling that one is in an atmosphere of saints, who are the more attractive the less they were conscious of their own saintliness. The only mistake, perhaps, was that the successors of these

"Chassidim or pious men of Germany" looked on many of the religious customs that were merely the voluntary expression of particularly devout souls as worthy of imitation by the whole community, and made them obligatory upon all.

This brings us to the question of the Code already mentioned (by R. Joseph Caro), with which Weiss's work concludes. I have already transgressed the limits of an essay, without flattering myself that I have done anything like justice to the greatest work on Jewish Tradition which modern Jewish genius has produced. But I should not like the reader to carry away with him the false impression that our author shares in the general cry, "Save us from the Codifiers." Weiss, himself a Rabbi, and the disciple of the greatest Rabbis of the first half of this century, is quite aware of the impossibility of having a law without a kind of manual to it, which brings the fluid matter into some fixed form, classifying it under its proper headings, and this is what we call codifying the law. And thus he never passes any attempt made in this direction without paying due tribute to its author — be it Maimonides or Caro. But however great the literary value of a code may be, it does not invest it with the attribute of infallibility, nor does it exempt the student or the Rabbi who makes use of it from the duty of examining each paragraph on its own merits, and subjecting it to the same rules of interpretation that were always applied to Tradition. Indeed, Weiss shows that Maimonides deviated in some cases from his own code, when it was required by circumstances.

Nor do I know any modern author who is more in favour of strong authority than Weiss. His treatment of the struggle between the Patriarch R. Gamaliel and his adversaries, which I have touched on above, proves this sufficiently. What Weiss really objects to, is a *weak* authority — I mean that phonograph-like authority which is always busy in reproducing the voice of others without an opinion of its own, without originality, without initiative and discretion. The real authorities are those who, drawing their inspiration from the past, also understand how to reconcile us with the present and to prepare us for the future.

VIII

THE DOCTRINE OF DIVINE RETRIBUTION
IN RABBINICAL LITERATURE

"Blessed be he who knows." These are the words
with which Nachmanides, in his classical treatise, *Gate of
Reward*, dismisses a certain theory of the Gaonim with
regard to this question; after which he proceeds to expound another theory, which seems to him more satisfactory. This mode of treatment implies that, unsatisfactory
as the one or other theory may appear to us, it would be
presumptuous to reject either entirely, there being only
One who knows the exact truth about the great mystery.
But we may indicate our doubt about one doctrine by putting by its side another, which we may affirm to be not
more absolutely true, but more probable. This seems to
have been the attitude, too, of the compilers of the ancient
Rabbinical literature, in which the most conflicting views
about this grave subject were embodied. Nor did the Synagogue in general feel called upon to decide between these
views. There is indeed no want of theodicies, for almost
every important expounder of Job, as well as every Jewish
philosopher of note, has one with its own system of retribution. Thus Judaism has no fixed doctrine on the subject.
It refused a hearing to no theory, for fear that it should

contain some germ of truth, but on the same ground it accepted none to the exclusion of the others.

These theories may, perhaps, be conveniently reduced to the two following main doctrines that are in direct opposition to each other, whilst all other views about the subject will be treated as the more or less logical results of the one or other doctrine.

1. There is no death without (preceding) sin, nor affliction without (preceding) transgression.[1] This view is cited in the name of R. Ammi, who quoted in corroboration the verses Ez. xviii. 20, and Ps. lxxxix. 33. Though this Rabbi flourished towards the end of the third century, there is hardly any doubt that his view was held by the authorities of a much earlier date. For it can only be under the sway of such a notion of Retribution that the Tannaim were so anxious to assign some great crime as the antecedent to every serious calamity by which mankind was visited. The following illustrations will suffice : — " Pestilence comes into the world for capital crimes mentioned in the Torah, which are not brought before the earthly tribunal. . . . Noisome beasts come into the world for vain swearing and for profanation of the name (of God). Captivity comes upon the world for strange worship and incest, and for shedding of blood and for (not) giving release to the land." As an example of the misfortune befalling the individual I will merely allude to a passage in another tractate of the Talmud, according to which leprosy is to be regarded as the penalty for immorality, slander, perjury, and similar sins.[2]

If we were now to complement R. Ammi's view by adding that there is no happiness without some preceding merit — and there is no serious objection to making this addition — then it would resolve itself into the theory of Measure for Measure, which forms a very common standard of reward and punishment in Jewish literature. Here are a few instances : — "Because the Egyptians wanted to destroy Israel by water (Exod. i. 22), they were themselves destroyed by the waters of the Red Sea, as it is said, Therefore I will *measure* their former work into their bosom (Is. lxv. 7);" whilst, on the other hand, we read, "Because Abraham showed himself hospitable towards strangers, providing them with water (Gen. xviii. 4), God gave to his children a country blessed with plenty of water (Deut. viii. 1)." Sometimes this form of retribution goes so far as to define a special punishment to that part of the body which mostly contributed to the committing of the sin. Thus we read, "Samson rebelled against God by his eyes, as it is said, Get her (the Philistine woman) for me, for she pleases *my eyes* (Judg. xvi. 21); therefore his *eyes* were put out by the Philistines (Judg. xviii. 9)"; whilst Absalom, whose sinful pride began by his *hair* (2 Sam. xiv. 25), met his fate by his *hair* (2 Sam. xviii. 9).[3] Nahum of Gemzo himself explained his blindness and the maimed condition of his arms and legs as a consequence of a specific offence in having neglected the duty of succouring a poor man. Addressing the dead body of the suppliant who perished while Nahum was delaying his help, he said, "Let my eyes (which had no pity for your pitiful gaze) become blind; may my hands and legs (that did not hasten to help thine) become maimed, and finally my whole body be covered with boils."[4] "This was the hand that wrote it," said Cranmer at the stake; "therefore it shall first suffer punishment."

It is worth noticing that this retribution does not always

consist in a material reward, but, as Ben Azzai expressed it: "The reward of a command is a command, and the reward of a transgression is a transgression."[5] So again: "Because Abraham showed himself so magnanimous in his treatment of the king of Sodom, and said, I will not take from thee a thread; therefore, his children enjoyed the privilege of having the command of Zizith, consisting in putting a thread or fringe in the border of their garments." In another passage we read, "He who is anxious to do acts of charity will be rewarded by having the means enabling him to do so."[6] In more general terms the same thought is expressed when the Rabbis explained the words, Ye shall sanctify yourselves, and ye shall be holy (Lev. xi. 44), to the effect that if man takes the initiative in holiness, even though in a small way, Heaven will help him to reach it to a much higher degree.[7]

Notwithstanding these passages, to which many more might be added, it cannot be denied that there are in the Rabbinical literature many passages holding out promises of *material* reward to the righteous as well as threatening the wicked with *material* punishment. Nor is there any need of denying it. Simple-minded men — and such the majority of the Rabbis were — will never be persuaded into looking with indifference on pain and pleasure; they will be far from thinking that poverty, loss of children, and sickness are no evil, and that a rich harvest, hope of posterity, and good health, are not desirable things. It *does* lie in our nature to consider the former as curses and 'the latter as blessings; "and if this be wrong there is no one to be made responsible for it but the Creator of nature." Accordingly the question must arise, How can a just and omnipotent God allow it to happen that men should suffer innocently? The most natural suggestion towards solving the difficulty would be that we are *not* innocent. Hence R. Ammi's assertion that affliction and death are both the outcome of sin and transgression; or, as R. Chanina ben Dossa expressed it, " It is not the wild beast but sin which kills." [8]

We may thus perceive in this theory an attempt "to justify the ways of God to man." Unfortunately it does not correspond with the real facts. The cry wrung from the prophets against the peace enjoyed by the wicked, and the pains inflicted on the righteous, which finds its echo in so many Psalms, and reaches its climax in the Book of Job, was by no means silenced in the times of the Rabbis. If long experience could be of any use, it only served to deepen perplexity. For all this suffering of the people of God, and the prosperity of their wicked persecutors, which perplexed the prophets and their immediate followers, were repeated during the death-struggle for independence against Rome, and were not lessened by the establishment of Christianity as the dominant religion. The only comfort which time brought them was, perhaps, that the long continuance of misfortune made them less sensible to suffering than their ancestors were. Indeed, a Rabbi of the first century said that his generation had by continuous experience of misery become as insensible to pain as the dead body is to a prick of a needle.[9] The anæsthetic effect of long suffering may, indeed, help one to endure pain with more patience, but it cannot serve as an apology for the deed of the inflictors of the pain. The question, then, how to reconcile hard reality with the justice of God, remained as difficult as ever.

The most important passage in Rabbinical literature relating to the solution of this problem is the following:— With reference to Exod. xxxiii. 13, R. Johanan said, in the name of R. José, that, among other things, Moses also asked God to explain to him the method of his Providence, a request that was granted to him. He asked God, Why are there righteous people who are prosperous, and righteous who suffer; wicked who are prosperous and wicked who suffer? The answer given to him was, according to the one view, that the prosperity of the wicked and the suffering of the righteous are a result of the conduct of their ancestors, the former being the descendants of righteous parents and enjoying their merits, whilst the latter, coming from a bad stock, suffer for the sins of those to whom they owe their existence. This view was suggested by the Scriptural words, "Keeping mercy for thousands (of generations) . . . visiting the iniquity of the fathers upon the children" (Exod. xxxiv. 7), which were regarded as the answer to Moses' question in the preceding chapter of Exodus.[10] Prevalent, however, as this view may have been in ancient times, the Rabbis never allowed it to pass without some qualification. It is true that they had no objection to the former part of this doctrine, and they speak very frequently of the "Merits of the Fathers" for which the remotest posterity is rewarded; for this could be explained on the ground of the boundless goodness of God, which cannot be limited to the short space of a lifetime. But there was no possibility of overcoming the moral objection against punishment of people for sins they have not committed.

It will suffice to mention here that, with reference to Joshua vii. 24, 25, the Rabbis asked the question, If he

(Achan) sinned, what justification could there be for putting his sons and daughters to death? And by the force of this argument they interpreted the words of the Scriptures to mean that the children of the criminal were only compelled to be present at the execution of their father.

Such passages, therefore, as would imply that children have to suffer for the sins of their parents are explained by the Rabbis as referring to cases in which the children perpetuate the crimes of their fathers.[11] The view of R. José, which I have already quoted, had, therefore, to be dropped, and another version in the name of the same Rabbi is accepted. According to this theory the sufferer is a person either "entirely wicked" or "not perfectly righteous," whilst the prosperous man is a person either "perfectly righteous," or "not entirely wicked."

It is hardly necessary to say that there is still something wanting to supplement this view, for the given classification would place the not entirely wicked on the same level with the perfectly righteous, and on a much higher level than the imperfectly righteous, who are undoubtedly far superior. The following passage may be regarded as supplying this missing something : — "The wicked who have done some good work are as amply rewarded for it in *this* world as if they were men who have fulfilled the whole of the Torah, so that they may be punished for their sins in the next world (without interruption); whilst the righteous who have committed some sin have to suffer for it (in this world) as if "they were men who burned the Law," so that they may enjoy their reward in the world to come (without interruption)."[12] Thus the real retribution takes place in the next world, the fleeting existence on earth not being the fit time either to compensate righteousness or to punish sin. But as, on the one hand, God never allows "that the merit of any creature should be cut short," whilst, on the other hand, He deals very severely with the righteous, punishing them for the slightest transgression; since, too, this reward and punishment are only of short duration, they must take place in this short terrestrial existence. There is thus established a sort of divine economy, lest the harmony of the next world should be disturbed.

Yet another objection to the doctrine under discussion remains to be noticed. It is that it justifies God by accusing man, declaring every sufferer as more or less of a sinner. But such a notion, if carried to its last consequences, must result in tempting us to withhold our sympathies from him. And, indeed, it would seem that there were some non-Jewish philosophers who argued in this way. Thus a certain Roman official is reported to have said to R. Akiba, "How can you be so eager in helping the poor? Suppose only a king, who, in his wrath against his slave, were to set him in the gaol, and give orders to withhold from him food and drink; if, then, one dared to act to the contrary, would not the king be angry with him?"[13] There is some appearance of logic in this notion put into the mouth of a heathen. The Rabbis, however, were inconsistent people, and responded to the appeal which suffering makes to every human heart without asking too many questions. Without entering here into the topic of charity in the Rabbinic literature, which would form a very interesting chapter, I shall only allude now to the following incident, which would show that the Rabbis did not abandon even those afflicted with leprosy, which, according to their own notion, given above, followed only as a punishment for the worst crimes. One Friday, we are told, when the day was about to darken, the Chassid Abba Tachnah was returning home, bearing on his shoulders the baggage that contained all his fortune; he saw a leprous man lying on the road, who addressed him : "Rabbi, do me a deed of charity and take me into the town." The Rabbi now thought, "If I leave my baggage, where shall I find the means of obtaining subsistence for myself and my family ? But if I forsake this leprous man I shall commit a mortal sin." In the end, he allowed the good inclination to prevail over the evil one, and first carried the sufferer to the town.[14] The only practical conclusion that the Rabbis drew from such theories as identify suffering with sin were for the sufferer himself, who otherwise might be inclined to blame Providence, or even to blaspheme, but would now look upon his affliction as a reminder from heaven that there is something wrong in his moral state. Thus we read in tractate *Berachoth :* [15] " If a man sees that affliction comes upon him, he ought to inquire into his actions, as it is said, Let us search and try our ways, and turn again to the Lord (Lam. iii. 40)." This means to say that the sufferer will find that he has been guilty of some offence. As an illustration of this statement we may perhaps consider the story about R. Huna, occurring in the same tractate.[16] Of this Rabbi it is said that he once experienced heavy pecuniary losses, whereupon his friends came to his house and said to him, " Let the master but examine his conduct a little closer." On this R. Huna answered, " Do you suspect me of having committed some misdeed ? " His friends rejoined, " And do you think that God would pass judgment without justice?" R. Huna then followed their hint, and found that he did not treat his tenant farmer so generously as he ought. He offered redress, and all turned out well in the end. Something similar is to be found in the story of the martyrdom of R. Simeon ben Gamaliel and R. Ishmael ben Elisha. Of these Rabbis we are told that on their way to be executed the one said to the other, "My heart leaves me, for I am not aware of a sin deserving such a death"; on which the other answered, "It might have happened that in your function as judge you sometimes — for your own convenience — were slow in administering justice." [17]

But even if the personal actions of the righteous were blameless, there might still be sufficient ground for his being afflicted and miserable. This may be found in his relations to his kind and surroundings, or, to use the term now more popular, by reason of human solidarity. Now, after the above remarks on the objections entertained by the Rabbis against a man's being punished for the sins of others, it is hardly necessary to say that their idea of solidarity has little in common with the crude notions of it current in very ancient times. Still, it can hardly be doubted that the relation of the individual to the community was more keenly felt by the Rabbis than by the leaders in any other society, modern or ancient. According to the view given by an ancient Rabbi whose name is unknown, it would, indeed, seem that to them the individual was not simply a member of the Jewish commonwealth, or a co-religionist, but a limb of the great and single body "Israel," and that as such he communicated both for good and evil the sensations of the one part to the whole. In the *Midrash*, where a parallel is to be found to this idea, the responsibility of the individual towards the community is further illustrated by R. Simeon ben Yochai, in the following way : "It is," we read there, "to be compared to people sitting on board a ship, one of the passengers of which took an awl and began to bore holes in the bottom of the vessel. Asked to desist from his dangerous occupation, he answered, 'Why, I am only making holes on my own seat,' forgetting that when the water came in it would sink the whole ship." Thus the sin of a single man might endanger the whole of humanity. It was in conformity with the view of his father that R. Eliezer, the son of R. Simeon (ben Yochai) said, "The world is judged after the merits or demerits of the majority, so that a single individual by his good or bad actions can decide the fate of his fellow-creatures, as it may happen that he is just the one who constitutes this majority." [18] Nor does this responsibility cease with the man's own actions. According to the Rabbis man is responsible even for the conduct of others — and as such liable to punishment — if he is indifferent to the wrong that is being perpetrated about him, whilst an energetic protest from his side could have prevented it. And the greater the man the greater is his responsibility. He may suffer for the sins of his family which is first reached by his influence ; he may suffer for the sins of the whole community if he could hope to find a willing ear among them, and he may even suffer for the sins of the whole world if his influence extend so far, and he forbear from exerting it for good.[19] Thus the possibility is given that the righteous man may suffer with justice, though he himself has never committed any transgression.

As a much higher aspect of this solidarity — and as may have already suggested itself to the reader from the pas-

sage cited above from the anonymous Rabbi — we may
regard the suffering of the righteous as an atonement for
the sins of their contemporaries.   "When there will be
neither Tabernacle nor the Holy Temple," Moses is said
to have asked God, "what will become of Israel?"   Whereupon God answers, "I will take from among them the
righteous man whom I shall consider as pledged for them,
and will forgive all their sins;" the death of the perfect
man, or even his suffering being looked upon as an expi-
ation for the shortcoming of his generation.[20]

It is hardly necessary to remind the reader of the affinity
of this idea with that of sacrifices in general, as in both
cases it is the innocent being which has to suffer for the
sins of another creature.   But there is one vital point which
makes all the difference.   It is that in our case the suffering is not enforced, but is a voluntary act on the part of
the sacrifice, and is even desired by him.   Without entering here on the often-discussed theme of the suffering of
the Messiah, I need only mention the words of R. Ishmael
who, on a very slight provocation, exclaimed, "I am the
atonement for the Jews," which means that he took upon
him all their sins to suffer for them.[21]   This desire seems
to have its origin in nothing else than a deep sympathy
and compassion with Israel.   To suffer *for*, or, at least
with Israel was, according to the Rabbis, already the ideal
of Moses.   He is said, indeed, to have broken the Two
Tables with the purpose of committing some sin, so that
he would have either to be condemned together with Israel
(for the sin of the golden calf), or to be pardoned together
with them.[22]   And this conduct was expected not only from
the leaders of Israel, but almost from every Jew.   "When
Israel is in a state of affliction (as, for instance, famine) one

must not say, I will rather live by myself, and eat and drink, and peace be unto thee, my soul. To those who do so the words of the Scriptures are to be applied : And in that day did the Lord God of Hosts call to weeping and to mourning, . . . and behold joy and gladness. . . . Surely this iniquity shall not be purged out from you till ye die " (Is. xxii. 12–14). Another passage is to the effect that, when a man shows himself indifferent to the suffering of the community, there come the two angels (who accompany every Jew), put their hands on his head, and say, " This man who has separated himself shall be excluded from their consolations." [23]

We might now characterise this sort of suffering as the chastisement of love (of the righteous) to mankind, or rather to Israel. But we must not confuse it with the Chastisement of Love often mentioned in the Talmud, though this idea also seems calculated to account for the suffering of the righteous. Here the love is not on the side of the sufferer, but proceeds from him who inflicts this suffering. " Him," says R. Huna, " in whom God delights he crushes with suffering." As a proof of this theory the words of Is. liii. 10 are given, which are interpreted to mean : him whom the Lord delights in He puts to grief. Another passage, by the same authority, is to the effect that where there is no sufficient cause for punishment (the man being entirely free from sin), we have to regard his suffering as a chastisement of love, for it is said : "Whom the Lord loveth He correcteth" (Proverbs iii. 11). [24] To what purpose He corrects him may, perhaps, be seen from the following passage : " R. Eleazar ben Jacob says : If a man is visited by affliction he has to be thankful to God for it : for suffering draws man to, and

Q

reconciles him with God, as it is said: For whom God loveth he correcteth." [25]

It is in conformity with such a high conception that affliction, far from being dreaded, becomes almost a desirable end, and we hear many Rabbis exclaim, "Beloved is suffering," for by it fatherly love is shown to man by God; by it man obtains purification and atonement, by it Israel came in possession of the best gifts, such as the Torah, the Holy Land, and eternal life.[26] And so also the sufferer, far from being considered as a man with a suspected past, becomes an object of veneration, on whom the glory of God rests, and he brings salvation to the world if he bears his affliction with joyful submission to the will of God.[27] Continuous prosperity is by no means to be longed after, for, as R. Ishmael taught, "He who has passed forty days without meeting adversity has already received his (share of the) world (to come) in this life."[28] Nay, the standing rule is that the really righteous suffer, whilst the wicked are supposed to be in a prosperous state. Thus, R. Jannai said, "We (average people) enjoy neither the prosperity of the wicked nor the afflictions of the righteous,"[29] whilst his contemporary, Rab, declared that he who experiences no affliction and persecution does not belong to them (the Jews).[30]

2. The second main view on Retribution is that recorded by the Rabbis as in direct opposition to that of R. Ammi. It is that there is suffering as well as death without sin and transgression. We may now just as well infer that there is prosperity and happiness without preceding merits. And this is, indeed, the view held by R. Meir. For in contradiction to the view cited above, R. Meir declares that the request of Moses to have

explained to him the mysterious ways of Providence was *not* granted, and the answer he received was, " And I will shew mercy on whom I will shew mercy " (Exod. xxxiii. 19), which means to say, even though he to whom the mercy is shown be unworthy of it. The old question arises how such a procedure is to be reconciled with the justice and omnipotence of God. The commentaries try to evade the difficulty by suggesting some of the views given above, as that the real reward and punishment are only in the world to come, or that the affliction of the righteous is only chastisement of love, and so on. From the passages I am about to quote, however, one gains the impression that some Rabbis rather thought that this great problem will indeed not bear discussion or solution at all. Thus .we have the legend: "The angels said to God, why have you punished Adam with death? He answered, On account of his having transgressed my commandment (with regard to the eating of the tree of knowledge). But why had Moses and Aaron to die? The reply given to them is the words, Eccl. ix. 2: 'All things come alike to all; there is one event to the righteous and to the wicked, to the good and to the clean and to the unclean.' " [31] Another legend records, "When Moses ascended to heaven, God showed him also the great men of futurity. R. Akiba was sitting and interpreting the law in a most wonderful way. Moses said to God: Thou hast shown me his worth, show me also his reward; on which he is bidden to look back. There he perceives him dying the most cruel of deaths, and his flesh being sold by weight. Moses now asks: Is this the reward of such a life? whereupon God answers him: Be silent; this I have determined." [32]

It is impossible not to think of the fine lines of the German poet : —

> Warum schleppt sich blutend, elend,
> Unter Kreuzlast der Gerechte,
> Während glücklich als ein Sieger
> Trabt auf hohem Ross der Schlechte?
>
> *   *   *   *   *
>
> Also fragen wir beständig,
> Bis man uns mit einer Handvoll
> Erde endlich stopft die Mäuler—
> Aber ist das eine Antwort?

Still, one might perhaps suggest that these passages when examined a little closer, not only contain a rebuke to man's importunity in wanting to intrude into the secrets of God, but also hint at the possibility that even God's omnipotence is submitted to a certain law — though designed by His own holy will — which He could not alter without detriment to the whole creation. Indeed, in one of the mystical accounts of the martyrdom of R. Akiba and other great Rabbis, God is represented as asking the sufferers to accept His hard decree without protest, unless they wish Him to destroy the whole world. In another place again, we read of a certain renowned Rabbi, who lived in great poverty, that once in a dream he asked the divine Shechinah how long he would have still to endure this bitter privation? The answer given to him was : "My son, will it please you that I destroy the world for your sake?"[33] It is only in this light that we shall be able to understand such passages in the Rabbinic literature as that God almost suffers Himself when He has to inflict punishment either on the individual or on whole communities. Thus God is represented as mourning for seven days (as in the case when one loses a child) before He brought the deluge on the world; He bemoans the fall of Israel and the destruction of the Temple, and the Shechinah laments even when the criminal suffers his just punishment. And it is not by rebelling against these laws that He tries to redeem His suffering. He himself has recourse to prayer, and says: "May it be my will that my mercy conquer my wrath, that my love over-rule my strict justice, so that I may treat my children with love." [34] If now man is equal to God, he has nevertheless, or rather on that account, to submit to the law of God without any outlook for reward or punishment; or, as Antigonos expressed it, "Be not as slaves that minister to the Lord with a view to receive recompense." [35] Certainly it would be hazardous to maintain that Antigonos's saying was a consequence of this doctrine; but, at any rate, we see a clear tendency to keep the thought of reward (in spite of the prominent part it holds in the Bible) out of view. Still more clearly is it seen when, with reference to Ps. cxii., "Blessed is the man . . . that delighteth greatly in his commandments," Rabbi Eleazar remarks that the meaning is that the man desires only to do His commandments, but he does not want the rewards connected with them. [36] This is the more remarkable, as the whole contents of this psalm are nothing else than a long series of promises of various rewards, so that the explanation of Rabbi Eleazar is in almost direct contradiction to the simple meaning of the words. On the other hand, also, every complaint about suffering must cease. Not only is affliction no direct chastisement by God in the way of revenge; but even when it would seem to us that we suffer innocently, we have no right to murmur, as

God himself is also suffering, and, as the Talmud expresses it, 'It is enough for the slave to be in the position of his master.'" [37]

This thought of the compassion — in its strictest sense of fellow-suffering — of God with His creatures becomes a new motive for avoiding sin. "Woe to the wicked," exclaims a Rabbi, "who by their bad actions turn the mercy of God into strict justice." [38] And the later mystics explain distinctly that the great crime of sin consists in causing pain, so to speak, to the Shechinah. One of them compared it with the slave who abuses the goodness of his master so far as to buy with his money arms to wound him. But, on the other hand, it becomes, rather inconsistently, also a new source of comfort; for, in the end, God will have to redeem Himself from this suffering, which cannot be accomplished so long as Israel is still under punishment.[39] Most interesting is the noble prayer by a Rabbi of a very late mystical school: "O God, speedily bring about the redemption. I am not in the least thinking of what I may gain by it. I am willing to be condemned to all tortures in hell, if only the Shechinah will cease to suffer." [40]

If we were now to ask for the attitude of the Synagogue towards these two main views, we should have to answer that — as already hinted at the opening of this paper — it never decided for the one or the other. R. David Rocca Martino dared even to write a whole book in Defence of Adam proving that he committed no sin in eating the fruit of the tree of knowledge against the literal sense of the Scriptures, which were also taken by the Rabbis literally.[41] By this he destroyed the prospects of many a theodicy, but it is not known to me that he was severely rebuked for it. It has been said by a great writer that the best theology is that which is not consistent, and this advantage the theology of the Synagogue possesses to its utmost extent. It accepted with R. Ammi the stern principle of divine retribution, in as far as it makes man feel the responsibility of his actions, and makes suffering a discipline. But it never allowed this principle to be carried so far as to deny the sufferer our sympathy, and by a series of conscious and unconscious modifications, he passed from the state of a sinner into the zenith of the saint and the perfectly righteous man. But, on the other hand, the Synagogue also gave entrance to the very opposite view which, abandoning every attempt to account for suffering, bids man do his duty without any hope of reward, even as God also does His. Hence the remarkable phenomenon in the works of later Jewish moralists, that, whilst they never weary of the most detailed accounts of the punishments awaiting the sinner and the rewards in store for the righteous, they warn us most emphatically that our actions must not be guided by these unworthy considerations, and that our only motive should be the love of God and submission to His holy will.

Nor must it be thought that the views of the Rabbis are so widely divergent from those enunciated in the Bible. The germ of almost all the later ideas is already to be found in the Scriptures. It only needed the process of time to bring into prominence those features which proved at a later period most acceptable. Indeed, it would seem that there is also a sort of domestication of religious ideas. On their first association with man there is a certain rude violence about them which, when left to the management of untutored minds, would certainly do great harm. But, let only this association last for centuries, during which these ideas have to be subdued by practical use, and they will, in due time, lose their former roughness, will become theologically workable, and turn out the greatest blessing to inconsistent humanity.

IX

THE LAW AND RECENT CRITICISM[1]

PROFESSOR TOY's work, *Judaism and Christianity*, gives
an admirable conspectus of the results of the modern
critical school in their bearing on the genesis of Christianity. The author takes various important doctrines of
Christianity, traces them back to their origin in Israelitism, pursues their course through their various phases
in Judaism, until they reach their final development in
the teaching of Jesus and His disciples, which, in the
author's judgment, is the consummation of that which
the prophets and their successors had to give to the
world. Laying so much stress as Professor Toy does on
the saying, "By their fruits shall ye know them," he
ought also, perhaps, to have told us what, in the course
of time, has become of these several doctrines. For
when, for instance, with regard to the doctrine of original sin, he remarks that "in certain systems of Christian
theology the human race is involved in the condem-
nation of the first man" (p. 185, *n.* 1); or that, in the
New Testament, "the demand for a mediating power between God and humanity is pushed to the farthest point
which thought can occupy consistently with the maintenance of the absoluteness of the one Supreme Deity"
(p. 121), he is rather evading a difficulty than answering
it. Such elaboration would, however, have been outside

the scope of Professor Toy's book, which claims only to be a sketch of the progress of thought from the Old Testament to the New. For his own solution of the indicated difficulty, Toy, to judge from his liberal stand-point, would probably refer us to Dr. Hatch's Hibbert lectures; the issue of such an appeal must, I imagine, remain for long doubtful and disputed.

A delightful characteristic of Toy's book is its trans-parent clearness and sobriety, which will make it inter-esting reading, even to those who are acquainted with the writer's authorities in their original sources. Almost entirely new, as well as most suggestive, is the justice which Toy does to the law in recognising it as a factor for good in the history of religion. In this point Toy is not only up to his date, but beyond it. It is true that even the Pharisees have made some advance in the esti-mation of the liberal school. They are no longer con-demned *en masse* as so many hypocrites. It is even admitted that there were a few honest men among them, such as Rabban Gamaliel, the teacher of Paul, or R. Akiba, the patriot of Bethar. We are now too polite to be personal. But with regard to the law, on the other hand, there is at present a markedly opposite tendency. The general idea seems to be that, as the doctrine of the resurrection of Christ must be loosely interpreted in a spiritual sense, it must logically have been preceded by a universal spiritual death, and the germs of the disease which brought this death about are to be sought for in the law. Hence the strained efforts to discover in the law the source of all religious evil, — cant, hypocrisy, formalism, externalism, transcen-dentalism, and as many "isms" more, of bad reputation.

It was probably with this current representation of the law in view that Toy, when speaking of the Levitical legislation, and of its fixing "men's minds on ceremonial details which, in some cases, it put into the same category and on the same level with moral duties," asks the question: "Would there not thence result a dimming of the moral sense and a confusion of moral distinctions? The ethical attitude of a man who could regard a failure in the routine of sacrifice as not less blameworthy than an act of theft cannot be called a lofty one" (p. 186). The answer which he gives is more favourable than such a leading question would induce us to expect. He tells us that, "in point of fact, the result was different" (*ibid*). "The Levitical law is not to be looked on as a mere extension and organisation of the ritual. . . . Its ritual was, in great part, the organised expression of the consciousness of sin" (p. 226). Of the law in general Toy says that it had "larger consequences than its mere details would suggest," for it "cultivated the moral sense of the people into results above its mechanical prescriptions," and "it developed the sense of sin, as Paul points out" (Gal. iii. 19), "and therewith a freer feeling, which brought the soul into more immediate contact with God" (p. 227); whilst in another place he reminds us "that much of the law is moral, and that no one could fail to see a spiritual significance beneath its letter" (p. 245), and he even admits that "the great legal schools which grew up in the second century, if we may judge by the sayings of the teachers which have come down to us, did not fail to discriminate between the outward and the inward, the ceremonial and the moral" (p. 186).

These and similar passages will suffice to show that

Toy's estimate of the law is a very different one from that of Smend and his school. However, it must not be supposed that he is not on the look-out for the germs of the disease. He must find these germs somewhere, or else the progress, which his book is intended to illustrate, would be difficult to detect. And thus he repeats the old accusations, though not without modification.

Professor Toy's objections may, perhaps, be summed up in the passage in which he represents the Jewish law as "an attempt to define all the beliefs and acts of life" (p. 239), or as "the embodiment of devotion to a fixed rule of belief and conduct" (p. 237). Toy does not entirely condemn this system, and even speaks of it as a "lofty attempt" (p. 239); but, on the whole, he considers that it must have resulted in bad theology, as well as in doubtful conduct. Without following Professor Toy over the whole area of his investigations, which would require a volume for itself, I will only take the opportunity of making a few general remarks upon the nature and character of this legal system, which seems to hold the key to the spiritual history of Judaism.

First, as to its theology, Toy's description of the law as an attempt to define all the *beliefs* of life — an assertion which is also made by Schürer — is not wholly accurate. For such an attempt was never made by Judaism. The few dogmas which Judaism possesses, such as the Existence of God, Providence, Reward, and Punishment — without which no revealed religion is conceivable — can hardly be called a creed in the modern sense of the term, which implies something external and foreign to man's own knowledge, and received only in deference to the weight of authority. To the Jew of the Christian era,

these simpler dogmas were so self-evident that it would
have cost him the greatest effort *not* to believe them.
Hence the fact that, whilst there have come down to us
so many controverted points between the Sadducees and
Pharisees with regard to certain juristic and ritual questions, we know of only one of an essentially dogmatic
character, viz. the dispute concerning the Resurrection.

It is thus difficult to imagine to what Professor Toy can
be alluding when he speaks of the "interest they (the
Jews) threw into the discussion and determination of
minutiæ of faith" (p. 241). Discussions upon *minutiæ*
of faith are only to be read in the works of the later
schoolmen (as Saadiah, Maimonides and their followers),
in which such subtle problems as *Creatio ex nihilo*, the
origin of evil, predestination, free will and similar subjects
are examined; but this period is very distant from that
with which Toy is concerned. The older schools and
the so-called houses of Shammai and Hillel, most of whose
members were the contemporaries of the Apostles, show
very little predilection for such *minutiæ*. Their discussions and differences of opinion about ritual matters are
very numerous, scattered as they are over the whole of
the ancient Rabbinic literature, but I can only remember
two of a metaphysical character, or touching upon the
minutiæ of faith. The one, dealing with the efficacy of
certain sacrifices, discusses whether it only extends to
the remission of the pending punishment for sins, or also
includes their purification and washing away; the other
considers the question whether it would not have been
better for man not to have been created.[2] But this latter
controversy, which is said to have lasted for two years
and a half, by no means led to any big metaphysical or

theological system, but only to the practical advice that, as we have been created, we ought to be watchful over our conduct. It is, indeed, a noteworthy feature of Judaism that theological speculations have never resulted in the formulation of any imposing or universal doctrine, but usually in divers ceremonial practices. To give one illustration: according to Professor Toy (p. 210) the conclusion which the author of 1 Tim. ii. 11–14 draws from the fact that woman was the immediate agent of the introduction of sin was the subordination of her sex. The Rabbis also noticed the same fact, and in their less abstract language speak of woman as having brought death and grief into the world; but the conclusion which they drew was that since woman had extinguished the "light of the world," she ought to atone for it by lighting the candles for the Sabbath.[3] Nor is Toy quite correct when he maintains that the conception of the Memra as Creator and Lord, etc., and as "representative of the immediate divine activity," did not keep its hold on Jewish thought, having been discarded in the later literature (p. 104). For the Shechinah of the Talmud, the *Metatron*[4] of the Gaonic-mystical literature, the Active Intelligence of the philosophical schools, as well as the Ten Sephiroth[5] (Emanations) of the Cabbalists, all owe their existence to the same theosophic scruples and subtleties in which the Logos of Philo and the Memra[6] of the Targums originated. Thus, they always kept — though under various forms — their hold on the Jewish mind. Judaism was always broad enough to accommodate itself to these formulæ, which for the one may mean the most holy mysteries, and for the other empty and meaningless catchwords. The objection — in fact, the active opposition — of the Synagogue began when these possible or impossible explanations of the universe tended to transgress the bounds of abstract speculation, and, passing over into real concrete beings, to be worshipped as such. An instance from comparatively modern times might be found in one of the vagaries of the followers of the Pseudo-Messiah, Shabbethai Tsebi. For many generations the controversy had raged among the Cabbalists, whether the first of the above-mentioned Ten Emanations (called by some *Original Adam*, by others, *Crown*[7]) is to be considered as a part of the Deity or as something separate, and so to speak, having a reality in itself. The danger of establishing a Being near the Deity, having an existence of its own and invested with divine attributes, could not have escaped the thoughtful, and there are indeed some indications to this effect. The Synagogue as such, however, remained during the whole controversy strictly neutral, and allowed these theosophists to fight in the air as much as they liked. But the moment that the sect of Shabbethai Tsebi identified the incarnate Original Adam with their leader, and worshipped him as a sort of God-Messiah, the Synagogue at once took up a hostile attitude against those who separated God from His world, and, declaring Shabbethai Tsebi and his followers to be apostates, excluded them from Judaism for ever.

Nor can it be proved that legalism or nomism has ever tended to suppress the spiritual side of religion, either in respect of consciousness of sin, or of individual love and devotion. With an equal logic quite the opposite might be argued. Professor Toy tells us himself that it is no "accident that along with this more definite expression of ethical-religious law we find the first traces of a more spiritual conception of righteousness in the 'new heart' of Jeremiah and Ezekiel" (p. 235), whilst in another passage we read that "a turning point is marked by the Deuteronomist Jeremiah and Ezekiel, who announce the principles of individual responsibility and inwardness of obedience" (p. 184). Now, two things are certain; first, that Ezekiel urges the necessity of the new heart as well as of individual responsibility more keenly than any of his predecessors; secondly, that in Ezekiel the legalistic tendency is more evident than in Deuteronomy and Jeremiah. The logical conclusion would thus be that the higher ideals of religion are not only not inconsistent with legalism, but are the very outcome of it, and the so-called Priestly Code, by the very fact of its markedly legalistic tendency, should be considered as a step in the right direction. The latter assertion sounds like a paradox, but it will seem less so when the prevailing characteristic of this portion of the Pentateuch, as given even by Kuenen, who is by no means a champion of the Law, is borne in mind. "The centre of gravity," according to the great Dutch critic, "lies for the priestly author elsewhere than for the prophet; it lies in man's attitude, not towards his fellow-men, but towards God; not in his social, but in his personal life" (*Hibbert Lectures*, p. 161). It is here that we seem to strike the keynote of the *Weltanschauung* of the Priestly Legislation. In it man is more than a social being. He has also an individual life of his own, his joys and sorrows, his historical claims, his traditions of the past, and his hopes for the future — and all these have to be brought under the influence of religion, and to become sanctified through their relation to God. Hence, the work of the Priestly narrator and legislator opens with a cosmogony of his own, in which we find the grand theological idea of man being created in the Divine image; hence, too, his religious conception of the history of the nation and the control claimed by him over all the details of human life, which became with him so many opportunities for the worship of God. To him, God is not a mere figurehead; He not only reigns, but governs. Everywhere, — in the temple, in the judge's seat, in the family, in the farm, and in the market-place, — His presence is felt in enforcing the laws bearing His *imprimatur*, "I am the Lord thy God." By thus diffusing religion over the whole domain of human life — not confining it to the social institutions which are represented only by a few personages, such as the king, the princes, the priests, the judges or elders —they made it the common good of the whole people, and the feeling of personal responsibility for this good became much deeper than before. Thus it came to pass that whilst, during the first temple, the apostasy of kings and aristocracy involved the entire people, so that the words "And he (the king) did evil in the sight of the Lord," embrace the whole nation, during the second temple it was no longer of much consequence which side the political leaders took. Both during the Hellenistic persecutions, as well as afterwards in the struggles of some Maccabean kings with the Pharisees, the bulk of the people showed that they considered religion as their own personal affair, not to be regulated by the conscience of either priest or prince. It is true that this success may be largely ascribed to such contemporary religious factors as the Synagogue with its minimum of form, the Scribes with their activity as teachers, and the Psalmists with their divine enthusiasm; but the very circumstance that

R

these factors arose and flourished under the influence of the Priestly Code would suffice to prove that its tendency was not so sacerdotal as some writers would have us believe. Jewish tradition indeed attributes the composition of the daily public prayers, as well as of others for private worship, to the very men whom modern biblical criticism holds responsible for the introduction of the Priestly Code. Now this fact may perhaps be disputed, but there is little doubt that the age in which these prayers were composed was one of flourishing legalism. Nor is there any proof that the synagogues and their ritual were in opposition to the temple. From the few documents belonging to this period, it is clear that there was no opposition to the legalistic spirit by which the Priestly Code was actuated. This would prove that legalism meant something more than tithes and sacrifices for the benefit of the priests.

Nor is it true that the legal tendency aimed at narrowing the mind of the nation, turning all its thoughts into the one direction of the law. Apart from the fact that the Torah contained other elements besides its legalism, the prophets were not forgotten, but were read and interpreted from a very early age. It was under the predominance of the Law that the Wisdom literature was composed, which is by no means narrow or one-sided, but is even supposed by some critics to contain many foreign elements. In the book of Job, the great problems of man's existence are treated with a depth and grandeur never equalled before or since. This book alone ought partly to compensate the modern school for the disappearance of prophecy, which is usually brought as a charge against the Law. Then, too, the Psalms, placed by the same school in the post-exilic period, are nothing but another aspect of prophecy, with this difference, perhaps, that in the Prophets God speaks to man, while in the Psalms it is man who establishes the same communion by speaking to God. There is no reason why the critical school, with its broad conception of inspiration, and with its insistence that prophecy does *not* mean prediction, should so strongly emphasise this difference. If "it is no longer as in the days of Amos, when the Lord Yahveh did nothing without revealing his counsel to his servants the prophets," there is in the days of the Psalmists nothing in man's heart, no element in his longings and meditations and aspirations, which was not revealed to God. Nay, it would seem that at times the Psalmist hardly ever desires the revelation of God's secrets. Let future events be what they may, he is content, for he is with God. After all his trials, he exclaims, "And yet I am continually with thee; thou hast taken hold of my right hand. According to thy purpose wilt thou lead me, and afterwards receive me with glory. Whom have I (to care for) in heaven? and possessing thee, I have pleasure in nothing upon earth. Though my flesh and my heart should have wasted away, God would for ever be the rock of my heart and my portion" (Ps. lxxiii. 23–26). How an age producing a literature containing passages like these — of which Wellhausen in his *Abriss* (p. 95) justly remarks, that we are not worthy even to repeat them — can be considered by the modern school as wanting in intimate relation to God and inferior to that of the prophets is indeed a puzzle.

Now a few words as to the actual life under the Law. Here, again, there is a fresh puzzle. On the one side, we hear the opinions of so many learned professors, proclaiming *ex cathedrâ*, that the Law was a most terrible burden, and the life under it the most unbearable slavery, deadening body and soul. On the other side we have the testimony of a literature extending over about twenty-five centuries, and including all sorts and conditions of men, scholars, poets, mystics, lawyers, casuists, schoolmen, tradesmen, workmen, women, simpletons, who all, from the author of the 119th Psalm to the last pre-Mendelssohnian writer — with a small exception which does not even deserve the name of a vanishing minority — give unanimous evidence in favour of this Law, and of the bliss and happiness of living and dying under it, — and this, the testimony of people who were actually living under the Law, not merely theorising upon it, and who experienced it in all its difficulties and inconveniences. The Sabbath will give a fair example. The law of the Sabbath is one of those institutions the strict observance of which was already the object of attack in early New Testament times. Nevertheless, the doctrine proclaimed in one of the Gospels — that the son of man is Lord also of the Sabbath — was also current among the Rabbis. They, too, taught that the Sabbath had been delivered into the hand of man (to break, if necessary), and not man delivered over to the Sabbath.[8] And they even laid down the axiom that a scholar who lived in a town, where among the Jewish population there could be the least possibility of doubt as to whether the Sabbath might be broken for the benefit of a dangerously sick person, was to be despised as a man neglecting his duty; for, as Maimonides points out, the laws of the Torah are not meant as an infliction upon mankind, "but as mercy, loving-kindness, and peace." [9]

The attacks upon the Jewish Sabbath have not abated

with the lapse of time. The day is still described by
almost every Christian writer on the subject in the most
gloomy colours, and long lists are given of minute and
easily transgressed observances connected with it, which,
instead of a day of rest, would make it to be a day of
sorrow and anxiety, almost worse than the Scotch Sunday as depicted by continental writers. But it so happens
that we have the prayer of R. Zadok, a younger contemporary of the Apostles, which runs thus: "Through the
love with which Thou, O Lord our God, lovest Thy people
Israel, and the mercy which Thou hast shown to the
children of Thy covenant, Thou hast given unto us in love
this great and holy Seventh Day." [10]   And another Rabbi,
who probably flourished in the first half of the second
century, expresses himself (with allusion to Exod. xxxi. 13:
Verily my Sabbaths ye shall keep . . . that ye may know
that I am the Lord that doth sanctify you) — "The Holy
One, blessed be He, said unto Moses, I have a good gift
in my treasures, and Sabbath is its name, which I wish
to present to Israel. Go and bring to them the good
tidings." [11]   The form again of the Blessing over the
Sanctification-cup [12] — a ceremony known long before the
destruction of the Second Temple — runs: " Blessed art
Thou, O Lord our God, who hast sanctified us by Thy
commandments, and hast taken pleasure in us, and in love
and grace hast given us Thy holy Sabbath as an inheritance." All these Rabbis evidently regarded the Sabbath
as a gift from heaven, an expression of the infinite mercy
and grace of God which He manifested to His beloved
children.

And the gift was, as already said, a *good* gift. Thus
the Rabbis paraphrase the words in the Scripture "See,

for that the Lord hath given you the Sabbath " (Exod. xvi.
29): God said unto Israel behold the gem I gave you, My
children I gave you the Sabbath for your good.   Sanctify
or honour the Sabbath by choice meals, beautiful garments;
delight your soul with pleasure and I will reward you (for
this very pleasure); as it is said : "And if thou wilt call
the Sabbath a delight and the holy of the Lord honourable
(that is honouring the Sabbath in this way) . . . then
shalt thou delight thyself in the Lord" (Is. lviii. 13, 14).[13]

The delight of the Sabbath was keenly felt. Israel
fell in love with the Sabbath, and in the hyperbolic language of the Agadah the Sabbath is personified as the
"Bride of Israel," whilst others called it "Queen Sabbath,"[14] and they are actually jealous of a certain class
of semi-proselytes who, as it seems, were willing to observe the Sabbath, but declined to submit to the covenant of Abraham.   The Gentile Sabbath-keepers — who,
like all the nations of the world, envy Israel their Sabbath — the Rabbis considered as shameless intruders deserving punishment.[15]   No, it was Israel's own Queen or
Bride Sabbath whose appearance in all her heavenly
glory they were impatiently awaiting.   Thus we are told
of R. Judah b. Ilai that when the eve of the Sabbath
came "he made his ablutions, wrapped himself up in his
white linen with fringed borders looking like an angel of
the Lord of Hosts," thus prepared for the solemn reception of Queen Sabbath.   Another Rabbi used to put on
his best clothes, and arise and invite the Sabbath with
the words: "Come in Bride, come in."[16]   What the Bride
brought was peace and bliss.   Nay, man is provided with
a super soul for the Sabbath, enabling him to bear both
the spiritual and the material delights of the day with

dignity and solemnity.[17] The very light (or expression) of man's face is different on Sabbath, testifying to his inward peace and rest. And when man has recited his prayers (on the eve of the Sabbath) and thus borne testimony to God's creation of the world and to the glory of the Sabbath, there appear the two angels who accompany him, lay their hands on his head and impart to him their blessing with the words: "And thine iniquity is taken away and thy sin purged" (Is. vi. 7).[18] For nothing is allowed to disturb the peace of the Sabbath; not even "the sorrows of sin," though the Sabbath had such a solemn effect on people that even the worldly man would not utter an untruth on the Day of the Lord. Hence it was not only forbidden to pray on Sabbath for one's own (material) needs, but everything in the liturgy of a mournful character (as for instance the confession of sin, supplication for pardon) was carefully avoided. It was with difficulty, as the Rabbis say, that they made an exception in the case of condoling with people who had suffered loss through the death of near relatives. There is no room for morbid sentiment on Sabbath, for the blessing of the Lord maketh rich, and He addeth no sorrow with it (Prov. x. 22).[19] The burden of the Sabbath prayers is for peace, rest, sanctification, and joy (through salvation) and praise of God for this ineffable bliss of the Sabbath.

Such was the Sabbath of the old Rabbis and the same spirit continued through all ages. The Sabbath was and is still celebrated by the people who did and do observe it, in hundreds of hymns, which would fill volumes, as a day of rest and joy, of pleasure and delight, a day in which man enjoys some foretaste of the pure bliss and happiness which are stored up for the righteous in the world to come. Somebody, either the learned professors, or the millions of the Jewish people, must be under an illusion. Which it is I leave to the reader to decide.

It is also an illusion to speak of the burden which a scrupulous care to observe six hundred and thirteen commandments must have laid upon the Jew. Even a superficial analysis will discover that in the time of Christ many of these commandments were already obsolete (as for instance those relating to the tabernacle and to the conquest of Palestine), while others concerned only certain classes, as the priests, the judges, the soldiers, the Nazirites, or the representatives of the community, or even only one or two individuals among the whole population, as the King and the High-Priest. Others, again, provided for contingencies which could occur only to a few, as for instance the laws concerning divorce or levirate marriages, whilst many — such as those concerning idolatry, and incest, and the sacrifice of children to Moloch — could scarcely have been considered as a practical prohibition by the pre-Christian Jew; just as little as we can speak of Englishmen as lying under the burden of a law preventing them from burning widows or marrying their grandmothers, though such acts would certainly be considered as crimes. Thus it will be found by a careful enumeration that barely a hundred laws remain which really concerned the life of the bulk of the people. If we remember that even these include such laws as belief in the unity of God, the necessity of loving and fearing Him, and of sanctifying His name, of loving one's neighbour and the stranger, of providing

for the poor, exhorting the sinner, honouring one's
parents and many more of a similar character, it will
hardly be said that the ceremonial side of the people's
religion was not well balanced by a fair amount of
spiritual and social elements. Besides, it would seem
that the line between the ceremonial and the spiritual
is too often only arbitrarily drawn. With many commandments it is rather a matter of opinion whether they
should be relegated to the one category or the other.

Thus, the wearing of Tephillin[20] or phylacteries has,
on the one hand, been continually condemned as a meaningless superstition, and a pretext for formalism and
hypocrisy. But, on the other hand, Maimonides, who
can in no way be suspected of superstition or mysticism, described their importance in the following words:
"Great is the holiness of the Tephillin; for as long as
they are on the arm and head of man he is humble and
God-fearing, and feels no attraction for frivolity or idle
things, nor has he any evil thoughts, but will turn his
heart to the words of truth and righteousness." The
view which R. Johanan, a Palestinian teacher of the
third century, took of the fulfilment of the Law, will
probably be found more rational than that of many a
rationalist of to-day. Upon the basis of the last verse
in Hosea, "The ways of the Lord are right, and the
just shall walk in them, but the transgressors shall fall
therein," he explains that while one man, for instance,
eats his paschal lamb with the purpose of doing the
will of God who commanded it, and thereby does an act
of righteousness, another thinks only of satisfying his
appetite by the lamb, so that his eating it (by the very
fact that he professes at the same time to perform a relig-

ious rite) becomes a stumbling-block for him.[21]   Thus all
the laws by virtue of their divine authority — and in this
there was in the first century no difference of opinion
between Jews and Christians — have their spiritual side,
and to neglect them implies, at least from the individual's
own point of view, a moral offence.

The legalistic attitude may be summarily described as
an attempt to live in accordance with the will of God, car-
ing less for what God is than for what He wants us to be.
But, nevertheless, on the whole this life never degenerated
into religious formalism.   Apart from the fact that during
the second temple there grew up laws, and even beliefs,
which show a decided tendency towards progress and
development, there were also ceremonies which were popular with the masses, and others which were neglected.   Men
were not, therefore, the mere soulless slaves of the Law ;
personal sympathies and dislikes also played a part in
their religion.   Nor were all the laws actually put upon
the same level.   With a happy inconsistency men always
spoke of heavier and slighter sins, and by the latter —
excepting, perhaps, the profanation of the Sabbath — they
mostly understood ceremonial transgressions.   The statement made by Professor Toy (p. 243), on the authority of
James (ii. 10), that "the principle was established that he
who offended in one point was guilty of all," is hardly correct; for the passage seems rather to be laying down a
principle, or arguing that logically the law ought to be
looked upon as a whole, than stating a fact.   The fact
was that people did not consider the whole law as of equal
importance, but made a difference between laws and laws,
and even spoke of certain commandments, such as those
of charity and kindness, as outweighing all the rest of the

Torah. It was in conformity with this spirit that in times of great persecution the leaders of the people had no compunction in reducing the whole Law to the three prohibitions of idolatry, of incest, and of bloodshed. Only these three were considered of sufficient importance that men should rather become martyrs than transgress them.

These, then, are some of the illusions and misrepresentations which exist with regard to the Law. There are many others, of which the complete exposure would require a book by itself. Meanwhile, in the absence of such a book to balance and correct the innumerable volumes upon the other side, Professor Toy has done the best he could with existing materials, and produced a meritorious work deserving of wide recognition and approval.

X

THE HEBREW COLLECTION OF THE BRITISH MUSEUM

THE Hebrew collection in the British Museum forms one of the greatest centres of Jewish thought. It is only surpassed by the treasures which are contained in the Bodleian Library at Oxford. The fame of these magnificent collections has spread far and wide. It has penetrated into the remotest countries, and even the Bachurim (*alumni*) of some obscure place in Poland, who otherwise neither care nor know anything about British civilisation, have a dim notion of the nature of these mines of Jewish learning.

All sorts of legends circulate amongst them about the "millions" of books which belong to the "Queen of England." They speak mysteriously of an autograph copy of the Book of Proverbs, presented to the Queen of Sheba on the occasion of her visit to Jerusalem, and brought by the English troops as a trophy from their visit to Abyssinia, which is still ruled by the descendants of that famous lady. They also talk of a copy of the Talmud of Jerusalem which once belonged to Titus, afterwards to a Pope, was presented by the latter to a Russian Czar, and taken away from him by the English in the Crimean war; of a manuscript of the book *Light is Sown*,[1] which is so large that no shelf can hold it, and which therefore hangs on iron chains. How they long to have a glance at these precious things! Would not a man get wiser only by looking at the autograph of the wisest of men?

But even the students of Germany and Austria, who are inaccessible to such fables, and by the aid of Zedner's, Steinschneider's, and Neubauer's catalogues have a fair notion of our libraries, cherish the belief that they would gain in scholarship and wisdom by examining these grand collections. How often have I been asked by Jewish students abroad: " Have you really been to the British Museum? Have you really seen this or that rare book or manuscript? Had you not great difficulties in seeing them? Is not the place where these heaps of jewels are treasured up always crowded by students and visitors? "

Yet how little does our English public know of these wonderful things! We are fairly interested in Græco-Roman art. We betray much curiosity about the different Egyptian dynasties. We look with admiration at the cuneiform inscriptions in the Nimrod room. We do not even grudge a glance at the abominable idols of the savage tribes. But as to the productions of Jewish genius, — well, it is best to quote here the words of Heine, who ridiculed this indifference to everything that is Jewish, in the following lines: —

> Alte Mumien, ausgestopfte,
> Pharaonen von Ægypten,
> Merowinger Schattenkön'ge,
> Ungepuderte Perücken,
>
> Auch die Zopfmonarchen China's
> Porzellanpagodenkaiser —

Alle lernen sie auswendig,
Kluge Mädchen, aber, Himmel!

Fragt man sie nach grossen Namen,
Aus dem grossen Goldzeitalter
Der arabisch-althispanisch
Jüdischen Poetenschule,

Fragt man nach dem Dreigestirn
Nach Jehuda ben Halevy,
Nach dem Salomon Gabirol
Und dem Moses Iben Esra.

Fragt man nach dergleichen Namen,
Dann mit grossen Augen schaun
Uns die Kleinen an — alsdann
Stehn am Berge die Ochsinnen.

Now Heine goes on to advise his beloved one to study
the Hebrew language. It would be indeed the best remedy against this indifference. But this is so radical a cure
that one cannot hope that it will be made use of by many.
A few remarks in English, trying to give some notion of
the Hebrew collection in the British Museum, may, therefore, not be considered altogether superfluous.

The Hebrew collection in the Museum may be divided
into two sections: Printed Books, and Manuscripts. The
number of the printed books amounted in the year 1867,
in which Zedner concluded his catalogue, to 10,100 volumes. Within the last twenty-eight years about 5000
more have been added.

This enormous collection has grown out of very small
beginnings. The British Museum was first opened to the
public in the year 1759. Amongst the 500,000 volumes
which it possessed at that time only a single Jewish work,
the *editio princeps* of the Talmud (Bomberg, Venice, 1520–

1523) was to be found on its shelves. According to an article by Zedner in the *Hebräische Bibliographie* (ii. p. 88), this copy of the Talmud once belonged to Henry VIII. But very soon the Museum was enriched by a small collection of Hebrew books, presented to it by Mr. Solomon da Costa, surnamed Athias, who had emigrated to England from Holland. The translation of the Hebrew letter with which the donor accompanied his present to the Trustees of the Museum was first published in the *Gentleman's Magazine*, February 1760, and was afterwards republished by the Rev. A. L. Green, in an article in the *Jewish Chronicle*, 1859. I shall only reproduce here the passage relating to the history of this collection. After expressing his gratitude to the "crowning city, the city of London, in which he dwelt for fifty-four years in ease and quietness and safety," and telling us that he bequeaths these books to the British nation as a token of his gratitude, Da Costa proceeds to say that they are 180 books, which had been gathered and bound for Charles II., with valuable bindings and marked with the king's own cipher. These books were intended as a present from the London Jewish community to Charles for certain privileges which he had bestowed on them. The sudden death of the king seems to have frustrated the intention of the first donors. The books were scattered, and Da Costa had to collect them again.

Small as this collection is, it is most valuable on account of its including many early editions of Venice, Constantinople, Naples, etc. The original letter of Da Costa, with a full list of the 180 books, is preserved in a MS. in the British Museum (Additional, 4710–11).

Of still greater importance is the Michaelis collection.

It consists of 4420 volumes, and was bought by the Trustees of the Museum in 1848. Other successive acquisitions, especially the purchase of a large number of printed books from the Almanzi collection, brought the Museum into possession of one of the most complete and one of the largest Hebrew libraries in the world.

After the foregoing remarks on the quantity of this collection, I shall now attempt to give some idea of its quality. The following table, taken from the Preface of Zedner's *Catalogue*, shows its manifold contents : —

1. Bibles	1260	8. Cabbalah	460
2. Commentaries on the Bible	510	9. Sermons	400
3. Talmud	730	10. Liturgies	1200
4. Commentaries on the Talmud	700	11. Divine Philosophy	690
5. Codes of Law	1260	12. Scientific works	180
6. Decisions	520	13. Grammars, Dictionaries	450
7. Midrash	160	14. History, Geography	320
		15. Poetry, Criticism	770

The reader can see that almost every branch of human thought, religious and secular, is amply represented in this collection. Looking at this table from a geographical point of view, we may perhaps classify the authors in the following way: — France and Germany in the Middle Ages, Poland and the East in modern times, are represented by the fourth, fifth, and sixth classes. The Rabbis of Spain and Italy would probably excel in the last five classes. In the productions of classes eight and nine all the before-mentioned countries would have an equal share. English Judaism, by reason of its large number of occasional prayers and wedding hymns (Zedner, pp. 472, 652), may perhaps be represented in the last class (criticism excluded). We in England are a pious, devotional people, and leave the thinking to others.

But what is still more welcome to the student is the fact that all these branches of Jewish learning are represented in the British Museum by the best editions. It would be a rather tedious task to enumerate here all the early editions of which this collection can boast. There is hardly any Hebrew book of importance from the Bible down to the Code of R. Joseph Caro of which the Museum does not possess the first printed edition. There are also many books and editions in the Museum of which no second copy is known to be in existence. An enumeration of these rare books and editions would require long lists, the perusal of which would be rather trying. But I shall say a few words to show the importance of such early editions for the student. They possess, first, the advantage of being free from the misprints which crept in with every fresh republication. The art of editing books in a correct and scientific way is of a very recent date. And even Hebrew literature does not find that support from the public which would enable scholars to edit Jewish books in such a way as Roman and Greek classics are prepared by Oxford and Cambridge students. A new edition of a Hebrew book meant therefore an addition of new mistakes and misprints. And it is only by examining the *editiones principes* that the scholar finds his way out of these perplexities.

Another advantage is the fact that these early editions escaped the hand of the censor, whose office was not introduced till a comparatively late date. The same advantage is also possessed by the Hebrew books published at Constantinople, Salonica, and other Mohammedan cities. Only

s

Christian countries indulged in the barbarous pleasure of burning and disfiguring Jewish books. It is one of the most touching points in the life of R. David Oppenheim, of Prague, who spent all his life and fortune in collecting Hebrew works, and whose collection now forms one of the greatest ornaments of the Bodleian Library, that he was not allowed by the censor to enjoy the use of his treasures. He had to put them under the protection of Lipman Cohen, his father-in-law in Hanover, many hundreds of miles from his own home. With the exception of the Bible hardly any Jewish books escaped mutilation. In certain Christian countries some books were not allowed to be published at all; of others, again, whole chapters had to be omitted, while of others many passages had to be expunged. The words Roman, Greek, Gentile, were strictly forbidden, and had to be changed into Turks, Arabs, Samaritans, or worshippers of the stars and planets. One can imagine what confusion such stupid alterations caused. Fancy what blunders would have been committed in history if the old chroniclers had been compelled to change the Pope into the Grand Turk or the Shah of Persia, the Christian rulers into as many califs and pashas, or Rome and Athens into Pekin and Mecca!

It may perhaps be interesting to learn that Jews sometimes imitated their bitter enemies in this work of mutilation. Thus in the later editions of the *Book of Genealogies* by Abraham Zacuto,[2] a passage was left out reproducing the evidence given by the widow of Moses de Leon to the effect that the cabbalistic work, the Zohar, was a forgery manufactured by her poor dear husband. Another omission of this kind is to be found in the Code of R. Joseph Caro, mentioned above. Here the earliest editions declare,

in the heading of section 605, " a certain religious usage "
to be "a custom of folly." In the republications, the last
three words were left out. From such nonsensical omis-
sions and changes only the earliest editions, which are
abundant in the Museum, were exempt.

A remarkable feature about the books of this Hebrew
collection also is that many of them are provided in the
margin with manuscript notes by their former possessors.
These often happen to bear very great names in literature.
I shall only mention here R. Jacob Emden, Almanzi,
Michael, Gerundi, and Heidenheim. Of the works written by R. Jacob Emden, the Museum possesses an almost
complete author's copy with abundant corrections, notes,
and emendations by the author himself. His works are
still very popular among Polish and Russian Jews, especially his Prayer-Book, and his Responses. It would be
advisable for publishers in these countries to avail themselves of this copy on the occasion of a new edition. Of
Christian scholars I should name here Isaac Casaubon. A
rather amusing mistake occurs in Ben-Jacob's *Treasure of
Books* in connection with this name. Among the many
valuable copies of Kimchi's grammatical work *Perfection*,[3]
possessed by the Museum, there is included one which
belonged to Casaubon, and is full of notes by him. The
author of the *Treasure* speaks of a *Perfection* with notes
by Rabbi Yitzchak Kasuban. I was at first at a loss to
guess who that Rabbi Casaubon might be. When examining Zedner I found it was no other than the famous
Christian scholar, Isaac Casaubon. It is not known that
Casaubon's ambition lay in this direction. But when
Philo was regarded as a Father of the Church, Ben Gabirol
quoted for many centuries as a Mohammedan philosopher,

why should not Casaubon obtain for once the dignity of a Rabbi ?

After having given the reader some notion of the collection of printed works, I should like now to invite him to accompany me through the Manuscript Department of the Museum. But I am afraid that I shall make a bad guide here ; for the Museum is still without a descriptive catalogue of the Hebrew manuscripts, which is the only means of enabling the student to obtain a general view of the number and nature of these works. The manuscript catalogue of Dukes goes only as far as 1856. It was, as we shall soon see, just after this time that the Museum made its largest and, to a certain degree also, its most valuable acquisitions in Hebrew manuscripts. The following remarks must, therefore, not be taken as the result of a systematic study of this collection, which would be quite impossible without the aid of a catalogue. They rest partly on the descriptions given of a certain number of manuscripts in the catalogue by Dukes, but for the greater part on occasional glances at this or that MS.

As to the history of the collection, it has grown out of small beginnings just as that of printed books. The collection of Dr. Sloane, which laid the foundation of the Museum Library, contained only nine Hebrew MSS. Later acquisitions, as the Harleian collection, the Cottonian collection, the Royal collection, and many other smaller collections marked as Additional up to 1854, increased the number of the Hebrew manuscripts to 232. Of much more importance was the Almanzi collection, bought by the trustees of the Museum in 1865, and consisting of 335 MSS. Of succeeding acquisitions I shall mention here only the Yemen MSS., which were brought

to this country by the famous Shapira. The number of
Hebrew MSS. at the present day is said to exceed one
thousand. But we must not forget that many MSS. contain more than one work; in some cases even three or
four, so that the number of Hebrew works is far greater
still.

I shall now speak of the nature and importance of these
MSS. As to their contents they may be easily grouped
under the following headings: Biblical MSS., Commentaries (to the Bible) and Super-Commentaries, parts of the
Talmud and their Commentaries, Theology, Philosophy
and Ethics, Massorah, Grammar and Lexicography, Cabbalah, Poetry, Mathematics, Astronomy, Astrology and
Magic, Historical and Polemical Literature, etc. All
these branches of theological and secular learning and even
of human folly are fairly represented in the collection of
Hebrew MSS. in the Museum, though often only by a
part or a fragment of a work.

Thus the Babylonian Talmud is to be found only in two
MSS. (Harl. 5508 and Add. 25,717) both of them including 11 Tractates, hardly a third part of the whole work.
Indeed poor "Rabbinus Talmud" had to go to the *auto de
fé* on so many occasions that one cannot wonder if only
disjointed limbs are to be found of him in libraries. The
only complete MS. copy which escaped this vandalism is
that in the Royal Library in Munich, from which Mr.
Rabbinowicz has edited his monumental work, *Variae
Lectiones of the Talmud.*

All other libraries, Oxford included, have to be satisfied
with fragments. Still worse, as it is seen, fared the Jerusalem Talmud, and excepting the well-known copy in
Leyden from which the Venice edition was prepared, not

even fragments of this Talmud are to be found in the majority of libraries. To my knowledge it is only the British Museum which can boast of the Jerusalem Talmud in MS. extending over *Order of Seeds* and one tractate of *Order of Festivals* [4] (Or. 2122–24) with commentaries of R. Solomon Syrillo, the first few pages of which were edited by Dr. Lehmann of Mayence. The Museum also possesses a great part of the Tosephta extending over 14 Tractates (Add. 27,296). Of Midrashim we find in the Museum two excellent manuscripts of the Genesis *Rabbah*, one of the Leviticus *Rabbah*, and one of the *Siphra* and the *Siphré* (Add. 27,169 and 16,406), besides two copies of the Midrash *Haggadol* and other Aagadic collections brought from Yemen. The *Midrash* by Machir b. Abba Mari to the minor prophets included in the Harleian collection (5704) is unique. Of Liturgies, besides a great umber of MSS. representing the most peculiar rites, I shall mention the Machzor [5] Vitri (Add. 27,200–1) composed by the disciples of R. Solomon b. Isaac, and forming in itself almost a small library. For, apart from the prayers for festivals and week days which gave it its title, it includes, besides the *Sayings of the Fathers* with a large commentary, three of the Minor Tractates of the Talmud, many responses by German and French Rabbis, and a whole series of religious hymns by German and Spanish authors, and many other literary pieces. Cabbalah is represented by various valuable writings of the pre-Zoharistic time (see for instance Add. 15,299) and the works of R. Moses de Leon and R. Abraham Abulafia. Of Poetry, I shall point here to the Tarshish of R. Moses Ibn Ezra, the Makames by Judah Al Charisi (Add. 27,122), and the Divan of R. Abraham of Bedres (Add. 27,188). Of works relating to grammar and lexicography, I may refer to a Codex (Add. 27,214) which contains the lexicon of R. Menahem ben Saruk, which is considered as the oldest Hebrew MS. in the Museum, dating from the year 1091. Of historical works, I mention the chronicle of R. Joseph the Priest (Add. 27,122) and the letter of R. Sherira Gaon (Arundel 51), the oldest existing copy of this work (1189), which was edited by Dr. Neubauer in his *Mediæval Jewish Chronicles*.

These examples will suffice to show the significance of the MSS. collection of this Library. And the student may rest assured that in whatever branch of Jewish thought he is interested, he will always find in the Museum some Hebrew manuscript useful for his purpose.

I ought now to say a few words as to the value of this collection of manuscripts. Now, if the work contained in a MS. has never been edited, as for instance the Machzor Vitri[6] and so many others, its value is established by the mere fact of its existence. For those who published MSS. were not always guided by the best literary motives. And while they published and republished many books of which one edition would have been more than enough, many other works of the greatest importance for Jewish literature and history remained in manuscript. As an instance, it will suffice to mention here the Zohar, which has passed through twenty-four editions since the sixteenth century, whilst the earliest Jewish Midrash, the *Pessikta de Rab Kahana*, had to linger in the libraries till the year 1868, when it was edited by Mr. S. Buber. Thus there are still many pearls of Jewish literature which exist only in MS. Likewise most publishers were careless in their choice of the manuscript from which our editions have been prepared. Almost the whole of Jewish litera-ture will have to be re-edited before a scientific study of it will be possible. But such critical editions can only be obtained by the aid of the MSS. not yet made use of, in which better readings are to be found. From this fact even those MSS. the contents of which have been several times reprinted, as for instance the MSS. of the Midrash *Rabbah*, gain the greatest literary importance. And the more MSS. the editor of a work has at his disposal, the more certain is he of being able to furnish us with a good text.

But even when the whole of Jewish literature lies before the student in the best of texts, there will still remain a great charm about manuscripts. Printed books, like the great mass of the modern society for which they are prepared, are devoid of any originality. They interest us only as classes, and it is very seldom that they have a story of their own to tell. It is quite different with manu-scripts, where the fact of their having been produced by a living being invests them with a certain kind of individual-ity. This is specially the case with Hebrew MSS., which were not copied by men shut up in cloisters, but by socia-ble people living in the world and sharing its joys and sorrows. Even women were employed in this art, and I remember to have read in some MS. or catalogue a post-script by the lady copyist, which, if I remember rightly, ran as follows: "I beseech the reader not to judge me very harshly when he finds that mistakes have crept into this work; for when I was engaged in copying it God blessed me with a son, and thus I could not attend to my business properly."

To be sure, some of these copyists were curious folk.

Their mind as well as that of the world around them must have been of a peculiar constitution hardly conceivable to us. Take, for example, Benjamin, the copyist of a certain Machzor in the Museum (Add. 11,639). This Machzor was written in times of bitter persecution. The copyist, who was himself a learned man, alludes in one place to the sufferings which the Jews in a certain French town had to undergo in the year 1276. On one of them, the martyr R. Samson, Benjamin the copyist composed a lamentation written in a most mournful strain. · But this lamentation is followed by a wine-song, one of the jolliest and wildest parodies for the feast of Purim.

Speaking of this Machzor I should like to remark that it forms one of the greatest ornaments of the Museum. Besides including the whole of the Pentateuch, the above-mentioned Tarshish by R. Moses Ibn Ezra, and many other smaller literary pieces which would require a small volume to describe them properly, this MS. is most richly illuminated, and contains very many illustrations. The subjects of these illustrations are biblical, sometimes also apocryphal, such as — Adam and Eve in Paradise, Noah in the Ark, Abraham meeting the angels, Sarah behind the door listening to the conversation of her husband with his guests, Moses with the rod in his hands dividing the Red Sea, Samson riding on the back of a lion, Solomon on his throne, Daniel in the lion's den, the king Ahasuerus holding out the golden sceptre to Esther, Judith addressing Holofernes, the Leviathan, the mythical bird Bar Yochni, and many other similar subjects. In passing I recommend these illustrations and illuminations to the attention of the artist as the most worthy examples of Jewish ecclesiastical art, — if there is such a thing as a special Jewish art. The artist will find the Museum best suited for this purpose, its collection being considered as the richest of the kind. Besides this Machzor I must also allude to the illuminated Bible (Or. 2226–28) written in Lisbon for R. Judah Alchakin — it is said to be one of the finest specimens of such works — and the illuminated Mishneh Torah of Maimonides, executed for R. Joseph of the famous Yachya family, also thought to be most artistically done. The liturgies for the Passover Eve service will also offer to the artist a rich harvest, especially Codex, Add. 27,210, which the wealthy Lady Rosa Galico presented to her son-in-law on his wedding-day, and Codex, Add. 14,762, even the binding of which is considered as an artistic curiosity.

Leaving now these marvels to the appreciation of the artist, the greatest wonder which suggests itself to us is how the Jews could maintain such a cultured taste in such unhappy times, and get the means of satisfying it. These reflections about the owners present themselves the more strongly to our mind when we meet with one of those old Jewish prayer-books, which in many cases formed the whole religious and literary treasure of the family. In their fly-leaves, in which the births and deaths of successive generations are very often registered, the *spiritus familiaris* seems to be still haunting the pages. When you turn them over and see the service for Passover Eve, are you not bound to think of the anxiety with which these poor creatures engaged in this ceremony lest they might be attacked suddenly by a fanatic mob? must you not ask how they could bear life under such circumstances? And when you turn a few more pages and arrive at the prayers read for the dead, must you not ask how did they die?

Were they perhaps burnt alive *ad majorem Dei gloriam*, or torn to pieces by a " saintly mob " ? Take again the illuminated copies of the Bible and the Mishneh Torah, both of which were finished only a few years before the great expulsion of the Jews from Spain and Portugal, times when the earth already "burnt under their feet, and the heaven was also very unkind to them." And nevertheless Jews were still, as these MSS. show us, cultivating science and art. Another instance of such a devotion to science in spite of the unfavourable times may be seen from a colophon to Codex Or. 39. It contains the book *Nissim*, a philosophical treatise on the fundamental teachings of Judaism, together with a philosophical commentary on the Pentateuch by R. Nissim of Marseilles, a contemporary of R. Solomon ben Adereth in the thirteenth century. The Museum copy was written by R. Jacob, the son of David, who also added some annotations to the book. At the end he says : " I have copied this book *Nissim* for my own use, that I may study in it, I and my children and my grandchildren. . . . I have finished it to-day, Sunday, the 28th of Ab, 5333 (1573), at Venice, in the year of the expulsion which befell us on account of our sins." Now, only observe this poor R. Jacob, who has to go through all these horrors, yet is still occupied in copying MSS. for his own pleasure, and in meditating on the most complicated problems of philosophy and religion.

But it is not always stories of this heroic nature that the MSS. tell us. They betray also very much of the instability of human affairs and their weakness. You find in many copies the words that they must not " be sold or given in mortgage." But scarcely a genera- tion has passed away, and they are already in the posses-

sion of a new owner, who writes the same injunction to
be broken again by his children in their turn. In Codex
27,122, we find commendatory letters for a worthy poor
man, who is so unhappy as to have two grown-up daughters, and not to have the means of supplying them with
marriage portions. Indeed, he must have been very poor,
not possessing even a book in his house, or else his
troubles could not have been so great. For in Codex
Harl. 5702, we find the owner saying: "To eternal
memory that I have acquired this *Third Book of Avicena*
from the hands of my father-in-law, R. Jekuthiel, as a
part of my dowry."

As a sign of human weakness I give the following two
instances. There lies before me a cabbalistic Codex (Add.
27,199), which acquired some notoriety from the fact of
its having been copied by the famous grammarian, R.
Elijah Levita, for his pupil Cardinal Aegidius. At the
end of this MS. we read: "I (Levita) have finished (the
copying of) this book on Wednesday, the day of Hoshana
Rabba,[7] 5277 (1516), on which day I have seen my head
in the shadow of the moon. Praised be God (for it), for
now I am sure not to die in the following year." These
words relate to a well-known superstition, according to
which, when a man is going to die in the course of the
next year his shadow disappears from him on the preceding Hoshana Rabba. But is it not humiliating to see
that the great Levita, who was superior to many prejudices of his time, and taught Christians Hebrew, and who
denied the antiquity of the vowels in the Bible, which was
considered by the great majority of his contemporaries
as a mortal heresy — is it not humiliating to see this
enlightened man trembling for his life on this night, and

anxiously observing his shadow? Another Codex lies before me (Add. 17,053), containing the Novellæ to three tractates of the Talmud. Its owner must accordingly have been a learned man. But in the fly-leaf of this MS. we read the following words: " Memorandum — Thursday, the 25th of Sivan, 5295 (1535), I have taken an oath in the presence of R. David Ibn Shushan and R. Moses de Castro, etc., not to play (cards) any more." I might perhaps suggest on this occasion that in our days when all sorts of Judaisms are circulating, a cooking Judaism, a racing Judaism, a muscular Judaism, and so many Judaisms more — it would be interesting to take up also the subject of playing Judaism, and to write its history.

In conclusion I shall mention the colophon to Codex Harl. 5713, which may have some interest for the English reader. It runs: " I have written it in honour of the noble and pious, etc., Humphrey Wanley, the noble Librarian of my Lord Treasurer. May his glory be increased. In the year 5474 (1714) in the holy community of London, under the reign of the noble and happy Queen Anne. May the Lord increase her splendour and glory." The signature of the copyist is " Aaron the son of Moses, born in the city of Navaschadok in Poland." By the way, we learn from this signature that the immigration of Polish Jews into this country had already begun in the time of Queen Anne, and perhaps still earlier.

Thus everything in a MS., the arrangement of the matter, the remarks of the owners, the signature of the copyist, sets the reader thinking, and contributes many a side-light to the history of the Jews.

XI

TITLES OF JEWISH BOOKS

It is now more than half a century since Isaac Reggio in his edition of Elijah Delmedigo's *Examination of Religion*, made the remark that this book adds to its other merits that of bearing a title corresponding to its contents, — a merit that is very rare in Jewish books. Reggio proceeds to give a few specimens confirming his assertion, and concludes his remarks with a eulogy on Delmedigo, who in this respect also had the courage to differ from his contemporaries. Zunz also once wrote an article on titles of books. But this article unfortunately appeared in some German periodical which the British Museum does not possess, and I could not even succeed in ascertaining whether Zunz treats at all of titles of Hebrew books, nor am I aware that the subject has been taken up by any other scholar, Isaac D'Israeli's few notes on the subject in his *Curiosities of Literature* being scarcely worth mention. It seems to me, however, interesting enough to deserve some illustration, though I can by no means hope to be complete.

The titles of the books contained in the Bible need not be discussed here; information concerning them is to be found in every critical introduction to the Old Testament. The Rabbinical works dating from antiquity also offer

270

little opportunity for reflection on their titles. The Tal-
mud, as a work, has no title at all; for Talmud simply
means "teaching" or "study." Sometimes it is termed
ShaSS, an abbreviation of *Shisha Sedarim*,[1] meaning the
Six Orders or divisions contained in the Mishnah. This
last word means, according to some authors, "Repetition."
Other Tannaitic collections of laws or expositions of the
Scriptures are called "the Book" (Siphra), "the Books"
(Siphré), or "Additions" (Tosephta to the Mishnah).
The word *Baraitha*[2] means the external Mishnah that
enjoyed less authority than the Mishnah of R. Judah the
Patriarch. Some approach to titles we find in the names
given to the different tractates included in the Mishnah,
as *Berachoth*, because it treats of Benedictions, *Peah*[3]
(Corner) which contains the particulars concerning the
law in Lev. xix. and so forth. Of the few works quoted
in the Talmud it will suffice to mention the *Seder Olam*,
the Order of the World, the name of which is very suitable to the chronological contents of the book. In general,
I may observe that as long as the law which prohibited
the writing down of the Oral teachings was in force, there
hardly existed Jewish books. But where there are no
books there is also no need for titles. The few titles,
however, which can be proved to be historical are simple
and to the point. It is not till about the beginning of the
Middle Ages, when this prohibitive law had, for reasons not
to be explained here, been abolished, that we can speak of
Hebrew books. But here also the Title-confusion begins.

In order that we may have some general view of the
thousands of titles that are catalogued by the Jewish
bibliographers, it will perhaps be well to arrange them
under the following six classes : —

I. *Simple titles*, that have no other object than that of indicating the subject matter of the book. These are, as we have just seen, the only kind of titles known to antiquity. The few books which the Gaonim left us bear such simple titles as could have served as models to later generations. Among them may be mentioned the *Halachoth* or collection of Laws, *Creeds and Opinions*, by R. Saadiah Gaon, the *Book on Buying and Selling*, by R. Hai Gaon, containing the laws relating to commercial transactions. It may be noticed that this last book is one of the best arranged in Jewish literature, and displays more systematising powers than even the Code of Maimonides. The greatest part of the literary activity of the Gaonim consists in their Responsa, in which they gave decisions on ritual questions, or explanations of difficult passages in the Talmud. The titles borne by the various collections of those Responsa belong to a period later than the author's. The great majority of the books produced by the Franco-German school may also be included in this class. They are termed "Commentaries," "Additions" or "Glosses," "Novellæ," or "Confirming Proofs," and similar modest titles which show both their relation to, and dependence on, another older authority. The largest collection of Midrashim we possess bears the simple title "Bag."[4] Many of the Responsa satisfy themselves with the words "Questions to, and Answers by."

II. *Titles taken from the first word with which the book begins*, or from the first word of the Scriptural verse occurring first in the book. This class is strongly represented by the Midrashim. Thus the Midrash to the Song of Songs is also quoted as the Midrash *Chazitha*,[5] "Midrash, Seest thou" (the first text with which this Midrash deals being Proverbs xxii. 28). The Midrash to the Psalms is called Midrash *Shocher Tob*,[6] "Midrash, He that diligently seeketh the good" (Prov. xi. 37). The Midrash containing the legendary story of the wars of the sons of Jacob with the Canaanites is quoted as Midrash *V'yisseu*,[7] "Midrash, And they journeyed," as the story begins with the verse from Gen. xxxv. 5. And this is the case with the titles of many other Midrashim. Whether the work cited under the strange name of *Meat on Coals* did not begin with those words, containing some law relating to the salting of meat, I do not venture to decide. Under this class we may also arrange those books that are called after a phrase which is often used in the book, *e.g.*, the Midrash *Yelamdenu* (He may teach us), or the *Vehizhir*, "And He commanded us," almost every paragraph in these books beginning with the phrases mentioned.[8] Probably all the books belonging to this class received from the hands of their authors or compilers no titles at all. The student who had to quote them gave them names after the phrase or word which first caught his eye. In later centuries this class disappears almost entirely (see, however, Ben-Jacob's *Treasure*, p. 201, No. 827).

III. *Pompous titles.* The largest contributions to this class were made by the mystical writers. Books which profess to know what is going on in the heavens above and the earth beneath cannot possibly be satisfied with modest titles. Thus we have the "Book of Brightness" (Zohar), "the shining book" (Bahir), "the Confidential Shepherd" (Moses).[9] The books which the Zohar quotes bear such titles as the Book of Adam, the Book of Enoch. The only excuse for the Zohar is that the manufacturing of such books with pseudo-epigraphical titles

T

had already begun in antiquity. It is not, however, till
the Gaonic period that a whole apocryphal literature suddenly emerges which perplexes the Gaonim themselves.
No one is spared. Angels, patriarchs, and martyrs are
called upon to lend their names to these books. What
one resents most is that history came within the range of
the forger's activity. There is, for instance, the Josippon,
which professes to be written by Josephus, the well-known
Jewish historian of the first century. But in spite of all
the care taken by the author to disguise himself in the
garb of antiquity, the Josippon is a forgery of the ninth
or tenth century. Of a similar kind is the Book of Jasher,
containing legendary stories relating to Biblical personages. It pretends to be identical with the Book of Jasher
quoted in Joshua x. 13 and 2 Sam. i. 18. Some sixty
years ago a certain Mr. Samuel of Liverpool had the misfortune to make himself ridiculous by maintaining the pretensions of this book; for, indeed, it does not require
much knowledge of the Agadic literature to see that the
Book of Jasher is only a compilation of comparatively late
Midrashim.

IV. *Titles suggested by other Titles.* As an instance of
this we may take Maimonides' great Code of Law, which
bears the title *Mishneh Torah.* The importance of the
book made it the object of study for hundreds of scholars,
who wrote their commentaries and glosses on it. Among
the titles of the commentaries such Title-genealogies may
be discovered as Maggid *Mishneh, Mishneh* Lammelech;
which last word again suggested such titles as Emek ha-
Melech, Shaar ha-*Melech,* and so on.[10]

The same process may be observed in other standard
works, the importance of which made them a subject of

investigation and interpretation as the "Prepared Table," one of the glosses to which is called *Mappah*, "Table-cloth," whilst others provided it with the *Shewbread* and with *New Fruit*.

V. *Euphemistic Titles*, as "The Tractate of Joys," treating of funeral ceremonies and kindred subjects. It does not seem that this title was known to antiquity, but it is certain that already the earlier authorities quoted it by this name. "The Book of Life" (the German Jewish title of which is *Alle Dinim, von Freuden*), is the name of a very popular book containing the prayers to be read in the house of mourning as well as in the cemetery, which is also called the House of Life.

VI. *Titles taken from the Bible*, or Fancy Titles. This is the largest class of all, though it was utterly unknown in antiquity. It will be, perhaps, convenient to arrange this class of titles under the following sub-divisions. (*a*) Titles taken from the Bible, but also fulfilling the purpose of indicating the name of the author. For instance, "Seed of Abraham" (Ps. cv. 6), is the title of nine different books, the name of whose authors happened to be Abraham; "And Isaac entreated" (Gen. xxv. 21), is by Isaac Satanow on the Prayers; "Then Isaac sowed" (*ibid.* xxvi. 12), edited by R. Isaac Perles, contains an index to the Zohar. "Jacob shall take root" (Is. xxvii. 6) is the name of a book on Grammar and Massorah by R. Jacob Bassani. R. Joseph of Posen left two collections of sermons and commentaries on the Pentateuch, of which the one is called "And Joseph nourished" (Gen. xlvii. 12), the other "And Joseph gathered" (*ibid.* 14). Authors with the name of Judah are represented among others by such titles as "And this of Judah"

(Deut. xxxiii. 7), a treatise on the laws concerning the killing of animals; or "Judah shall go up" (Judges i. 2), a pamphlet containing a collection of prayers to be said on a journey. "Moses began" (Deut. i. 5) forms the title of three different books on various subjects, the authors of which had the name Moses. "Moses shall rejoice," a phrase occurring in the morning prayer for Sabbaths, is also the title of two books, the authors of which were named Moses. The "Rod of Aaron" enjoyed, as it seems, a goodly popularity; there are four bearing this name, not to speak of a fifth, "The Rod of Aaron brought forth buds" (Exod. xvii. 23), which is the name of a collection of Responsa by R. Aaron ben Chayim. But other Rods also were fashionable; there are, besides the five Rods of Moses, also Rods of Ephraim, Dan, Judah, Joseph, Naphtali, and Manasseh. By authors of the name of David we find books with the title "And David said," or a "Prayer of David," and other phrases occurring in the Psalms relating to David; whilst the "Tower of David" became the stronghold of other writers, and the "Shield of David" protected as many as nine more. The "Chariot of Solomon" (Cant. iii. 9) adorns the title-pages of five books by authors named Solomon. The Caraite Solomon Troki was so fond of that title that he called his two polemical treatises "He made himself a chariot," while R. Solomon of Mir's collection of sermons has the title, "This Bed which is Solomon's" (Cant. iii. 7). As to family names, there were not many authors in the enjoyment of that luxury (especially among the German Jews), but we find them indicating the fact of their being Priests or Levites. Among such books are the collection of Responsa, by R. Raphael Cohen, which has the title

"And the Priest shall come again" (Lev. xiv. 39), and the Cabbalistic treatise by R. Abraham Cohen, of Lask, with the title "And the Priest shall reckon unto him" (Lev. xxvii. 18). Probably the author deals with numbers. R. Hirsch Horwitz, the Levite, called his Novellæ to the Talmud "The Camp of Levi." The title "The Service of the Levite" (with allusion to Exodus xxxviii. 21) is borne by five other books by authors who were Levites. And there may be found hundreds of books with titles suggesting the Priestly or Levitical descent of their authors. Most anxious is Joseph Ibn Kaspi (Joseph the Silvern, so called after his native place Argentière, in the south of France) to provide most of his numerous books with some Biblical titles combined with silver, as a "Bowl of Silver" (Numb. vii. 13), or "Points of Silver" (Song of Songs i. 11), or "Figures of Silver" (Prov. xxv. 10), and other similar phrases. On the other hand Azulai manages to indicate at least one of his three Hebrew names, Chayim Joseph David, in most of his works, of which the number exceeds seventy, as Chayim Shaal,[11] "He asked Life" (Ps. xxi. 4), or "The knees of Joseph" (alluding to Gen. xlviii. 12), and "Truth unto David" (Ps. cxxxii. 11).

(*b*) The Tabernacle with its furniture was also a great favourite with many authors. There are not only six tabernacles (two on Cabbalah, two on grammar, and two on Talmudical subjects), but also three "Arks of the Testimony," two "Altars of gold," two "Tables of Shewbread," four "Candlesticks of the Light," two "Sockets of Silver," and two "Pillars of Silver." Others again preferred the vestments of the priests as the "Plate of Judgment," the "Robe of the Ephod," the "Mitre of Aaron," the "Plate of Gold," the "Bell and Pomegranate," "Wreathen Chains," and the "Arches of Gold." Many of these books were written by authors claiming to be priests. (*c*) But besides the canonical, other costumes were also fashionable. R. Mordecai Yafeh composed ten books, every one of them bearing the name of some garment or apparel, as "Apparel of Royalty," "Apparel of Blue," "Apparel of White," and so the whole suit with which Mordecai went out from the presence of the king (Esther viii. 15). These ten works range from codifications of the law and occasional sermons to philosophy, astronomy, and Cabbalah. By other writers we have three "Coats of many colours" (Gen. xxxvii. 4), one "Bridal Attire," and the "Thread of Scarlet" is not missing. (*d*) The ingredients for incense as well as other articles used in the Tabernacle or in the Temple were also fancied by some authors, and we have two books with the title of "Principal Spices," two "Pure Myrrh," three "Arts of the Apothecary," one "Oil of Holy Ointment," five "Meat Offerings mingled or dry," three or four "Flour of the Meat Offering," and also one "Two Young Pigeons" (Bene Yonah) by R. Jonah Zandsopher. But the appetite of the authors did not stop at these holy things. It extended also to such lay articles as "Spiced Wine," "Juice of Pomegranate" (Cant. viii. 2), "Forests of Honey," the "Book of the Apple," and "Seven Kinds of Drink."

(*e*) Field and flock also suggested to Hebrew writers as well as to Mr. Ruskin such titles as "The Fruit of the Hand," the "Rose of Sharon," the "Lily of the Valleys," or "The Shepherds' Tents," and "In the Green Pastures" (Ps. xxiii. 2).

The specimens given for every class may with very little trouble be doubled and redoubled. But it is not my inten-

tion to reproduce here whole catalogues. Reggio thinks
all such titles, which do not correspond with the context
of the book, absurd and confusing. He suggests that
the Jews followed in this respect the Arabic writers. There
is no doubt that Reggio is not altogether wrong in his
complaint. Almost all the titles included in class vi., as
the reader might have observed, never indicate to the
student the subject of which the books treat. How can
one guess that the Responsa, the Dance of Mahanaim
(two companies), is of a polemical nature against the tendencies of reform? This list may be lengthened by hundreds of titles. But even these incomprehensible titles
are better than the *Chad Gadyah Lo Israel* (One Kid No
Israel),[12] the un-Hebrew title of a pamphlet trying to prove
the un-Jewish origin of the well-known folk-song sung on
Passover Eve. But, on the other hand, it must not be
overlooked that even this class has, though not always,
something suggestive and even practical about it. The
"Choice of Pearls" is undoubtedly more attractive than
the prosaic "Collection of Proverbs and Sayings," which
is what the book contains. "Understanding of the Seasons" (1 Chr. xii. 32), sounds also better than the simple
"Collection of Sermons on different occasions." "The
Lips of those who Sleep" recommends itself as a very
suggestive title for a catalogue, especially when one thinks
of the Agadic explanation given to Cant. vii. 10, according
to which the study of the book of a departed author
makes the lips of the dead man to speak. Such titles as
"Bunch of Lilies" for a collection of poems are still usual
with us. Such a title as the "Jealousy Offering," or the
"Law of Jealousies," in polemical literature is very appro-
priate for its subject. R. Jacob Emden, who named one

of his pamphlets " Rod for the fool's back " (Prov. xxvi. 3), will be envied for his choice by many a controversialist even to-day. Wittily devised is the pun-title, " City of Sihon " for a mathematical book by R. Joseph Tsarphathi, alluding to Numb. xxi. 27, " For Hesbon (reckoning) is the City of Sihon."

Other titles were probably intended more as mottoes than titles. " Go forth and behold, ye daughters of Zion " (Cant. iii. 11), is put in the title-page of R. Jacob's German-Jewish paraphrase of the Pentateuch, which was written chiefly for the use of ladies. " Let another man praise thee and not thine own mouth, a stranger and not thine own lips " (Prov. xxvii. 2), forms the title of a book extending over only one and a half page in quarto. It contains letters by seven Rabbis (among them R. Liva of Prague) recommending the Ascetic, R. Abraham Wangos, who has a daughter to marry, and wants also to make a pilgrimage to the Holy Land, as deserving the support of his brethren.

There is also another objection to these titles. It is that they seem sometimes not quite consonant with our notions of modesty. Thus we have " Desirable and Sweet " on astronomy, " Sweeter than Honey " or "He shall comfort us," and many others of this kind. But it must not be thought that we have a right to infer from the title to the author. There is, indeed, an anecdote that three authors were rather too little careful about the choice of their titles, namely Maimonides in calling his Code *Mishneh Torah* (which is the traditional title of the Book of Deuteronomy), R. Moses Alshech in calling his homiletical commentaries *Torah* of Moses, and R. Isaiah Horwitz in calling his book *Shene Luchoth ha-*

Berith (The Two Tables of the Covenant). These authors, as the story goes, had for their punishment that their works are never quoted by the titles they gave to them, the former two being usually cited as Rambam or Alshech, whilst the last is more known by its abbreviated title of SHeLa[13] than by its full name.

I do not remember where I have read this story, but I am quite sure that its pious author would have been more careful about repeating it had he known that this accusation against Maimonides was a favourite topic with apostates, who thought to hit Judaism in the person of its representative Maimonides. But, as R. Solomon Duran in his polemical work remarks, Maimonides was too much of a truly great man to find any satisfaction in such petty vanity. Nor do I believe that even the character of less-known authors can in any way be impugned by the seemingly conceited titles of their books; just as on the other hand the humility of the author is not proved by calling his book "The Offering of the Poor," or other modest titles. The fancy title was in common use, and was therefore a commonplace with no significance whatever. The real disadvantage of such titles lies in the fact that, as already pointed out, they conceal from the student the contents of the book which he might otherwise consult in the course of his researches.

Did these authors perhaps foresee that there would come a time in which index-knowledge would pass for deep scholarship? and did they thus by using these obscure titles try to put a check on the dabblers who speak the more of a book the less they have read of its contents? If this be the case we can only admire their foresight.

XII

THE CHILD IN JEWISH LITERATURE

" I saw a Jewish lady only yesterday with a child at her knee, and from whose face towards the child there shone a sweetness so angelical that it seemed to form a sort of glory round both. I protest I could have knelt before her, too, and adored in her the divine beneficence in endowing us with the maternal *storgé* which began with our race and sanctifies the history of mankind." These words, which are taken from Thackeray's *Pendennis*, may serve as a starting-point for this paper. The fact that the great student of man perceived this glory just round the head of a Jewish lady rouses in me the hope that the small student of letters may, with a little search, be able to discover in the remains of our past many similar traces of this divine beneficence and sanctifying sentiment. Certainly the glimpses which we shall catch from the faded leaves of ancient volumes, dating from bygone times, will not be so bright as those which the novelist was so fortunate as to catch from the face of a lady whom he saw but the previous day. The mothers and fathers, about whom I am going to write in this essay, have gone long ago, and the objects of their anxiety and troubles have also long ago vanished. But what the subject will lose in brightness, it may perhaps gain in reality and intensity. A few moments of enraptured devotion do not make up the saint. It is a whole series of feelings and sentiments betrayed on different occasions, expressed in different ways, a whole life of sore troubles, of bitter disappointments, but also moments of most elevated joys and real happiness.

And surely these manifestations of the divine beneficence, which appear in their brightest glory in the literature of every nation when dealing with the child, shine strongest in the literature of the Jewish nation. In it, to possess a child was always considered as the greatest blessing God could bestow on man, and to miss it as the greatest curse. The patriarch Abraham, with whom Israel enters into history, complains — "Oh Lord, what wilt Thou give me, seeing I go childless!"

The Rabbis regarded the childless man as dead, whilst the Cabbalist in the Middle Ages thought of him who died without posterity as of one who had failed in his mission in this world, so that he would have to appear again on our planet to fulfil this duty. To trace out the feelings which accompanied the object of their greatest anxiety, to let them pass before the reader in some way approaching to a chronological order, to draw attention to some points more worthy of being emphasised than others, is the aim of this essay.

I said that I propose to treat the subject in chronological order. I meant by this that I shall follow the child in the different stages through which it has to pass from its birth until it ceases to be a child and attains its majority. This latter period is the beginning of the thirteenth year in the case of a female, and the beginning of the fourteenth year in the case of a male. I shall have occasion later on to examine this point more closely.

But there is the embryo-period which forms a kind of preliminary stage in the life of the child, and plays a very important part in the region of Jewish legends. Human imagination always occupies itself most with the things of which we know least. And so it got hold of this semi-existence of man, the least accessible to experience and observation, and surrounded it by a whole cycle of legends and stories. They are too numerous to be related here. But I shall hint at a few points which I regard as the most conspicuous features of these legends.

These legends are chiefly based on the notion of the pre-existence of the soul on the one hand, but on the other hand they are a vivid illustration of the saying of the Fathers, "Thou art born against thy will." Thus the soul, when it is brought before the throne of God, and is commanded to enter into the body, pleads before Him: "O Lord, till now have I been holy and pure; bring me not into contact with what is common and unclean." Thereupon the soul is given to understand that it was for this destiny alone that it was created. Another remarkable feature is the warning given to man before his birth that he will be responsible for his actions. He is regularly sworn in. The oath has the double purpose of impressing upon him the consciousness of his duty to lead a holy life, and of arming him against the danger of allowing a holy life to make him vain. As if to render this oath more impressive, the unborn hero is provided with two angels who, besides teaching him the whole of the Torah, take him every morning through paradise and show him the glory of the just ones who dwell there. In the evening he is taken to hell to witness the sufferings of the reprobate. But such a lesson would make free will impossible. His future conduct would only be dictated by the fear of punishment and hope of reward. And the moral value of his actions also depends, according to Jewish notions, upon the power to commit sin. Thus another legend records: "When God created the world, He produced on the second day the angels with their natural inclinations to do good, and the absolute inability to commit sin. On the following days again He created the beasts with their exclusively animal desires. But He was pleased with neither of these extremes. If the angels follow my will, said God, it is only on account of their impotence to act in the opposite direction. I shall therefore create man, who will be a combination of both angel and beast, so that he will be able to follow either the good or evil inclination. His evil deeds will place him beneath the level of animals, whilst his noble aspirations will enable him to obtain a higher position than angels." Care is therefore taken to make the child forget all it has seen and heard in these upper regions. Before it enters the world an angel strikes it on the upper lip, and all his knowledge and wisdom disappear at once. The pit in the upper lip is a result of this stroke, which is also the cause why children cry when they are born.

As to the origin of these legends, the main features of which are already to be found in the Talmud, I must refer the reader to the researches of Löw and others.[1] Here we have only to watch the effect which these legends had upon the minds of Jewish parents. The newly born child was in consequence looked upon by them as a higher being, which, but a few seconds before, had been convers-

ing with angels and saints, and had now condescended
into our profane world to make two ordinary mortals
happy.　The treatment which the child experienced from
its parents, as well as from the whole of the community,
was therefore a combination of love and veneration.　One
may go even further and say that the belief in these
legends determines greatly the destination of the child.
What other destination could a being of such a glorious
past have than to be what an old German Jewish poem
expressed in the following lines : —

> Geboren soll es wehren
> Zu Gottes Ehren.

" The child should be born to the honour of God."　The
mission of the child is to glorify the name of God on earth.
And the whole bringing up of the child in the old Jewish
communities was more or less calculated to this end.　The
words of the Bible, " And ye shall be unto me a kingdom
of priests," were taken literally.　Every man felt it his
duty to bring up his children, or at least one member of
his family, for this calling.　How they carried out this
programme we shall see later on.

Now, regarding almost every infant as a predestined
priest, and thinking of it as having received a certain
preparation for this calling before it came into this world,
we cannot wonder that the child was supposed to show
signs of piety from the days of its earliest existence, and
even earlier.　Thus we read that even the unborn children
joined in with the chorus on the Red Sea and sang the
Song (of Moses).　David, again, composed Psalms before
perceiving the face of this world.　On the Day of Atonement they used to communicate to the unborn child,

through the medium of its mother, that on this great day it had to be satisfied with the good it had received the day before. And when a certain child, afterwards named Shabbethai, refused to listen to such a request, R. Johanan applied to it the verse from the Psalm, "The wicked are estranged from the womb." Indeed, Shabbethai turned out a great sinner. It will perhaps be interesting to hear what his sin was. It consisted in forestalling the corn in the market and afterwards selling if to the poor at a much higher price. Of a certain child the legend tells that it was born with the word *emeth* (truth) engraved on its forehead. Its parents named it Amiti,[2] and the child proved to be a great saint.

The priest, however, could not enter into his office without some consecration. As the first step in this consecration of the child we may consider the Covenant of Abraham. But this was prefaced by a few other solemn acts which I must mention. One of the oldest ceremonies connected with the birth of a child was that of tree-planting. In the case of a boy they planted a cedar, in that of a girl a pine ; and on their marriage they cut branches from these trees to form the wedding-canopy. Other rites followed, but they were more of a medical character, and would be better appreciated by the physician. In the Middle Ages superstition played a great part. To be sure, I have spoken of saints ; but we ought not to forget that saints, too, have their foolish moments, especially when they are fighting against hosts of demons, the existence of which is only guaranteed by their own over-excited brains. Jewish parents were for many centuries troubled by the fear of Lilith,[3] the devil's mother, who was suspected of stealing children and killing them. The precautions they took to prevent this atrocity were as foolish as the object of their fear. I do not intend to enumerate here all these various precautions. Every country almost has its own usages and charms, one more absurd than the other. It will suffice to refer here to the most popular of these charms, in which certain angels are invoked to protect the child against its dangerous enemy Lilith. But of whatever origin they may be, Judaism could do better without them. The only excuse for their existence among us is to my mind that they provoked the famous Dr. Erter to the composition of one of the finest satires in the Hebrew language.

Of a less revolting character was the so-called ceremony of the "Reading of the Shema."[4] It consisted in taking all the little children of the community into the house of the newly-born child, where the teacher made them read the Shema, sometimes also the ninety-first Psalm. The fact that little children were the chief actors in this ceremony reconciles one a little to it despite its rather doubtful origin. In some communities these readings took place every evening up to the day when the child was brought into the covenant of Abraham. In other places they performed the ceremony only on the eve of the day of the *Berith Milah*[5] (Ceremony of the Circumcision). Indeed, this was the night during which Lilith was supposed to play her worst tricks, and the watch over the child was redoubled. Hence the name "Wachnacht," or the "Night of Watching." They remained awake for the whole night, and spent it in feasting and in studying certain portions of the Bible and the Talmud, mostly relating to the event which was to take place on the following day. This ceremony was already known to Jewish

writers of the thirteenth century. Nevertheless, it is considered by the best authorities on the subject to be of
foreign origin. Quite Jewish, as well as entirely free from
superstitious taint, was the visit which was paid to the
infant-boy on the first Sabbath of his existence. It was
called "Shalom Zachar,"[6] probably meaning "Peace-
boy," in allusion to a well-known passage in the Talmud
to the effect that the advent of a boy in the family brings
peace to the world.

At last the dawn of the great day of the Berith came.
I shall, however, only touch here on the social aspects of
this rite.

Its popularity began, as it seems, in very early times.
The persecutions which Israel suffered for it in the times
of Antiochus Epiphanes, "when the princes and elders
mourned, the virgins and the young men were made
feeble, and the beauty of women was changed, and when
certain women were put to death for causing their children to be circumcised," are the best proof of the attachment of the people to it. The repeated attempts against
this law, both by heathen and by Christian hands, only
served to increase its popularity. Indeed R. Simeon ben
Eleazar characterised it as the law for which Israel
brought the sacrifice of martyrdom, and therefore held
firmly by it. In other words they suffered for it, and it
became endeared to them. R. Simeon ben Gamaliel declares it to be the only law which Israel fulfils with joy
and exultation. As a sign of this joy we may regard the
eagerness and the lively interest which raised this ceremony from a strictly family affair to a matter in which the
whole of the community participated. Thus we find that
already in the times of the Gaonim the ceremony was

U

transferred from the house of the parents to the synagogue. Here it took place after the prayers, in the
presence of the whole congregation. The synagogue
used to be specially illuminated in honour of the event.
Certain pieces of the daily prayer, of a rather doleful
nature, such as the confession of sins, were omitted, lest
the harmony of the festival should be disturbed. As a
substitute for these prayers, various hymns suitable for
the occasion were composed and inserted in the liturgy
for the day. As the most prominent members among
those present figured the happy father of the child and
the medical man who performed the ceremony, usually
called the Mohel or Gozer,[7] both wearing their festal
garments and having certain privileges, such as being
called up to the Reading of the Law and chanting certain
portions of the prayers. It is not before the tenth century
that a third member suddenly emerges to become almost
as important as the father of the child. I refer to the
Sandek or Godfather. In some countries he was also
called the Baal Berith (Master of the Covenant). In Italy
they seemed to have had two Sandeks. This word was
for a long time supposed to be the Greek word σύνδικος.
But it is now proved beyond doubt that it is a corruption
of the word σύντεκνος used in the Greek church for godfather. In the church he was the man who lifted the
neophyte from the baptismal waters. Among the Jews,
the office of the Sandek was to keep the child on his
knees during the performance of the rite. The Sandek's
place was, or is still, near the seat of honour, which is
called the Throne of Elijah, who is supposed to be the
angel of the covenant. Other angels, too, were believed
to officiate at this rite. Thus the angel Gabriel is also

said to have performed the office of Sandek to a certain child. According to other sources the archangel Meta-tron himself attended. Probably it was on this account that later Rabbis admonished the parents to take only a pious and good Jew as Sandek for their children. Christian theologians also declared that no good Christian must render such a service to a Jew. The famous Bux-torf had to pay a fine of 100 florins for having attended the Berith of a child, whose father he had employed as reader when editing the well-known Basel Bible. The poor reader himself, who was the cause of Buxtorf's offence, was fined 400 florins. Of an opposite case in which a Jew served as godfather to a Christian child, we find a detailed account in Schudt's *Merkwürdigkeiten der Juden*, a very learned and very foolish book. When the father was summoned before the magistrate, and was asked how he dared to charge a Jew with such a holy Christian ceremony, he coolly answered, because he knew that the Jew would present him with a silver cup. As to the present, I have to remark that with the Jews also the godfather was expected to bestow a gift on the child. In some communities he had to defray the expenses of the festival-dinner, of which I shall speak presently. In others, again, he had also to give a present to the mother of the child.

Much older than the institution of the Sandek is the festival-dinner just alluded to, which was held after the ceremony. Jewish legend supplies many particulars of the dinner the patriarch Abraham gave at the Berith of his son Isaac. This is a little too legendary, but there is ample historical evidence that such meals were already customary in the times of the Second Temple. The

Talmud of Jerusalem gives us a detailed account of the proceedings which took place at the Berith dinner of Elisha ben Abuyah, who afterwards obtained a sad celebrity as Acher. Considering that Elisha's birth must have fallen within the first decades after the destruction of the Temple, and that these sad times were most unsuitable for introducing new festivals, we may safely date the custom back to the times of the Temple. The way in which the guests entertained themselves is also to be gathered from the passage referred to. First came the dinner, in which all the guests participated; afterwards the great men of Jerusalem occupied one room, indulging there in singing, hand clapping, and dancing. The scholars again, who apparently did not belong to the great men, were confined to another room, where they employed themselves in discussing biblical subjects. In later times special hymns, composed for this festival, were inserted in the grace after dinner. After the dinner, sermons or speeches used also to be given, the contents of which were usually made up of reflections on biblical and Talmudical passages relating to the event of the day. Sometimes they consisted of a kind of learned puns on the name which the child received on this occasion.

With this meal the first consecration of the child-priest was concluded. In some places they used to come to the father's house on the third day after the circumcision with the purpose of making inquiries after the child's health. In the case when the child was the first-born the ceremony of " redeeming the child " [8] in accordance with Exodus xiii. used to take place. The details of this ceremony are to be found in almost every prayer-book, and there is nothing fresh to add. But perhaps I may be allowed to draw

attention to another distinction that the first-born received
in the Middle Ages. I refer to an account given by the
author of the book, *The Ordinance of the Law*,[9] who
flourished in the thirteenth century. He says : Our predecessors made the rule to destine every first-born to God,
and before its birth the father had to say, " I take the vow
that if my wife presents me with a son, he shall be holy
unto the Lord, and in His Torah he shall meditate day and
night." On the eighth day after the Berith Milah they
put the child on cushions, and a Bible on its head, and
the elders of the community, or the principal of the college, imparted their blessings to it. These first-born sons
formed, when grown up, the chief contingent of the Yeshiboth (Talmudical Colleges), where they devoted the
greatest part of their lives to the study of the Torah. In
later centuries the vow was dropped, but from the abun-
dance of the Yeshiboth in Poland and elsewhere it seems
as if almost every child was considered as having no other
calling but the study of the Torah. Indeed, the growing
persecutions required a strengthening of the religious
force.

With these ceremonies the first act of consecration
ended in the case where the new-born child was a boy.
I will now refer to the ceremony of the name-giving, which
was common to males and females. In the case of the
former this ceremony was connected with the Berith
Milah. The oldest formula, which is already to be found
in the *Ritual Rab Amram Gaon*, is composed in Aramaic.
It is, like many prayers in that language, a most beautiful
composition, and very suitable for the occasion. Our
present Hebrew prayer is far less beautiful, and dates
from a much later age. In some countries the ceremony

of naming was repeated in the house of the parents. It took place on the Sabbath, when the mother returned home from her first visit to the synagogue after her recovery. Here the friends and relatives of the family assembled, and after arranging themselves round the cradle of the child they lifted it three times, shouting the new name at every lifting. This name was the so-called "profane" name, whilst the name it received in the synagogue was the "sacred" or Hebrew name. The ceremony concluded with the usual festival-dinner. By the way, there was perhaps a little too much feasting in those days. The contemporary Rabbis tried indeed to suppress some of the banquets, and put all sorts of restrictions on dinner-hunting people. But considering the fact that, as Jews, they were excluded from every public amusement, we cannot grudge them the pleasure they drew from these semi-religious celebrations. For people of an ascetic disposition it was, perhaps, the only opportunity of enjoying a proper meal. In the same way, in our days, the most severe father would not deny his lively daughter the pleasure of dancing or singing charitably for the benefit of suffering humanity. The ceremony described was known to the authors of the Middle Ages by the name of *Holle Kreish*. These words are proved by Dr. Perles to be of German origin, and based on some Teutonic superstition into the explanation of which I cannot enter here.

Of much more importance was the ceremony of name-giving in the case of a girl, it being the only attention the female child received from the synagogue. The usages varied. In some countries the name was given on the first Sabbath after the birth of the child. The father was "called up to the Reading of the Law," on which followed the formula, "He who blessed our ancestors Abraham," etc., "may He also bless," etc., including the blessing and announcement of the child's name. After the prayer the congregation assembled in the house of the parents to congratulate them. In other countries the ceremony took place on the Sabbath when the mother attended the synagogue after the recovery. The ceremony of Holle Kreish seems to have been especially observed in the case of a girl.

Though the feasting was now over for the parents, the child still lived in a holiday atmosphere for a long time. In the legend of the "Ages of Man" the child is described in the first year of its existence as a little prince, adored and petted by all. The mother herself nourished and tended the child. Although the Bible already speaks of nurses, many passages in the later Jewish literature show a strong aversion to these substitutes for the mother. In the event of the father of the child dying, the mother was forbidden to marry before her suckling infant reached the age of two years, lest a new courtship might lead to the neglect of the child.

More difficult is it to say wherein the other signs of loyalty to the little prince consisted; as, for instance, whether Jews possessed anything like lullabies to soothe the little prince into happy and sweet slumber. At least I am not aware of the existence of such songs in the ancient Jewish literature, nor are they quoted by mediæval writers. The "Schlummerlied," by an unknown Jewish bard, about which German scholars wrote so much, contains more heathen than Jewish elements. From the protest in *The Book of the Pious*, against using non-Jewish cradle-songs, it seems that little Moshechen was

lulled to sleep by the same tunes and words as little
Johnny. The only Jewish lullaby of which I know, is
to be found in the work of a modern writer who lived
in Russia. How far its popularity goes in that country
I have no means of ascertaining. This jingle runs as
follows : —

> O! hush thee, my darling, sleep soundly my son,
> Sleep soundly and sweetly till day has begun ;
> For under the bed of good children at night
> There lies, till the morning, a kid snowy white.
> We'll send it to market to buy Sechora,[10]
> While my little lad goes to study Torah.
> Sleep soundly at night and learn Torah by day,
> Then thou'lt be a Rabbi when I have grown gray.
> But I'll give thee to-morrow ripe nuts and a toy,
> If thou'lt sleep as I bid thee, my own little boy.[11]

But naturally the holiday atmosphere I spoke of was
very often darkened by clouds resulting from the illness
of the child. Excepting small-pox, the child was subject
to most of those diseases which so often prove fatal to
our children. These diseases were known under the collective name of " the difficulties (or the pain) of bringing
up children." These difficulties seem to have been still
greater in Palestine, where one of the old Rabbis exclaimed that it was easier to see a whole forest of young
olive trees grow up than to rear one child.[12] To avoid
so mournful a subject, I refrain from repeating the touching stories relating to the death of children. The pain
was the more keenly felt since there was no other way
of explaining the misfortune which befell the innocent
creature than that it had suffered for the sins of the
parents ; and the only comfort the latter had was that

the child could not have lost much by its being removed from this vale of tears at such an early period. A remarkable legend describes God Himself as giving lessons so many hours a day to these prematurely deceased children.[18] Indeed, to the mind of the old Rabbis, the only thing worth living for was the study of the Law. Consequently the child that suffered innocently could not have a better compensation than to learn Torah from the mouth of the Master of masters.

But even when the child was healthy, and food and climate proved congenial to its constitution, there still remained the troubles of its spiritual education. And to be sure it was not an easy matter to bring up a " priest." The first condition for this calling was learning. But learning cannot be acquired without honest and hard industry. It is true that R. Akiba numbers wisdom among the virtues which are hereditary from father to son. Experience, however, has shown that it is seldom the case, and the Rabbis were already troubled with the question how it happens that children so little resemble their fathers in respect of learning.

Certainly Jewish legends can boast of a whole series of prodigies. Thus a certain Rabbi is said to have been so sharp as to have had a clear recollection of the mid-wife who made him a citizen of this world. Ben Sira again, instantly after his birth, entertains his terrified mother with many a wise and foolish saying, refuses the milk she offers him, and asks for solid food. A certain Nachman was born with a prophecy on his lips, predicting the fate of all nations on earth, as well as fixing the date for the advent of the Messiah. The youngest of seven sons of Hannah, who became martyrs under the reign of Antio-

chus Epiphanes, was according to one version aged two
years, six months, six hours, and thirty minutes. But the
way in which he defied the threats of the tyrant was
really worthy of one of seventy. R. Judah de Modena is
said to have read the lesson from the prophets in the
synagogue at the age of two years and a half. A famous
Cabbalist, Nahum, at the age of three, gave a lecture on
the decalogue that lasted for three days. The Chassidim
pretended of one of their Zaddikim that he remembered
all that he had been taught by the angels before his birth,
and thus excused their Zaddik's utter neglect of studying
anything. Perhaps I may mention in this place a sentence from Schudt, which may reconcile one to the harmless exaggerations of the Chassidim. It relates to a case
where a Jewish girl of six was taken away by a Christian
with the intention of baptising her, for he maintained that
this was the wish and pleasure of the child. Probably
the little girl received her instruction from the Christian
servant of the house, as has happened many times.
Schudt proves that this wish ought to be granted in spite
of the minority of the child. He argues: As there is a
maxim, "What is wanting in years may be supplied by
wickedness," why could not also the reverse be true that
"What is wanting in years can be supplied by grace"?
Of a certain R. Meshullam, again, we know that he
preached in the synagogue at Brody, at the age of nine,
and perplexed the chief Rabbi of the place by his deep
Talmudical learning. As the Rabbi had a daughter of
seven, the cleverness exhibited by the boy Rabbi did not
end without very serious consequences for all his life.

Happily all these prodigies or children of grace are
only exceptional. I say happily, for the Rabbis them-

selves disliked such creatures. They were more satisfied
with those signs of intelligence that indicate future greatness. The following story may serve as an instance : —
R. Joshua ben Hananiah once made a journey to Rome.
Here he was told that amongst the captives from Jerusalem there was a child with bright eyes, its hair in
ringlets, and its features strikingly beautiful. The Rabbi
made up his mind to redeem the boy. He went to the
prison and addressed the child with a verse from Isaiah,
" Who gave Jacob for a spoil and Israel to the robbers?"
On this the child answered by continuing the second half
of the same verse, " Did not the Lord, He against whom
we have sinned? For they would not walk in His ways,
neither were they obedient unto His law" (Isaiah xlii.
24). The Rabbi was so delighted with this answer, that
he said : " I am sure he will grow up to be a teacher in
Israel. I take an oath to redeem him, cost what it
may." The child was afterwards known under the name
of R. Ishmael ben Elisha. Such children were ideals
of the Rabbis, but they hated the baby scholar, who
very often grew impertinent and abused his elders. The
Rabbis much preferred the majority of those tiny creatures, who are characterised by the already mentioned
legends on the "Ages of Men" as little animals playing, laughing, crying, dancing, and committing all sorts
of mischief.

But these children must be taught. Now, there is the
well-known advice of Judah ben Tema, who used to say
that the child at five years was to be taught Scripture,
at ten years Mishnah, at thirteen to fulfil the Law, etc.
This saying, incorporated in most editions in the fifth
Chapter of the *Sayings of the Fathers*, is usually con-

sidered as the programme of Jewish education. But, like so many programmes, this tells us rather how things ought to have been than how they were. In the times of the Temple, the participation of the youth in religious actions began at the tenderest age. As soon as they were able to walk a certain distance with the support of their parents, the children had to accompany them on their pilgrimages to Jerusalem. In the Sabbatical year they were brought to the Temple, to be present at the reading of Deuteronomy by the king.[14] The period at which the child's allegiance to the Synagogue began is still more distinctly described. Of the many Talmudical passages relating to this question, I shall select the following quotation from a later Midrash, because it is the most concise. In allusion to Leviticus xix. 23, 24, concerning the prohibition of eating the fruits of a tree in the first three years, this Midrash goes on to say: "And this is also the case with the Jewish child. In the first three years the child is unable to speak, and therefore is exempted from every religious duty, but in the fourth year all its fruits shall be holy to praise the Lord, and the father is obliged to initiate the child in religious works." Accordingly the religious life of the child began as soon as it was able to speak distinctly, or with the fourth year of its. life. As to the character of this initiation we learn from the same Midrash and also from other Talmudical passages, that it consisted in teaching the child the verses, "Hear, O Israel: the Lord our God *is* One" (Deut. vi. 4), and "Moses commanded us a Torah, the inheritance of the congregation of Jacob" (Deut. xxxiii. 4). It was also in this year that the boys began to accompany their parents to the synagogue, car-

rying their prayer-books. At what age the girls first
came out — not for their first party, but with the purpose of going to the synagogue — is difficult to decide
with any degree of certainty. But if we were to trust a
rather doubtful reading in Tractate *Sopherim*,[15] we might
maintain that their first appearance in the synagogue was
also at a very tender age. I hope that they behaved there
more respectfully than their brothers, who played and
cried instead of joining in the responses and singing
with the congregation. In some communities they proved
so great a nuisance that a certain Rabbi declared it would
be better to leave them at home rather than to have the
devotion of the whole congregation disturbed by these
urchins. Another Rabbi recommended the praiseworthy
custom of the Sephardim,[16] who confined all the boys
in the synagogue to one place, and set a special over-
seer by their side, with a whip in his hands, to compel
them to keep quiet and to worship with due devotion.

A strange custom is known among the Arabian and Palestinian Jews under the name of *Chalaka*. It means the
first hair-cutting of the boy after his fourth birthday. As
on this occasion loyalty to the Scripture is shown by not
touching the " corners " (Lev. xix. 17), the whole action is
considered a religious ceremony of great importance. In
Palestine it usually takes place on the second day of the
Feast of the Passover when the counting of the seven
weeks begins. On this day friends and relatives assemble
at the house of the parents. Thither the boy is brought,
dressed in his best garments, and every one of the as-
sembly is entrusted with the duty of cutting a few hairs,
which is considered a great privilege. The ceremony is as
usual followed by a dinner given to the guests. The Jews

in Safed and Tiberias perform the ceremony with great pomp in the courtyard surrounding the (supposed) grave of R. Simeon ben Yochai, in one of the neighbouring villages.

Another custom already mentioned in the Talmud, but which quite disappeared in later times, is that of weighing the child. It would be worth reviving if performed in the way in which the mother of Doeg ben Joseph did it. This tender-hearted mother weighed her only son every day, and distributed among the poor, in gold, the amount of the increased weight of her child.

I pass now to the second great consecration of the boy, — the rites performed on the day when the boy went to school for the first time. This day was celebrated by the Jews, especially in the Middle Ages, in such a way as to justify the high esteem in which they held the school. The school was looked upon as a second Mount Sinai, and the day on which the child entered it as the Feast of Revelation. Of the many different customs, I shall mention here that according to which this day was fixed for the Feast of Weeks. Early in the morning, while it was still dark, the child was washed and dressed carefully. In some places they dressed it in a "gown with fringes." As soon as day dawned the boy was taken to the synagogue, either by his father or by some worthy member of the community. Arrived at their destination, the boy was put on the Almemor, or reading-dais, before the Scroll of the Law, from which the narrative of the Revelation (Exod. xx. 2–26) was read as the portion of the day. From the synagogue the boy was taken to the house of the teacher, who took him into his arms. Thereupon a slate was brought, containing the alphabet in various combinations,

the verse, " Moses has commanded," etc. in Deut. xxxiii. 4,
the first verse of the Book of Leviticus, and the words,
" The Torah will be my calling." The teacher then read
the names of the letters, which the boy repeated. After
the reading, the slate was besmeared with honey, which the
boy licked off. This was done in allusion to Ezekiel iii.
3, where it is said : " And it (the roll) was in my mouth
as honey for sweetness." The boy was also made to eat
a sweet cake, on which were written passages from the
Bible relating to the importance of the study of the Torah.
The ceremony was concluded by invoking the names of
certain angels, asking them to open the heart of the boy,
and to strengthen his memory. By the way, I am very
much afraid that this invocation was answerable for the
abolition of this ceremony. The year in which this ceremony took place is uncertain, probably not before the fifth,
nor later than the seventh, according to the good or bad
health of the child.

The reverence for the child already hinted at was still
further increased when the boy entered the school. " The
children of the house (school) of the master " is a regular
phrase in Jewish literature. It is on their pure breath
that the existence of the world depends, and it is their
merit that justifies us in appealing to the mercy of God.
Words of Scripture, uttered by them quite innocently,
were considered as oracles ; and many a Rabbi gave up
an undertaking on account of a verse pronounced by a
schoolboy, who hardly understood its import. Take only
one instance : R. Johanan was longing to see his friend
Mar Samuel in Babylon. After many disturbances and
delays, he at last undertook the journey. On the way he
passed a school where the boys were reciting the verse

from I Samuel xxviii. 3, "And Samuel died." This was accepted by him as a hint given by Providence that all was over with his friend.

Especially famous for their wisdom and sharpness were the children of Jerusalem. Of the many illustrative stories given in the Midrash to Lamentations, let the following suffice: R. Joshua was one day riding on his donkey along the high road. As he passed a well, he saw a little girl there, and asked her to give him some water. She accordingly gave water to him and to his animal. The Rabbi thanked her with the words: "My daughter, you acted like Rebecca." "To be sure," she answered, "I acted like Rebecca; but you did not behave like Eleazar." I must add that there are passages in Jewish literature from which, with a little ingenuity, it might be deduced that Jewish babies are the most beautiful of their kind. The assertion made by a monk that Jewish children are inferior to Christian children is a dreadful libel. The author of the *Old Victory*,[17] in whose presence this assertion was made, was probably childless, or he would have simply scratched out the eyes of this malicious monk, instead of giving a mystical reason for the superior beauty of any other children than his own.

Another point to be emphasised is that the boys were not confined all day long to the close air of the schoolroom. They had also their hours of recreation. This recreation consisted chiefly, as one can imagine, in playing. Their favourite game was the ball, boys as well as girls being fond of this form of amusement. They did not deny themselves this pleasure even on festivals. They were also fond of the kite and games with nuts, in which their mothers also took part. Letter-games and riddles also occupied their minds in the recreation hours. The angel Sandalphon,[18] who also bears in the Cabbalah the name of "Boy," was considered by the children as their special patron, and they invoked him in their plays, addressing to him the words: "Sandalphon, Lord of the forest, protect us from pain." Speaking generally, there are very few distinctively Jewish games. From the researches of Zunz, Güdemann, and Löw on this subject, it is clear that the Jews always adopted the pastimes of the peoples among whom they dwelt.

But it must not be thought that there was too much playing. Altogether, Jewish education was far from spoiling the children. And though it was recommended — if such recommendation were necessary — to love children more than one's own soul, the Rabbis strongly condemned that blind partiality towards our own offspring, which ends in burdening our world with so many good-for-nothings. The sad experience of certain biblical personages served as a warning for posterity. Even from the quite natural behaviour of Jacob towards his son Joseph, which had the best possible results in the end, they drew the lesson that a man must never show to one of his children marks of greater favour than to the others. In later times they have been even anxious to conceal this love altogether, and some Rabbis went so far as to refrain from kissing their children. The severity of Akabya ben Mahalaleel is worth mentioning, if not imitating. When this Rabbi, only a few minutes before his death, was asked by his son to recommend him to his friends and colleagues, the answer the poor boy received was: "Thy conduct will recommend thee to my friends, or will estrange thee from them." Another Rabbi declared (with reference to Prov.

x

xxviii. 27) that it is life-giving to a youth to teach him temperance in his diet, and not to accustom him to meat and wine. R. Judah, the Pious, in the Middle Ages, gives the advice to rich parents to withdraw their resources from their sons if they lead a disorderly life. The struggle for their existence, and the hardship of life, would bring them back to God. When the old Rabbi said that poverty is a most becoming ornament for Israel, his remark was probably suggested by a similar thought. And many a passage in the Rabbinic literature gives expression to the same idea as that in Goethe's divine lines: —

> Wer nie sein Brot mit Thränen ass,
> Wer nie die kummervollen Nächte
> Auf seinem Bette weinend sass,
> Der kennt Euch nicht, Ihr himmlischen Mächte.

I have spoken of a kingdom of priests, but there is one great disadvantage of such a polity. One or two priests in a community may be sustained by the liberality of the congregation. But if a community consisted of only priests, how could it then be maintained? Besides, the old Jewish ideal expected the teacher to be possessed of a divine goodness, imparting his benefits only as an act of grace. Salaries, therefore, either for teaching or preaching, or for giving ritual decisions, were strongly forbidden. The solution of the question put by the Bible, "And if ye shall say, What shall we eat?" is to be found in the law that every father was obliged to teach his son a handicraft, enabling him to obtain a living.

I have now to speak of the time when childhood is brought to a conclusion. It is, as I stated above, in the case of a girl at the beginning of the thirteenth year, and in that of a boy at the beginning of the fourteenth year. As a reason for this priority I will reproduce the words of R. Chisda, who said that God has endowed woman with a greater portion of intelligence than man, and therefore she obtains her maturity at an earlier period than man does. A very nice compliment, indeed; but like all compliments it is of no practical consequence whatever. It is not always the wiser who get the best of it in life. Whilst the day on which the girl obtained her majority passed unnoticed either by her or by her family, it was marked in the case of the boy as the day on which he become a Son of the Law,[19] and was signalised by various rites and ceremonies, and by the bestowing on him of beautiful presents. I miss only the wig, which used to form the chief ornament of the boy on this happy day.

Less known, however, is the origin of this ceremony, and the reason for fixing its date. It cannot claim a very high antiquity. I may remark that in many cases centuries elapse before an idea or a notion takes practical shape and is crystallised into a custom or usage, and still longer before this custom is fossilised into a law or fixed institution. As far as the Bible goes, there is not the slightest indication of the existence of such a ceremony. From Lev. xxvii. 5, and Num. xiv. 29, it would rather seem that it was not before the twentieth year that the man was considered to have obtained his majority, and to be responsible for his actions. It was only in the times of the Rabbis, when Roman influence became prevalent in juristic matters at least, that the date of thirteen, or rather the *pubertas*, was fixed as giving the boy his majority. But it would be a mistake to think that before having obtained this majority the boy was considered as under age in every respect. Certainly the law made every possible effort to connect him with the synagogue, and to initiate him in his religious duties long before the age of thirteen.

We have seen that the boy's first appearance in the synagogue was at the beginning of the fourth year. We have noticed the complaints about his troublesome behaviour. But how could we expect the poor child to be attentive to things which quite surpassed the intellectual powers of his tender age? There was no better reason for this attendance either in the Temple or in the synagogue than that the parents might be rewarded by God for the trouble of taking their children there. These cares, by the way, fell most heavily upon the women. The mother of R. Joshua enjoyed this burden so much that she carried her boy, when still in the cradle, to the "House of Study of the Law," in order that his ears might be accustomed to the sound of the Torah. In later times there was another excuse for taking the little children to the synagogue. They were there allowed to sip the wine of the Sanctification Cup,[20] which was the exclusive privilege of the children; an easy way of worshipping, but, as you can observe, it is a method that they enjoy and understand most excellently. They did not less enjoy and understand the service with which they were charged on the day of "The Rejoicing of the Law."[21] On this feast they were provided with flags, which they carried before the bearers of the Torah, who feasted them after the service with sweets. Another treat was that of being called up on this day to the Torah, a custom that is still extant. In the Middle Ages they went in some countries so far as to allow these little fellows who did not wear caps "to be called up" to say the blessings over the Law bare-headed. A beautiful custom was that every Sabbath, after finishing the weekly lesson and dressing the Scroll of the Law, the children used to come up to the Almemor and kiss the Torah. Leaving the synagogue they kissed the hands of the scholars. At home the initiation began with the blessing the child received on every eve of the Sabbath, and with its instruction in " Hear O Israel" and other verses as already mentioned. Short prayers, consisting of a single sentence, were also chosen for children of this age. The function of the child on the eve of the first day of Passover is well known. Besides the putting of the four questions for the meaning of the strange ceremony (Exod. xiii. 14), the boy had also to recite, or rather to sing, the " Praise." [22] But I am afraid that they enjoyed better the song of " One Kid," which was composed or rather adapted for their special entertainment from an old German poem.

Within three or four years after entering the synagogue, and with the growth of intellect and strength, the religious duties of the boy increased, and became of a more serious character. He had not only to attend the school, which was troublesome enough, but he was also expected to attend the services more regularly, and to gain something by it. Yet the Rabbis were not so tyrannical as to put unjust demands on the patience of the child. The voice of God on Mount Sinai, the Rabbis said, was adapted to the intellect and powers of all who witnessed the Revelation — adapted, as the Midrash says, to the powers of old and young, children and women. It was in accordance with tnis sentiment that the Rabbis suited their language to the needs of the less educated classes. Thus we read in the Tractate *Sopherim* that according to the law the portion of the week, after hav-

ing been recited in Hebrew, must be translated into
the language of the vernacular for the benefit of the unlearned people, the women, and the children. Another
consideration children experienced from the Rabbis was
that at the age of nine or ten the boy was initiated into
the observance of the Day of Atonement by fasting a
few hours. Lest, however, this good work might be over-
done, and thus endanger the child's health, the sage R.
Acha used to tell his congregation after the Addition-
Prayer " My brethren, let every one of you who has a
child go home and make it eat." In later centuries,
when the disease of small-pox became so fatal, some
Rabbis declared it to be the duty of every father to
leave the town with his children as soon as the plague
showed itself. The joy with which the Rabbis hailed
Dr. Jenner's discovery deserves our recognition. None
of them perceived in vaccination a defiance of Providence. R. Abraham Nansich, from London, wrote a
pamphlet to prove its lawfulness. The Cabbalist Buzagli
disputed Dr. Jenner's priority, but nevertheless approved
of vaccination. R. Israel Lipschütz declared that the
Doctor acquired salvation by his new remedy.

With his advancing age, not only the boy's duties but
also his rights were increased. An enumeration of all
these rights would lead me too far, but I shall mention
the custom which allowed the boy the recital of " Magnified "[25] and " Bless ye "[24] in the synagogue. Now this
privilege is restricted to the orphan boy. It is interesting to hear that girls were also admitted to recite the
Magnified in the synagogue, in cases where their parents
left no male issue. I have myself witnessed such a case.
In some countries the boy had the exclusive privilege of

reading the prayers on the evenings of the festivals and Sabbaths. R. Samson ben Eleazar, in the fifteenth century, received his family name Baruch Sheamar[25] from the skill with which he recited this prayer when a boy. He chanted it so well that he was called by the members of the community Master Baruch Sheamar. As to the question whether the boy, while under age, might lawfully be considered as one of the Ten when such a quorum was required, or one of the three in the case of grace after meals, I can only say that the authorities never agreed in this respect. Whilst the one insisted upon his having obtained his majority, the other was satisfied with his showing such signs of intelligence as would enable him to participate in the ceremony in question. Here is an instance of such a sign. Abaye and Raba, the two celebrated heroes of the Babylonian Talmud, were sitting at the table of Rabbah. Before saying grace he asked them, " Do you know to whom these prayers are addressed?" Thereupon one boy pointed to the roof, whilst the other boy went out and pointed to the sky. The examiner was satisfied with their answer.

The privilege of putting on the phylacteries forms now in most countries the chief distinction of "The Son of the Law"; in olden times, however, every boy had claim to it as soon as he showed himself capable of behaving respectfully when wearing the holy symbol. It even happened that certain honours of the synagogue were bestowed on boys, though under age. We possess a copy of a Jewish epitaph dating from about the third century, which was written in Rome for a boy of eight years, who is there designated as archon. The fact is the more curious, as on the other hand the Palestinian R. Abuha, who lived in the same century, maintained that no man must be elected as Warden before he has achieved his fiftieth year. That boys were admitted to preach in the synagogue I have already mentioned.[26]

From all these remarks it will easily be seen that in olden times the boy enjoyed almost all the rights of majority long before the day of his being "The Son of the Law." The condition of the novice is hardly distinguishable from that of the initiated priest. The Talmud, the Gaonim, and even R. Isaac Alfasi and Maimonides knew neither the term "The Son of the Law" (in our sense of the word) nor any ceremony connected with it. There is only one slight reference to such an institution, recorded in the Tractate *Sopherim*, with the quotation of which I shall conclude this paper. We read there: "In Jerusalem there was the godly custom to initiate the children at the *beginning* of the thirteenth year by fasting the whole Day of Atonement. During this year they took the boy to the priests and learned men that they might bless him, and pray for him that God might think him worthy of a life devoted to the study of the Torah and pious works." For, this author says, "they were beautiful, and their lives harmonious and their hearts directed to God."

XIII

WOMAN IN TEMPLE AND SYNAGOGUE

THE learned Woman has always been a favourite subject with Jewish students; and her intellectual capabilities have been fully vindicated in many an essay and even fair-sized book. Less attention, however, has been paid to woman's claims as a devotional being whom the Temple, and afterwards the Synagogue, more or less recognised. At least it is not known to me that any attempt has been made to give, even in outline, the history of woman's relation to public worship. It is needless to say that the present sketch, which is meant to supply this want in some measure, lays no claim to completeness; but I venture to hope that it will help to direct the attention of the friends of research to the matter, and that it may induce others to deal more fully with the subject and do it the justice it deserves.

The earliest allusion to women's participation in *public* worship, is that in Exodus xxxviii. 8, to the women who assembled to minister at the door of the "tent of meeting," of whose mirrors the lavers of brass were made (cf. I Sam. ii. 22). Philo, who is not exactly enamoured of the emancipation of women, and seeks to confine them to the "small state," is here full of their praise. "For," he says, "though no one enjoined them to do so, they of

313

their own spontaneous zeal and earnestness contributed the mirrors with which they had been accustomed to deck and set off their beauty, as the most becoming first-fruits of their modesty, and of the purity of their married life, and, as one may say, of the beauty of their souls." In another passage Philo describes the Jewish women as "competing with the men themselves in piety, having determined to enter upon a glorious contest, and to the utmost extent of their power to exert themselves so as not to fall short of their holiness."

It is, however, very difficult to ascertain in what this ministry of women consisted. The Hebrew term "Zo-beoth"[1] would suggest the thought of a species of religious Amazons, who formed a guard of honour round the Sanctuary. Some commentators think that the ministry consisted in performing religious dances accompanied by various instruments. The Septuagint again speaks "of the women who fasted by the doors of the Tabernacle." But most of the old Jewish expositors, as well as Onkelos, conceive that the women went to the tent of meeting to pray. Ibn Ezra offers the interesting remark, "And behold, there were women in Israel serving the Lord, who left the vanities of this world, and not being desirous of beautifying themselves any longer, made of their mirrors a free offering, and came to the tabernacle every day to pray and to listen there to the words of the commandments." When we find that in 1 Sam. i. 12, "Hannah continued to pray before the Lord," she was only doing there what many of her sisters did before and after her. We may also judge that it was from the number of these noble women, who made religion the aim of their lives, that the "twenty-two" heroines and prophetesses sprang who form part of the glory of Jewish history. Sometimes it even happened that their husbands derived their religious inspiration from them. Thus the husband of the prophetess Deborah is said to have been an unlettered man. But his wife made him carry to the Sanctuary the candles which she herself had prepared, this being the way in which she encouraged him to seek communion with the righteous.

The language in which the husband of the "Great Woman" of Shunem addresses his wife: "Wherefore wilt thou go to him" (the prophet)? "it is neither New Moon nor Sabbath" (2 Kings iv. 23), proves that on Festivals and Sabbaths the women used to attend some kind of worship, performed by the prophet, though we cannot say in what this worship consisted. The New Moon was especially a woman's holiday, and was so observed even in the Middle Ages, for the women refrained from doing work on that day. The explanation given by the Rabbis is that when the men broke off their golden earrings to supply material for the golden calf, the women refused to contribute their trinkets, for which good behaviour a special day of repose was granted to them. Some Cabbalists even maintain that the original worshippers of the golden calf continue to exist on earth, their souls having successively migrated into various bodies, while their punishment consists in this, that they are ruled over by their wives. Rather interesting as well as complimentary to women is the remark which the Rabbis made with regard to the "Great Woman." As will be remembered, it is *she* who says, "I perceive that this (Elisha) is a holy man of God" (2 Kings iv. 19). In allusion to this verse the Talmud says: "From this fact we may infer that woman is quicker in recognising the worth of a stranger than man."

The great woman, or women, continued to pray and to join in the public worship also after the destruction of the first Temple. Thus Esther is reported by tradition to have addressed God in a long extempore prayer before she presented herself before the throne of Ahasuerus to plead her people's cause; and women were always enjoined to attend the reading of the Book of Esther. When Ezra read the Law for the first time, he did so in the presence of the men and the women (Neh. viii. 3). In the Book of the Maccabees we read of "The women girt with sackcloth . . . and the maidens that ran to the gates . . . And all holding their hands towards heaven made supplication." In the Judith legend, mention is also made of "Every man and woman . . . who fell before the Temple, and spread out their sackcloth before the face of the Lord . . . and cried before the God of Israel." In the second Temple, the women, as is well known, possessed a court reserved for their exclusive use. There the great illuminations and rejoicings on the evening of the Feast of Tabernacles used to be held. On this occasion, however, the women were confined to galleries specially erected for them. It was also in this Women's Hall that the great public reading of certain portions of the Law by the king, once in seven years, used to take place, and women had also to attend at the function. On the other hand, it is hardly necessary to say that women were excluded from performing any important service in the Temple. If we were to trust a certain passage in the "Chapters of R. Eliezer," we might perhaps conclude that during the first Temple, the wives of the Levites formed a part of the choir, but the meaning of the passage is too obscure and doubtful for us to be justified in basing on it so important an inference. Nor can the three hundred maidens who were employed for the weaving of the curtains in the Temple, be looked upon as having stood in closer connection with the Temple, or as having formed an order of women-priests or girl-devotees (as one might wrongly be induced to think by certain passages in Apocryphal writings of the New Testament). But on the other hand, it is not improbable that their frequent contact with the Sanctuary of the nation produced in them that religious enthusiasm and zeal which may account for the heroic death which — according to the legend — they sought and found after the destruction of the Temple. It is to be remarked that, according to the law, women were even exempted from putting their hands on the head of the victim, which formed an important item in the sacrificial worship. It is, however, stated by an eye-witness, that the authorities permitted them to pèrform this ceremony if they desired to do so, and that their reason for this concession was " to give calmness of the spirit, or satisfaction, to women."

Still greater, perhaps, was " the calmness of spirit " given to women in the synagogue. We find in ancient epitaphs that such titles of honour were conferred upon them as " Mistress of the Synagogue," and " Mother of the Synagogue," and, though they held no actual office in the Synagogue, it is not improbable that they acquired these titles by meritorious work connected with a religious institution, viz. : Charity. There was, indeed, a tendency to exclude women from the synagogue at certain seasons, but almost all the authorities protest against it, many of them declaring such a notion to be quite un-Jewish. Some

Jewish scholars even think that the ancient synagogues knew of no partition for women. I am rather inclined to think that the synagogue took for its model the arrangements in the Temple, and thus confined women to a place of their own. But, whether they sat side by side with the men or occupied a special portion of the edifice, there can be no doubt that the Jewish women were great synagogue-goers. To give only one instance. One Rabbi asks another: Given the case that the members of the synagogue are all descendants of Aaron, to whom then would they impart their blessing? The answer is, to the women who are there.

Of the sermon they were even more fond than their husbands. Thus one woman was so much interested in the lectures of R. Meir, which he was in the habit of giving every Friday evening, that she used to remain there so long that the candles in her house burnt themselves out. Her lazy husband, who stopped at home, so strongly resented having to wait in the dark, that he would not permit her to cross the threshold until she gave some offence to the preacher, which would make him sure that she would not venture to attend his sermons again.

The prayers they said were the Eighteen Benedictions which were prescribed by the Law. But it would seem that occasionally they offered short prayers composed by themselves as suggested by their personal feelings and needs. Thus, to give one instance, R. Johanan relates that one day he observed a young girl fall on her face and pray: "Lord of the world, Thou hast created Paradise, Thou hast created hell, Thou hast created the wicked, Thou hast created the righteous; may it be Thy will that I may not serve as a stumbling-block to them."

The fine Hebrew in which the prayer is expressed, and the notion of the responsibility of Providence for our actions, manifest a high degree of intelligence and reflection. It would also seem that some women went so far in their religious sensibility as to lead a regular ascetic life, and, according to the suggestion of some scholars, even took the vow of celibacy. Of these the Rabbis did not approve, and stigmatised them as the "destroyers of the world." Perhaps it was just at this period that Judaism could not afford to give free play to those morbid feelings, degenerating into religious hysterics, which led some to join rival sects, and others to abandon themselves to the gross immorality we read of in the history of the Gnostics.

The same circumstances may have been the cause of public opinion being led to accept the view of R. Eliezer, who thought it inadvisable — it would seem on moral grounds — to permit woman to study the Law. This opinion was opposed to that of Ben Azzai, who considered it incumbent upon every father to teach his daughter Torah. But justified as the advice of R. Eliezer may have been in his own time, it was rather unfortunate that later generations continued to take it as the guiding principle for the education of their children. Many great women in the course of history indeed became law-breakers and studied Torah; but the majority were entirely dependent on men, and became in religious matters a sort of appendix to their husbands, who by their good actions insured salvation also for them, and sometimes the reverse. Thus there is a story about a woman which, put into modern language, would be to the effect that she married a minister and copied his sermons for him; he died, and she then married a cruel usurer, and kept his accounts for him.

The fact that women were exempted from certain affirmative laws, which become operative only at special seasons — *e.g.*, the taking of the palm branch on the Feast of Tabernacles — must also have contributed to weaken their position as a religious factor in Judaism. The idea that women should vie with men in the fulfilment of every law, became even for the Rabbis a notion connected only with the remotest past. This is the impression one gains when reading the legend about Michal, the daughter of Saul, putting on phylacteries, or the wife of the prophet Jonah making a pilgrimage to Jerusalem at the three Festivals. It would indeed seem as if women were led to strive for the satisfaction of their religious wants in another direction. Yet it was said of Jewish women, " The daughters of Israel were stringent and laid certain restrictions on themselves." They were also allowed to form a quorum by themselves for the purpose of saying the Grace, but they could not be counted along with males for this end. It was also against the early notion of the dignity of the congregation that women should perform any public service for men.

One privilege was left to women — that of weeping. In Judges xi. 40, we read of the daughters of Israel that went yearly to lament the daughter of Jephthah; while in 2 Chronicles xxxv. 25, we are told how "all the singing men and the singing women spake of Josiah in their lamentations." Of this privilege they were not deprived, and if they were not allowed to sing any longer, they at least retained the right to weep as much as they pleased. Even in later times they held a public office as mourning

women at funerals. In the Talmud fragments of compositions by women for such occasions are to be found. Indeed, woman became in these times the type of grief and
sorrow. She cannot reason, but she feels much more
deeply than man. Here is one instance from an old
legend: Jeremiah said, " When I went up to Jerusalem
(after the destruction of the Temple) I lifted my eyes and
saw there a lonely woman sitting on the top of the mountain, her dress black, her hair dishevelled, crying, ' Who
will comfort me?' I approached her and spake to her,
' If thou art a woman, speak to me. If thou art a ghost,
begone.' She answered, ' Dost thou not know me? . . .
I am the Mother, Zion.'"

In general, however, the principle applied to women
was: The king's daughter *within the palace* is all glorious
(Psalm xlv. 14), but *not* outside of it. In the face of the
" Femina in ecclesia taceat," which was the ruling maxim
with other religions, Jewish women could only feel flat-
tered by this polite treatment by the Rabbis, though it
meant the same thing. We must not think, however,
that this prevented them from attending the service of the
synagogue. According to the Tractate *Sopherim*, even
" the little daughters of Israel were accustomed to go to
the synagogue." In the same tractate we find it laid
down as " a duty to translate for them the portion (of the
Law) of the week, and the lesson from the prophets " into
the language they understand. The " King's daughter "
occasionally asserted her rights without undue reliance on
the opinion of the authorities. And thus being ignorant
of the Hebrew language women prayed in the vernacular,
though this was at least against the letter of the law.
And many famous Rabbis of the twelfth and thirteenth

Y

centuries express their wonder that the "custom of women praying in other (non-Hebrew) languages extended over the whole world." It is noteworthy that they did not suppress the practice, but on the contrary, they endeavoured to give to the Law such an interpretation as would bring it into accord with the general custom. Some even recommended it, as, for example, the author of *The Book of the Pious*, who gives advice to women to learn the prayers in the language familiar to them.

At about the same period a lengthy controversy was being waged by the commentators of the Talmud and the codifiers, about woman's partaking in the fulfilment of the laws for special seasons, from which, as already remarked, they were exempted. To the action itself there could not be much objection, but the difficulty arose when women also insisted on uttering the blessing. Now the point at issue was whether they could be permitted to say, for instance, " Blessed art Thou, O Lord our God, etc., who hast sanctified us by Thy Commandments, and *hast commanded us*, concerning the taking of the Palm branch," since in reality the women had *not* been commanded to do it. To such logical and systematic minds as Maimonides and R. Joseph Caro, the difficulty was insurmountable, and they forbade women to use the formula; but with the less consistent majority women carried their point. Rather interesting is the answer received by R. Jacob, of Corbeil, with regard to this question. This Rabbi is said to have enjoyed the mysterious power which enabled him to appeal in cases of doubt to the celestial authorities. Before them he put also this women's case for decision. Judgment was communicated to him in the verse from the Scriptures, " In all that Sarah saith unto Thee, hearken

unto her voice" (Gen. xxi. 12). Nor was it unknown for
a pious Jew to compose a special hymn for his wife's use
in honour of the Sabbath.

How long this custom of women praying in the vernacular lasted, we have no means of ascertaining. Probably
was already extinct about the end of the fifteenth century.
For R. Solomon Portaleone, who lived in the sixteenth
century, already regrets the abolition of "this beautiful
and worthy custom." "When they prayed in the vernacular," he says, "they understood what they were saying, whilst now they only gabble off their prayers." As
a sort of compromise we may regard the various "Sup-
plications";[2] they form a kind of additional prayers supplementary to the ordinary liturgy, and are written in
German. Chiefly composed by women, they specially answer the needs of the sex on various occasions. These
prayers deserve a full description by themselves, into
which I cannot enter here; I should like only to mention
that in one of these collections in the British Museum, a
special supplication is added for servant-maids, and if I
am not quite mistaken, also one for their mistresses.

It is also worth noticing that the manuals on the
"Three Women's Commandments" (mostly composed in
German, sometimes also in rhymes), contained much more
than their titles would suggest. They rather served as
headings to groups of laws, arranged under each commandment. Thus the first (about certain laws in Lev. xii.
and xv.) becomes the motto for purity in body and soul;
the second (the consecration of the first cake of the
dough) includes all matters relating to charity, in which
women were even reminded to encourage their newly
married husbands not to withhold from the poor the

tithes of the bridal dowry, as well as of their future yearly income ; whilst the third (the lighting of the Sabbath lamp) becomes the symbol for spiritual light and sweetness in every relation of human life.

As another compromise may also be considered the institution of "Vorsugern" (woman-reader) or the "Woilkennivdicke" (the well-knowing one) who reads the prayers and translates them into the vernacular for the benefit of her less learned sisters. In Poland and in Russia, even at the present time, such a woman-reader is to be found in every synagogue, and from what I have heard the institution is by no means unknown in London. The various prayer-books containing the Hebrew text as well as the Jewish-German translation, which appear in such frequent editions in Russia, are mostly intended for the use of these praying women. Not uninteresting is the title-page of R. Aaron Ben Samuel's Jewish-German translations and collections of prayers which appeared in the beginning of the eighteenth century. He addressed the Jewish public in the following terms : " My dear brethren, buy this lovely prayer-book or wholesome tonic for body and soul, which has never appeared in such German print since the world began ; and make your wives and children read it often, thus they will refresh their bodies and souls, for this light will shine forth into your very hearts. As soon as the children read it they will understand their prayers, by which they will enjoy both this world and the world to come."

An earlier translator of the prayer-book addresses himself directly to the " pious women " whom he invites to buy his book, " in which they will see very beautiful things." Recent centuries seem, on the whole, to have been dis-

tinguished for the number of praying-women they produced.   The virtues which constituted the claim of women
to religious distinction were modesty, charity, and daily attendance at the synagogue morning and evening.   In the
memorial books of the time hundreds of such women are
noticed.   Some used also to spin the " Fringes," which
they presented to their friends; others fasted frequently,
whilst " Old Mrs. Hechele " not only attended the synagogue every day, and did charity to poor and rich, but also
understood the art of midwifery, which she practised in the
community without accepting payment for her services.
According to R. Ch. J. Bachrach women used also to say
the " Magnified " prayer in the synagogue when their
parents left no male posterity.

In bringing to a close this very incomplete sketch, perhaps I ought to notice the confirmation of girls introduced
during this century in some communities in Germany,
which the " Reformed " Rabbis recommended, but of which
the " Orthodox " Rabbis disapproved.   It would be well if
in the heat of such controversies both sides would remember the words of R. Zedekiah b. Abraham, of Rome, who
with regard to a certain difference of opinion on some
ritual question, says : " Every man receives reward from
God for what he is convinced is the right thing, if this
conviction has no other motive but the love of God."

XIV

THE EARLIEST JEWISH COMMUNITY
IN EUROPE

ROMAN Judaism has disappeared from our guide-books.
Civilisation has levelled down the walls of the Ghetto, and
its former inhabitants are not any longer "a people that
dwell alone." But with this well-deserved destruction
a good deal of the interest was also destroyed which the
traveller used to attach to "the peculiar people" enclosed
in that terrible slum of Rome.

Still, if there is anything eternal in the "eternal city,"
which was neither reconstructed by the Cæsars, nor im-
proved upon by the Popes, it is the little Jewish community at Rome. It has survived the former; it has suffered
for many centuries under the latter, and, partaking in the
general revival which has come upon the Italian nation,
it may still be destined for a great future. Indeed, the
history of the relation of Israel to Rome is so old that it is
not lacking even in legendary elements. On the day on
which King Solomon married the daughter of Pharaoh,
the Rabbis narrate, there came down the angel Gabriel.
He put a reed into the sea, which, by means of the slime
that adhered to it, formed itself, in the course of time,
into a large island, on which the city of Rome was built—
an event with which the troubles of Israel began. These

were the evil consequences of the first *mésalliance*. Even
more unfortunate for Israel (and it is not impossible that
this is the meaning of the legend) were the results of that
spiritual mixed marriage between Judaism and paganism
which took place at a much later period, whereat a blunt
soldier, who sympathised with neither, and "who dealt in
salvation as he dealt in provinces," acted as best man.
As a fact, the parties concerned never understood each
other properly. The declaration of love, and the final
proposal, were made in an Alexandrine jargon, strange to
both, the obscurities of which only grew with the commentaries each successive generation added to them.
Under such circumstances, a happy union was not to be
expected, and the family quarrel which fills the annals of
civilised Europe soon broke out. Judaism, more particularly Roman Judaism, witnessed this struggle from the
beginning, and its fortunes were greatly dependent on
the chance which of these two elements, the Jewish or the
pagan, won the ascendency.

However, I am theologising too much, whilst I am
deviating from the subject of these lines. Nor could I
think of giving here, even in outline, the history of the
oldest Jewish community in Europe. This has been
already admirably done by Dr. A. Berliner, who has made
the history of the Jews of Rome the subject of his studies
for nearly a quarter of a century. I intend only to reproduce here, in a stray fashion, some of those impressions
and reflections which, I am certain, must occur to every
Jewish traveller in Italy.

Now I do not think for a moment that we Jews should
have a point of view of our own for looking at things and
men in this paradise of Europe. It would be as silly to

have a Jewish Baedeker as to think of orthodox mathematics or an ecclesiastical logic or a racial morality —
though unfortunately there exist such things.   But on the
other hand, if we have not, like the fox in the fable, left
our heart at home, let us not do violence to our feelings by
passing over everything Jewish, over sights which might
remind us of our history, with a certain indifference which
would be affected on our part.   We are not all little
Goethes, nor even little Ruskins, and our artistic enjoyment is hardly so intense as to shut our hearts against
impressions which force themselves upon us either by
the way of remembrance of the past, or even as a living
contrast in the present.

It so happened that my first visit to the Vatican was
on a Friday.   After doing my work in the Vatican
Library, which is open till noon, I went into the adjoining
Church of St. Peter.

One should be, like the angel of death in the legend,
full of eyes, properly to see all the wonders of art and
marvels of architecture at which human genius and piety
laboured busily through centuries, in adorning the grand-
est of sacred buildings in the world.   But there is Baedeker or Murray serving at least as a pair of good specta-
cles to the layman, and it was by their aid that I made my
round in St. Peter.   But lo, whilst you are observing the
celebrated Pietà by Michael Angelo, and, according to
the instruction of your guides, admiring both the grief
of the Mother and the death of the Son, you notice in its
vicinity a little column, surrounded by rails to which the
pilgrims approach with a certain awe ; for "Tradition
affirms it to have been brought from Jerusalem."   Naturally, one is instantly reminded of the report, given by the

famous traveller of Tudela, of the curiosities of Rome,
which among other things records, "That there are also
to be seen in St. Giovanni in Porta Latina (probably
meant for Lateran) the two brazen pillars, constructed
by King Solomon of blessed memory, whose name,
Solomon, the son of David, is engraved upon each; of
which he was also told that every year about the 9th
of Ab (the anniversary of the destruction of Jerusalem),
these pillars sweat so much that water runs down from
them." So far Benjamin of Tudela in the twelfth century. In our days pillars weep no longer, and even of
men it is considered a special sign of good breeding to
behave pillar-like; but a sigh is still permissible at the
sight of this temple-column, which in its captivity sym-
bolises, not less than the Pietà, the grief of a whole
people. Of course, not possessing on the spot either
the *Itinerary* or even Urlick, one is unable to establish
the connection between these two traditions and their
claim to authenticity. Perhaps one may even comfort
oneself on the same ground on which the famous curé
tried to appease his flock who were sobbing bitterly at
his telling them the Passion story. He exclaimed: "My
children, do not weep so much; it happened long ago,
and even perhaps is not quite true."

However, the Vatican is the last place in the world to
exercise your critical faculties; you are so deeply absorbed
in seeing, that you have no time to think. So on I went,
from aisle to aisle, from niche to niche, from chapel to
chapel, looking, staring, and admiring, till of a sudden my
eyes were struck by a large statue, on which the words,
"Thou shalt have no other God before me," are engraved.
There I stood before a question of exegesis, where one is

permitted to use his right senses without any regard to the æsthetic side. Yet not all the manifold expositions of the Decalogue, nor all the talk about the subjective-objective, the absolute and the real, with which metaphysicians have tried to confuse the notion of the Unity of God, will reconcile one to the meaning which Mediæval Art has impressed upon the Ten Commandments. The truth has to be sought elsewhere, and thus my thoughts were turned to the synagogue, and thither I went.

The day was already drawing to its close, and, by a marvellous coincidence, I arrived at the synagogue just as the congregation was intoning the words: " The Lord is one, and His name is one to His renown and glory." Here was sound, simple exegesis, though sadly lacking in the illustrative matter in which the Vatican is so rich. But what need was there of any real or artificial "aid to the believer," in the presence of such a living faith, as enabled this little community to maintain its protesting position in the teeth of the mistress of the world! And this even at a time, when it only required a hint from the successors of the old Roman Emperors to make the whole world renounce its right of thinking and judging, and, were we to believe Herr Janssen, even to feel perfectly happy in this torpor.

But, by the way, are our own times much better? As I write these lines (October 1893) I hear that a Bill has been brought into the German Diet, asking that the Talmud should be submitted to a Commission (which *en pas-sant*, has been sitting in unbroken session in that country since the days of Pfefferkorn in the fifteenth century) with the purpose of examining its contents, while in the Vatican the very pupils of Loyola are offering every convenience and comfort to the student who should care to devote his time to Rabbinic literature. Does not the work of a great number of our poets, historians, theologians, and so-called seers in this blessed century of ours, in many respects prove but a strained effort to destroy the few humanitarian principles which were established a few generations ago, as well as to deify every brutal warrior who was successful in his day? Again, is the national idea so much sublimer, so much grander, than that of a universal religion, that we would willingly permit the former to employ the means which have been denied to the latter as inhuman and barbarous? Every age has its own idolatry, and the eternal wandering Jew will always be the chosen victim of the Moloch in fashion.

Let us, however, return to the synagogue, which withstood many a cruelty, both ancient and modern. The place where the synagogue stands is near the Ghetto, now called Piazza di Scuola. It is, besides a few other communal houses, the only building left there, — all those narrow, dirty, and typhoid-breeding streets which formed the old Ghetto having been demolished by a sage and humane government, which by this action wiped out the last stain from its history. There, on this vast blank is the synagogue, a comparatively small, insignificant building, laden with heavy age and looking down on her children whom she has been nursing, consoling, and protecting for centuries, but who, now grown old, have forsaken her and scattered to all the ends of the city. Of all her former acquaintances there appears to be left only father Tiber, who would seem to be murmuring to her many an old tale of the times before she was called into existence. And if he listened to the special prayers recited within her walls by the deputies of the Jewish communities, when preparing themselves to go to the court of the Pope, the Tiber heard many a sigh and cry, wrung out from the heart of a Jewish captive who, preferring death to slavery even under the masters of the world, found his last repose in its waters. But insignificant as this synagogue appears, she proved the spiritual bulwark against all the attacks of the time, and you admire her brave resistance all the more when you look at that multitude of churches and cloisters in the closest vicinity of the Ghetto, impressing you as so many intrenchments, all directing their missiles and weapons against this humble, defenceless building, threatening it with death and destruction. One of these churches, probably founded by some Jewish convert, who gained in it both salvation and a good living, bears on its gates in Hebrew letters the inscription : " I have spread out my hands all the day unto a rebellious people, which walketh in the way that was not good, after their own thoughts. A people that provoketh me to anger continually to my face " (Isaiah lxv. 2, 3). Menace is followed by persuasion, the cited verses being accompanied by the Latin words : " Indulgentia plenaria quotodiana perpetua pro vivis et defunctis." Theologians who like to quarrel most about things they can know least, have for ages discussed the question, whether prayers for the dead are of any use; here the matter is decided by a simple advertisement. It is not to be denied that one would enjoy the fortunes accumulated by one's late sinner of an uncle all the better for being sure that a few pennyworths of prayer enable the legatee to make one's benefactor in Hades comfortable and happy.

The thought is very consoling indeed, and it is not to be wondered at that the Roman synagogue could not entirely withstand its temptations, and introduced into the offering-blessing after one is called up to the Torah, the words: "To the advancing of the soul of the departed." Of course much of this tendency may be attributed to the Ford Jabbok,[1] which was and is still very popular in that country; but the fact that the author of this Jewish "Book of the Dead" was an Italian (from Modena), shows clearly that there was some Catholic influence at work, from which even the fellow-countrymen of Azariah de Rossi and Judah Messer Leon could not entirely emancipate themselves.

I ought to have spoken of Roman synagogues, since the building in the Ghetto to which I have been constantly alluding comprises four prayer-houses devoted to Spanish and Italian rites. It says much for Roman Judaism, that they did not consider ritual differences of such importance as to prevent them from forming one community for all charitable and congregational purposes. In Verona and in Modena some congregations even retained the German rite, which their ancestors who immigrated from the Rhine provinces brought with them, whilst they accepted the Spanish pronunciation. I wish that the Anglo-Jewish community could see their way to imitate their example. Not that I think for a moment that the Spanish pronunciation is more correct than the German. Each system has its own mistakes and corruptions; and it is more than probable that the prophet Isaiah, or even the author of Ecclesiastes, would be as little able to follow the prayers in Bevis Marks as in Duke's Place. But since the non-Jewish scientific world has, though only by pure accident, accepted the Spanish way of reading the Hebrew, I should like to see this trifling difference of *Ba*ruch over *Bu*ruch at last disappear, by pronouncing the camets-vowel *a* instead of *o*, and accepting similar little changes, which are of no real importance to us.

The inside of these synagogues is even more simple than their outside. I was told that the synagogue which was burned down last winter, and which also formed a part of this building, could boast of many fine decorations and carvings, etc., but I could observe nothing of the kind in the synagogues I had occasion to frequent. Nor is there much of natural decorum in them, and they reconcile one perfectly to the worst of the Small Synagogues elsewhere. I venture to think that in this respect, too, we have to recognise Catholic influence. It was, I think, one of the leaders in the Oxford Movement who expressed his delight at seeing in Italy a woman poorly-dressed coming into the church, who, after putting down the basket from her back, kneels before one of the many altars and says her prayers. A good deal of this familiarity in the place of worship may also be noticed in the Roman synagogues, where I have seen a woman come into the partition for men, notwithstanding their having a separate gallery, without bonnet or hat on her head, and with an infant in her arms, and listen there to the prayers, till she walked home with her husband. The other people were also very restless, coming and going often, whilst, as soon as the reading of the Law was over, the greater part of the worshippers left the synagogue. It was not a very delightful sight. A minus of decorum does not always mean a plus of devotion; just as little as a maximum of respectability and stiffness are to be taken as signs of true piety.

It is not uninteresting to notice that the Roman synagogue, in spite of its old traditions, did not entirely shut itself against modern reforms. Among them there is that of "calling up the people to the Torah" by the simple formula, "Let the Priest" (or "the Levite") "step forth," [2] and so on, not mentioning either names or titles, which I should like to recommend most strongly to our congregations. I hope that no man will suspect me of such heresy as that of questioning the wisdom of the Synagogue Regulations. But I am inclined to think that the business of conferring the degrees of *Rabbi*, "Associate" or "Master," does not exactly fall within the sphere of activity of the Wardens. The matter could only be decided by a proper Board of examination. As the Council is not provided with such a Board, nor is every aspirant to this honour prepared to undergo the examination required, the wisest course would be to give up titles altogether, calling up all people alike in the way indicated.

The robes the ministers wear (somewhat similar to those of the Greek clergy), are probably also an innovation of modern date, — the old orthodox Rabbis looking at any special vestment for the Preacher or Reader with the same feeling of disgust which the old Puritans entertained for surplice or mitre. But the principle of "The Beauty of Holiness" proved too strong for resistance, and it was only a pardonable vanity when the reformers applied it to their own persons; "Vanity of vanities," saith the preacher, so often, that he gets rather to like it. This vanity is greatly redeemed by the fact that the preacher does not grudge his uniform to his humbler brother, the beadle, who is in most cases to be distinguished from the officiating ministry only by the brass-plate on his breast,

on which the word "Servant" is engraved. Considering
the great confusion arising from the meaningless " Rever-
end" and the universal white neck-tie, such a label, indicating the proper office of the bearer, might, perhaps,
prove as useful among the English Jews as it is among
the Jews of Rome.

It was with a pupil of the Rabbinical College, in company with his friends, that I took my first walk through
ancient Rome. I felt attracted to him by his striking face
of that peculiar fine Jewish type, which is more common
among the Jews in the East than among us. And when
he was reading the lesson from the Prophets in the synagogue, where I made his acquaintance, he reminded me of
that Jewish boy with bright eyes, black curls, and features
strikingly beautiful walking as a captive from Jerusalem
through the streets of Rome some seventeen centuries ago,
whose proficiency in the words of Isaiah caused his redemption. It would be an exaggeration to say that my
companion's remarks were very instructive from an artistic
point of view. Being born and bred in Rome, he passed
with utter indifference many objects which we are bidden
to admire, whilst at others he actually shouted out "Image," or made some other prosaic remark. But in a country where one is determined to play the heathen for so
many weeks, to worship superannuated deities, to get into
raptures at every reminiscence of superseded and vanishing religions, and to be delighted at the sights of "greasy
saints and martyrs hairy," there can be no great harm in
being called back to one's true nature.

The feelings crowding upon one, when entering that
part of the ancient city which probably was in the mind
of the Rabbis when they spoke of "Guilty Rome," are

of a conflicting nature. Every stone and every brick there saw the humiliation of Israel, in every theatre and every circus the Jew served as a comic figure, and was held up to ridicule, whilst there was, perhaps, hardly a single lane or gate through which those who resented the yoke of the "anti-Semites of Antiquity" did not pass, in order to "be butchered to make a Roman holiday." What concerns a Jew most in this perished world of ruins, and at the same time causes him the deepest grief, is the triumphal arch of Titus, "commemorating the defeat of the Jews, and dedicated to him by his successor, Domitian." Enough has been said and written about it both by antiquarians and theologians, the former admiring the workmanship of the reliefs, the latter perceiving in it a proof of the fulfilment of the well-known passages in the New Testament about the destruction of the Temple, which came to pass in spite of the efforts made by Titus to save it. Those who have read Bernay's essay on the "Chronik des Sulpicius Severus" know that the behaviour of "the delight of the human species" on that occasion is rather open to doubt, and it is more probable that, instead of trying to rescue it, he commanded that it should be set on fire. Josephus, who witnessed the shame of his compatriots and co-religionists, has left us a full account of the triumphal procession. Only a flunkey like Josephus could maintain that calm indifference with which he describes the events of the "bitter day," the perusal of which makes one's blood boil. His description fairly agrees with the famous relief on the arch, showing that part of the procession in which the table with the shewbread, the candlestick with the seven lamps, and the golden trumpets figure as the chief ob-

z

jects. The only thing which we miss is the "Law of the Jews," which, according to Josephus, was carried in the triumph as "the last of all the spoils." Was it only an oversight of the artist, or had he no place for it, or is it Josephus who committed the error, mistaking some other object for the Scroll of the Law? I dearly hope that this last was the case, and that Heine was under the impulse of a true and real and poetic inspiration when he wrote (speaking of the Holy Scripture to which he owed his conversion): "The Jews, who appreciate the value of precious things, knew right well what they did when, at the burning of the second temple they left to their fate the golden and silver implements of sacrifice, the candlesticks and lamps, even the breastplate of the High Priest adorned with great jewels, but saved the Bible. This was the real treasure of the temple, and, thanks be to God! it was not left a prey to the flames, nor to the fury of Titus Vespasian, the wretch, who, as the Rabbi tells us, met with so dreadful a death."

However, there were others who brought the glad tidings of the Old Testament to Rome long before there existed a New one. And this is, on the other side, what makes Rome a sort of Terra Sancta even to the Jew. It is true that we have not to look for the footprints of the prophets, for whom even tradition never claimed "the gift of missionary-travelling." But might not the ground there have received a sort of consecration by the fact that it was traversed by the ambassadors of Judas Maccabæus (about 161 B.C.) "to make a league of amity and confederacy" with the Roman Senate? Of the embassy of Simon the Maccabee (about 140 B.C.) there is actual historical evidence that they began to propagate in Rome the Jewish

religion. Some seventy or eighty years later the Jews
had already their own quarter in Rome, with their own
synagogues, which they were in the habit of visiting,
"most especially on the sacred Sabbath days, when they
publicly cultivate their national philosophy." That many
of the oldest teachers of Israel, the Tannaim, went to
Rome as deputies, and that one of them (R. Mathia ben
Chares) founded a school there early in the second century, is also an authenticated fact. One would like to
know what they taught, and in what way they expounded
their *national philosophy*. Most of all one would like to
know what were the spiritual means they employed in
their proselytising work, in which they were, according to
the testimony of history, so successful. Did they preach
in the streets? Or did they hold public controversies?
Or did they even send out Epistles which, in form at least,
served as a model to apostles of another creed? How
many a problem would be solved; how many a miracle
would disappear; how many a book would become superfluous, if we could obtain certainty about these points!
The Talmud tells us little, almost nothing, about these
important things, whilst we get from the Roman writers
only sneers and raillery. To these respectable Romans
the Jews were only a mob of unlettered atheists. Indeed,
to a good orthodox heathen, a religion without images and
statues, with a God without a pedigree and without a
theogony, was an impossible thing. Those poor metaphysicians!

However, why dwell so long on a past world? A
famous Rabbi once exclaimed: "If a man would ask thee,
'Where is thy God?' answer him: 'In the great city of
Rome.'" The underlying idea was the mystical notion

that wherever Israel had to migrate, they were accompanied by the Divine presence. And Rome was, in the times of the Rabbis, the point to which the streams of Jewish migration from the Holy Land chiefly converged. But now, instead of to Rome, might we not point to London and New York as centres of Jewish migrations?

NOTES

I. THE CHASSIDIM

1. SUBJOINED IS A LIST OF SELECTED AUTHORITIES ON THE SUB-
JECT OF THE CHASSIDIM. — *Historical and Bibliographical Works:*
Graetz (xi. including the polemical literature quoted in the Appendix),
Jost, Peter Beer, M. Bodek (סדר הדורות החדש, Lemberg, 1865), A. Wal-
den (שם הגדולים החדש, Warschau, 1864), Finn (קריה נאמנה, Wilna, 1860),
D. Kahana (אבן אופל in the periodical השחר, iv.), Zederbaum (כתר כהונה,
Odessa, 1868). *Essays and Satires:* T. Erter (הצופה, Wien, 1858),
S. Szantó (*Jahrbuch für Israeliten*, p. 108–178, 1867), A. Gottlober
(in his periodical הבוקר אור, iii.), L. Löw (Ben Chananjah, ii.), Ruder-
mann (השחר, vi.), Rapoport (נחלת יהודה, Lemberg, 1873, p. 10), Fröhlich
(המדריך, Warschau, 1876, p. 63 *seq.*), S. Maimon (*Autobiographie*,
Berlin, 1792). Compare also the Hebrew novels by P. Smolensky,
L. Gordon, M. Brandstätter, A. Gottlober and B. Horowitz (German).
Occasional references to the liturgy or the system of the Chassidim in
the "Responses" of R. Ezechiel Landau, Moses Sopher, E. Flekeles
and T. Steinhart, and in the works of Israel Samostsch, Salomon
Chelma and Chayim Walosin. Compare also Zunz (*Gottesdienstliche
Vorträge*, p. 477) and L. Löw (*Mannheimer Album*, Wien, 1874),
Senior Sachs (ההחיה, i. 61) and B. L. Zeitlin (חזות קשה, Paris, 1846).
The best book on the whole subject is E. Zweifel's work שלום על ישראל
(Zitomyr 1868, three parts), which I strongly recommend to students.
The books written by the Chassidim would amount to more than 200.
They are catalogued by Bodek and Walden. I shall only draw the
attention of the student to the works of Beer, Salomon Ladier, and
Mendel Witipsker on one side, who developed the theory of the
Immanence, and those of Nachman Braslaw and Melech Liezensker,
who, on the other hand, carried the theory of Zaddikism to its utmost
consequences. The student will find a fair collection of sayings and
sentences arranged according to theological subjects in the books דרך
חסידים and לשון חכמים (Anon., Lemberg, 1876).

2. הסידים, "pious ones" (Ps. xxxvii. 28, lxx. 2, etc.). The reader is probably acquainted with the term from the Maccabean history (1 Macc. ii. 42, vii. 13), in which the strict party, opposed to all Hellenistic influence, are called "Assideans" [R.V. "Hasidaeans"], Gr. Ἀσιδαῖοι.

3. בעל שם, "The Master of the Name," a term usually applied to exorcists, who cast out devils and performed other miracles through adjuration by the name of God (or angels). The unbelieving Rabbis maintained indeed that in his exorcisms Baalshem employed "impure names" (of devils), whilst the Chassidim, on the other hand, declared that their Master never used "names" at all, his miracles being performed by the divine in Baalshem to which all nature owes obedience. Occasionally the Chassidim call him בעל שם טוב (The Man of Good Name), in allusion to Eccles. vii. 1, shortened by some into *Besht*.

4. בית המדרש — "House of Research" or of "study" (of the Law), but in which also divine service is held thrice a day.

5. תלמיד חכם — "Disciple of the Wise," the usual title of a scholar or student.

6. A Jewish sect, so called after their founder Jacob Leibovicz Frank, who was himself one of the apostles of the pseudo-Messiah Shabbethai Tsebi of Smyrna in Turkey. Among his other doctrines he taught also a sort of Trinity, consisting of the Holy Ancient One, the Holy King or the Messiah, and a feminine person in the Godhead, in which he, like his master, represented the Second Person. The sect ultimately abolished the Law, and, after many controversies with the Rabbinic Jews, went over to Catholicism, the dominant religion in Poland, by which they were soon absorbed. Eybeschütz, chief Rabbi of Prague and Hamburg, was suspected by Emden to be a secret adherent of Shabbethai Tsebi, which was tantamount to apostasy from Judaism. Eybeschütz protested. The litigants excommunicated each other, and the Rabbis divided into two camps, taking sides either with Emden or with his antagonist.

7. The works of Maimonides or Moses b. Maimon (1135–1204) are too many to be enumerated here. The most important are the *Guide of the Perplexed* (מורה נבוכים) and his *Compendium of the Law* (משנה תורה). Judah Hallevi or Abul Hassan flourished in the first half of the twelfth century. He is well known as a poet by his *Divan* and as a

deep religious thinker by his *Cusari*. The former contains also many
songs of a secular nature. Isaac Alfasi (died 1103) is best known by
his Compendium of the Talmud, which was so greatly admired by his
contemporaries that they declared it could never have been composed
"without the aid of the Holy Spirit." R. Solomon b. Isaac, also
called by his initials Rashi (1040–1105), is well known by his commentaries on the Bible and the Talmud.

8. ‏רבי‎, ‏רבינו‎.

9. ‏ספר‎, *Sepher*.

10. The Hebrew word is ‏פלפול‎, meaning subtle discussion and sharp
distinction. The word is closely related to ‏פלפל‎ or ‏פלפלא‎, which means
"pepper" or "seasoning."

11. ‏מהרם שיף‎ = R. Meir Shiff, whose *novellæ* on the Talmud are of a
very subtle kind, and were very popular with the students of this work.

12. ‏תנאים‎—‏אמוראים‎, "The Repeaters," and "The Interpreters." The
sayings and statements of the former are embodied in the Mishnah, a
work compiled by R. Judah the Saint about 220 A.C., and covering a
period of about 250 years (30 B.C.–220 A.C.). The latter occupied
themselves mainly with the interpretation of the Mishnah, and their
discussions and controversies are incorporated in the Talmud of Jerusalem and that of Babylon, and extend over the period from 220–500
A.C. The Talmud of Jerusalem is mostly the product of the schools
of Palestine. The Talmud of Babylon is a growth of that country.
The authorities of this latter Talmud being far away from the place
where the first great Rabbis lived and laboured, their traditions are
naturally not so historically reliable as those of the Talmud of Jerusalem. The authorities of Palestine were also simpler in their method
of interpretation. These again are followed by the Babylonian schools
of new interpreters (of the Talmud).

13. ‏שדין יהודאין‎, an expression that goes back as far as to the *Zohar*.

14. ‏זוהר‎, "Brightness." Cf. Dan. xii. 3, — the authors of "The
Brightness" pretending to be the *Maskilim* or "Wise Ones" mentioned in this verse.

15. ‏שפלות‎.

16. ‏שמחה‎.

17. ‏התלהבות‎.

18. ‏צדיק‎, pl. ‏צדיקים‎.

II. NACHMAN KROCHMAL

1. R. Johanan b. Zaccai was a contemporary of the Apostles, and died about 110 A.D. He belonged to the peace party in opposition to the Zealots, and obtained permission from the Roman government to establish the school of Jamnia, which, after the destruction of the Temple, became the centre of Jewish religious life. See also p. 188.

2. R. Saadiah Gaon was born in Egypt in 892, and died as the head of the school of Sura in Babylon in 942. He is known by his translations of and commentaries on the Bible, and many other works, especially his philosophical treatise *Creeds and Opinions*. He was also a great controversialist. Most of his polemical writings are directed against the Caraites (קראים) or "Scripturalists," a Jewish sect founded by Anan in the eighth century. They protested against the Oral Law, and denied Tradition. On the title "Gaon," see note 1 to Elijah Wilna.

3. מורה נבוכים, *Moreh Nebuchim*, generally considered to be the greatest philosophical work by any Jewish thinker.

4. R. Abraham Ibn Ezra, who spent some time in London, died about 1161. He is best known by his commentaries on the Bible. He was the first writer who doubted the unity of the book of Isaiah.

5. תלמיד חבר.

6. עיר מלאה חכמים וסופרים, meaning "sages" and "scribes," but used by later writers in the sense given in the text.

7. בכורים, dealing with the laws relating to the firstfruits which were brought to the temple (Ex. xxiii. 19). The processions formed by the pilgrims are very vividly described after the said tractate by Delitzsch in his *Iris*, p. 190 *sq.* (English ed.). See also by the same author, *Jüdisches Handwerkerleben zur Zeit Jesu*, p. 66 *seq.*

8. תענית, "Fast," or תעניות, "Fasts."

9. סדר נזיקין, "Order of Damages," treating of the civil law of the Jews, the procedure of courts of justice, and kindred subjects. This Order also includes the tractate אבות, *Aboth* or "Sayings of the Fathers," which is very important for the study of Rabbinic doctrine and ethics.

10. סדר טהרות, "Order of Purities," dealing with the laws regarding Levitical purity.

11. ‏מכילתא, ספרי, (תורת כהנים or ספרא. These three works form the oldest Rabbinic commentary on Exodus, Leviticus, Numbers, and Deuteronomy. The authorities cited in these commentaries all belong to the period of the Tannaim. See above, note 12 to the Chassidim. Constituting as they do, to a certain extent, one of the sources used by the *Gemara*, they are naturally indispensable for a scientific study of the Talmud.

12. הצופה, "*Hatsophe*," a spirited satire against the orthodox and especially against the then prevailing belief in the transmigration of souls taught by the mystical schools. The book is written in the purest biblical Hebrew.

13. מורה נבוכי הזמן.

14. מדרש, pl. מדרשים (*Midrashim*), "Research," "Researches," a name usually applied to the homiletical part of the Rabbinic literature. The most important collection of this kind is the *Midrash Rabbah* to the Pentateuch. The usual way of quoting it is *Genesis Rabbah, Exodus Rabbah*, and so on.

15. See above, note 12 to the Chassidim.

16. מינים, "Heretics," applied to the first Christians, and more so to certain Gnostic sects.

17. הלכה למשה מסיני, see below, p. 186 and *note*.

18. הלכה — אנדה or הגדה, "rule," "method," — "narrative." The former deals with the legal side of the Scriptures, and is thus more of a juristic nature; the latter represents a collection of homilies having mostly as their text the historical and exhortatory parts of the Bible, and is thus more of an edifying character. The theological side of Judaism, as well as its ideal aspirations and Messianic hopes, find their expression in the Agadah. The two words are also used as adjectives, as *Halachic* (legalistic, juristic, and obligatory) and *Agadic* (poetic, edifying, and hyperbolic).

19. ערך מלין, a sort of encyclopædia to the Talmud, of which only the first letter appeared.

20. Menahem Azariah de Rossi, an Italian Jew who flourished in the first half of the sixteenth century. His great work, מאור עינים, *Meor Enayim*, "Light of the Eyes," is the first attempt made by a Jew to

submit the statements of the Talmud to a critical examination, and to question the value of tradition in its historical records.

21. ‏פרקי דר״ אליעזר‎.

22. Italian Jews of the fifteenth and seventeenth centuries. The one, Elijah Delmedigo, wrote an Examination of Religion, whilst his grandson, Joseph Solomon Delmedigo, wrote various pamphlets of a deeply sceptical character. See Geiger's Introduction to his *Melo Chofnayim* (Berlin, 1840).

III. ELIJAH WILNA

1. ‏גאון‎, "The Great One." The authorities of the Babylonian schools after the sixth century were also called the Gaonim (‏גאונים‎), "[their] Eminences." The title was also given afterwards to great Rabbis distinguished for their learning.

2. R. Joseph Caro (1488–1575) lived in Safed. The title of his code is ‏שלחן ערוך‎, *Prepared Table*. This is a code of the Oral Law compiled from the Rabbinic literature.

3. ‏קריה נאמנה‎, containing an account of the Jewish worthies of that city.

4. ‏עלית אליהו‎.

5. A famous mystic of the sixteenth century, from Safed, who was the more admired the less his pupils understood him.

6. Hai was the last of the authorities called Gaon. With his death (1038) the schools of Babylon fell into decay and soon disappeared.

7. ‏הגיגה‎, treating of the voluntary offerings brought by the pilgrims to Jerusalem.

8. ‏גמרא‎, "Perfection or Supplementary Explanations." By this is understood the interpretation given to the Mishnah by the schools in Palestine and Babylon. See above, note 12 to the Chassidim.

9. See Dean Church's *St. Anselm*, from which this story is taken.

10. ‏תוספתא‎, "Addition" (to the Mishnah), but also containing only the sayings and discussions of the period of the Tannaim.

11. ‏סדר עולם‎, "Order of the World," dealing with the Chronology of the Bible, and dating from about the end of the second century.

12. These "Minor Tractates" include, among others, treatises on proselytes, on the laws concerning funerals, the writing of the Law,

and the like. Others are more of an edifying nature, treating of good manners, conduct, etc.

13. ‏קבלת גלות‎.

14. ‏שמונה עשרה‎, "Eighteen." They are recited thrice a day, and form the original germ of the prayers, from which a very rich liturgy developed in the course of time.

15. The titles of the old authorities from 70 B.C. to 500 A.C. See above, note 12 to the Chassidim.

16. ‏נשיא, אב בית דין‎, "Prince," or "Patriarch," religious head, of the Jews (not political), and "Father (or president) of the Court of Justice."

17. ‏זבחים, מנחות‎, "Sacrifices," "Offerings." They treat of the laws relating to sacrifices and meal-offerings.

18. ‏כלאים‎, the laws relating to diverse seeds and garments of diverse sorts. Cf. Deut. xxii. 9–11.

19. ‏מגיד‎, "Teller," a sort of travelling preacher.

20. ‏לולב‎, "palm branch." Cf. Lev. xxiii. 40.

21. ‏ישיבה‎, "High School," or "Academy," in which the Rabbinic literature is studied.

22. ‏ישיבת עץ חיים‎.

23. ‏סמבטיון‎, a mythical river which is supposed to stop its course on Sabbath.

24. ‏בחורים‎, sing. ‏בחור‎, "Young man," by which term the Jews usually understand the *alumni* of their Talmudical schools.

25. Levi b. Gershom (1286–1344) is generally regarded as the greatest successor of Maimonides. Besides his rationalistic commentaries on the Bible, he wrote various treatises on metaphysics, mathematics, astronomy, medicine, etc.

26. ‏בחינת עולם‎.

IV. NACHMANIDES

1. In Steinschneider's *Catalogue of the Bodleian Library*, under the name of Moses Nachmanides, pp. 1947–1965, all the works which are ascribed to this author are put together, and also discussed as to their authenticity. There are only to be added the new edition of the *Derasha* by Jellinek (Vienna, 1872), in which the variants from Schorr's MS. (‏החלוץ‎, viii. 162) are already incorporated; a new edi-

348 STUDIES IN JUDAISM

tion of the ויכוח, and the commentary to Is. lii.–liii. by Steinschneider (Berlin, 1860) ; a *Sermon* for the New Year, ed. by H. Berliner (*Libanon*, v. 564) ; and another Sermon at a wedding (?), ed. by Schorr (*Hechaluz*, xii. 3). For the literature on Nachmanides, besides the references given by Steinschneider, in his *Catalogue,* and the Addenda, p. cxviii. (cf. also the pedigree in the *Catalogue* 2305), see also Graetz, *Geschichte*, vii., pp. 112–143, and p. 147 *seq.* ; Michael, אור החיים, No. 1125, and Weiss, דור דור ודורשיו, v. 4 *seq.* ; Perles' *Monatsschrift*, 1860, p. 175 ; Zomber, *ibid.* 421 ; and Z. Frankel, *ibid.* 1868, p. 449, and *The Jewish Quarterly Review*, iv. 245 *seq.* For Nachmanides' disputation we have to add M. Loeb in the *Révue des Études Juives*, xv. 1 *seq.*, and xviii. 52 (about Abner), and Dr. Neubauer's Essay on Jewish Controversy in the *Expositor*, vol. vii. (third series), p. 98 *seq.*, with the references given there. See also his article on the Bahir and the Zohar in *The Jewish Quarterly Review*, iv. 357. With regard to Nachmanides' mystical system see the references to S. Sachs (whose remarks are most suggestive), Krochmal, and Jellinek in Steinschneider, col. 1949 and 1964, Perles' *Monatsschrift*, 1858, p. 83 *seq.*, and Steinschneider in the Heb. *Bibliographie*, i. 34. See also Professor Kaufmann's *Die Geschichte der Attributenlehre*, and the references given in the index under this name. The *Novellæ* by his son R. Nachman, alluded to in the text, are in the University Library, Cambridge (Add. 1187, 2). The קץ הגאולה is extant in the British Museum, MS. Add. 26,894, and the passage quoted by De Rossi is to be found on p. 163*b*, but a few words are erased by the censor. As to the poem given at the end of this paper, see Zunz, *Synagogale Poesie*, p. 478 ; Landshut, *Amude ha-Abodah s.v.*, the references in Sachs' *Religiöse Poesie der Juden*, and Luzzatto in the *Ozar Nechmad*, ii. 27. Compare also Professor Cheyne's *The Origin of the Psalter*, p. 421.

2. New Year's Day, on the first of Tishri. It is in autumn.

3. A famous Rabbi of the fifteenth century, known by his various casuistical and philosophical works.

4. Chiefly known through his controversial writings against the adherents of the pseudo-Messiah Shabbethai Tsebi. He was for some time the Rabbi of the Portuguese congregation in London.

5. The main objections of the opponents of Maimonides were directed against his rationalistic notions of Revelation, and his allegoris-

ing interpretation of the Scriptures, which amounted in some places to a denial of miracles. He was also suspected of having denied bodily resurrection. A history of Jewish rationalism is still a desideratum. I am certain that it would prove at least as interesting as Reuter's *Geschichte der religiösen Aufklärung im Mittelalter* (Berlin, 1845–60).

6. רבינו משה.

7. אגדות, "Homilies." See above, p. 64 and *note*.

8. קץ הגאולה, "The end of the Redemption," that is the time when the advent of the Messiah is to be expected.

9. This patriarch is famous in Jewish legend for his hospitality. See Beer's *Leben Abrahams*, pp. 37 and 56.

10. This is the quorum necessary to form a congregation (עדה) for the purpose of holding divine service.

11. By *Zobah*, or *Aram Zobah*, the Jews of the Middle Ages usually understood Aleppo. See Benjamin of Tudela's *Itinerary*, i. 88, ii. 124 (London and Berlin, 1840–41).

12. See below, p. 141, where a full translation of the letter is given.

13. הלכות גדולות, a compendium of the Law, dating from the ninth century, by R. Simon Caro.

14. R. Simlai flourished in Palestine in the third century. He is best known as an Agadic teacher and a great controversialist. According to him, 613 commandments were given to Moses on Mount Sinai, of which 365 are prohibitive laws, whilst the remaining 248 are positive injunctions.

15. שער הגמול, "Treatise on Reward (and Punishment)."

16. עלם הבא.

17. Ps. cix. 4; ואני תפלה.

18. אצילות.

19. נפש חיה.

20. ידיעה, "Knowledge," "Foreknowledge," "Omniscience."

21. שכינה, כבוד.

22. סגולה. See Exod. xix. 5

23. חקים.

24. קרבן, קרב.

25. According to a Jewish tradition (the date of which is uncertain) the advent of the Messiah, the Son of David, will be preceded by that of the Messiah, the Son of Joseph. The latter will perish in the battle

against Gog and Magog (the Antichrist of Jewish literature), but will soon be brought back to life on the appearance of the former. Cf. G. H. Dalman's *Der leidende und der sterbende Messias der Synagoge* (Berlin, 1881).

26. בראשית, "In the beginning," Gen. i. 1.

27. מאין; Job xxvii. 12.

28. *Chagigah* 14*b*. The activity of these four Rabbis falls chiefly in the second century. R. Akiba died as a martyr in the Hadrianic persecution (about 130). Elisha b. Abuyah, the apostate, was usually called אחר, *Acher*, "the other one."

29. The former lived in the twelfth, the latter in the sixteenth, century. They are both known for their hostility to philosophy.

30. Bachya wrote in the eleventh century a famous book called חובות הלבבות, *The Duties of the Heart*. For the others see above, p. 13 and *note*, p. 49 and *note*, p. 102 and *note*, p. 97 and *note*, p. 71 and *note*. They all belong to the rationalistic school.

31. A younger contemporary of Maimonides, who translated the *Guide* from Arabic into Hebrew.

32. ספר המשקל. See above, p. 18. R. Moses Cordovora, the author of the פרדס, lived in Safed in the sixteenth century. For R. Isaac Loria, the author of the עץ החיים, see above, note 5 to Elijah Wilna.

33. שושן סודות.

34. ספר הבהיר, a forgery by a Provençal Jew of the thirteenth century, who attributed it to a Rabbi of the first century.

35. This hymn is now incorporated in her excellent little book, *Songs of Zion*, pp. 13-15.

36. זהוב, a gold piece. The country and the date of the writer not being certain, it is impossible to determine the value of this coin.

37. The lawfulness of eating this fish (= sturgeon?) was contested for many centuries, and the controversy still continues.

38. פשוט, a smaller coin than the Zehub.

39. שמע, "Hear," the verses from Deut. vi. 4–9, xi. 13–21, and Num. xv. 37–41, recited twice a day by the Jews.

V. A JEWISH BOSWELL

1. *Sabbath*, 30*b*.

2. מנהג, pl. מנהגים (*Minhagim*), applied usually to those ritual customs and ceremonies for which there is no distinct authority in the Scriptures or even in the Talmud.

VI. THE DOGMAS OF JUDAISM

1. *Jerusalem*, in Mendelssohn's *Sämmtliche Werke* (Vienna, 1838), especially from p. 264 onwards, and a letter by him published in Frankel-Graetz's *Monatsschrift*, 1859, p. 173. For Mendelssohn's position, see Graetz's *Geschichte*, xi. 86 *seq.*, especially p. 88 and note 1; Kayserling, *Leben und Werke* of M., 2d ed., p. 394; Steinheim, *Moses Mendelssohn* (Hamburg, 1840), p. 30 *seq.*; Holdheim, *Moses Mendelssohn* (Berlin, 1859), p. 18 *seq.*; Leopold Löw's pamphlet, *Jüdische Dogmen* (Pesth, 1871).

2. See the Commentaries on Maimonides' ספר המצות, especially R. Simeon Duran's זוהר הרקיע; cf. also ancient and modern commentaries on Exod. xx. 2.

3. See *Siphra* (ed. Weiss), pp. 86*b*, 93*b*.

4. *Baba Bathra*, 14*b*; cf. Fürst's *Kanon*, p. 15.

5. See *Sanhedrin*, 38*b*, and *Pseudo-Jonathan* to Gen. iv. 8.

6. *Mechilta*, 33*b*.

7. אפיקורוס, Lat. Epicurus.

8. See *Mishnah, Sanhedrin*, x. e, § 1, and Talmud, *ibid.* 90*a* and *b*, and Rabbinowicz's *Variae Lectiones*, ix. p. 247 notes. Besides the ordinary commentaries on the Talmud, account must also be taken of the remarks of Crescas, Duran, Albo, and Abarbanel on the subject. Cf. also Kämpf in the *Monatsschrift* (1863), p. 144 *seq.*; Oppenheim, *ibid.* (1864), p. 144; Friedmann in the *Beth Talmud*, i. p. 210 *seq.* See also Talmudical Dictionaries, *s.v.* אפיקורוס. The explanation I have adopted agrees partly with Friedmann's and partly with Oppenheim's views.

9. *Sayings of the Fathers*, iii. § 9, and iv. § 22.

10. See אדרת אליהו (Jovslow, 1835), p. 48. In my exposition of the dogmas of the Caraites I have mainly followed the late Dr. Frankl's

article "Karaiten" in Ersch u. Gruber's *Encyclopädie* (sec. ii. vol. xxxvi. pp. 12–18). See also his *Ein mutazilitischer Kalam* and his *Beiträge zur Literaturgeschichte der Karäer* (Berlin, 1887) on Bashazi. Cf. also Jost's *Geschichte*, ii. c. 13.

11. Kairowan was one of the greatest centres of Jewish learning in North Africa during that period.

12. See, however, Professor D. Kaufmann's note in the *Jewish Quarterly Review*, i. p. 441. From this it would seem that the creed of R. Judah Hallevi may be formulated in the following articles : — The conviction of the existence of God, of His eternity, of His guidance of our fathers, of the Divine Origin of the Law, and of the proof of all this, the pledge or token of its truth, the exodus from Egypt.

13. אמונה רמה, *Emunah Ramah*, pp. 44 and 69; cf. Gulmann, *Monatsschrift*, 1878, p. 304.

14. For the various translations of the Thirteen Articles which were originally composed in Arabic, see Steinschneider, Cat. Bodl. col. 1887. Cf. Rosin, *Ethik des Maimonides*, p. 30 ; Weiss, *Beth Talmud*, i. p. 330, and *Ben Chananjah*, 1863, p. 942, and 1864, pp. 648 and 697, and Landshut, עמודי העבודה, p. 231.

15. מנחת קנאות. See pp. 1–16.

16. See *Hammaskir*, viii. pp. 63 and 103.

17. See Steinschneider, *Cat. München*, No. 210.

18. See the Collection דברי חכמים, by Ashkenazi, pp. 56*b seq.*

19. See Albo, c. iii. Probably identical with the author mentioned by Duran, 13*b*.

20. ספר נצחון, "Sepher Nizzachon."

21. See אור ה' (ed. Johannisburg), preface, and pp. 20*a*, 44*b*, 59*b*, and elsewhere. The style of this author is very obscure. Cf. Joel's pamphlet on this author (Breslau, 1874).

22. See the first pages of the מגן אבות (Leghorn, 1758), and his אוהב משפט, pp. 13 *seq.*

23. עקרים, *Ikkarim*, "Fundamentals."

24. See *Ikkarim*, i. c. 23, and Maimonides' *Commentary on the Mishnah* (end of tractate Maccoth). On Albo compare Schlesinger's Introduction and notes to the *Ikkarim*, Joel's pamphlet, p. 82 ; Paulus, *Monatsschrift*, 1874, p. 463, and Brüll's *Jahrb.* iv. p. 52.

25. I know his work from a MS. in the British Museum, Orient. 39.

26. ‏דרך אמונה‎, *Derech Emunah.* Cf. Steinschneider, *Monatsschrift,* 1883, p. 79 *seq.*

27. See ‏עקירת יצחק‎, gate 55.

28. See his ‏יסוד האמונה‎ and ‏מאמר האחדות‎.

29. ‏ראש אמנה‎.

30. See ‏בחינת הדת‎, ed. Reggio, p. 28.

31. See ‏מעשה טוביה‎ (Venice, 1707), 16a and 23a. His language is very vague.

32. See the Collection by Ashkenazi (as above, note 18), p. 29b.

33. See his ‏בשמים ראש‎, p. 331.

34. See Weiss's admirable monograph on Maimonides, published in the *Beth Talmud,* i.

VII. THE HISTORY OF JEWISH TRADITION

1. The Hebrew title of the work is ‏דור דור ודורשיו‎.

2. That is, vows of an ascetic nature (not vows or oaths enforced by a court of justice), which the tribunal could annul when there was sufficient reason for it.

3. The ten Rabbis who are named as the bearers of tradition during the period between 170 and 30 B.C. The "pair" in each case is supposed to have consisted of the president and the vice-president of the Sanhedrin for the time being. See, however, Kuenen, *Gesammelte Schriften,* p. 49 *seq.*

4. ‏דרשנים גדולים‎.

5. ‏הלכות למשה מסיני‎. They amount, in the whole of Rabbinic literature, to about forty, of which more than ten concern the preparation of the phylacteries, whilst others relate to the libations of water at the Feast of Tabernacles and similar subjects.

6. This is the time when the school of R. Johanan b. Zaccai began its activity. Others place the Tannaitic age in Hillel's time (30 B.C.).

7. ‏בת קול‎.

8. ‏בית דין‎, lit. "Court of Justice," as above, note 16 to Elijah Wilna, but it means also a sort of permanent Synod, in which of course justice was also administered as a part of religion.

9. ‏עדיות‎, "Evidences given by Witnesses." The tractate consists

mostly of a number of laws attested by various Rabbis as having come down to them as old traditions.

10. The family of Hillel, which was supposed to be descended from the house of David, supplied the Jews with patriarchs for many gen-·erations. Gamaliel II. flourished about 120 A.C., whilst Simon b. Gamaliel's activity as Patriarch falls about 160 A.C.

11. שמחות, *Semachoth*. It is a euphemistic title, the tractate dealing with the laws relating to funeral ceremonies and mourning.

12. סבוראי, " Elucidators " or " Explainers." The heads of the schools in Babylon during the fifth and sixth centuries were so designated.

13. The Rabbinic Jews of the dispersion add one day to each festival, and thus celebrate the Passover eight days, the Feast of Weeks two days, etc. The custom arose out of the uncertainty about the first day of the month, the prerogative of fixing the New Moon resting with the great *Beth Din* in Palestine, which had not always the means of communicating in time the evidence given before them that the New Moon had been seen by qualified witnesses. The prerogative was abolished in the fourth century, and the calendar fixed for all future time, but the additional day is still kept by the Rabbinic Jews as the " Custom of their Fathers."

14. היכלות, שיעור קומה, " Chambers (of Heaven) " and the " Measure of the Stature," mystical works in which occasionally gross anthropomorphisms are to be found. Their authorship is unknown.

III. THE DOCTRINE OF DIVINE RETRIBUTION IN RABBINICAL LITERATURE

1. *Sabbath*, 55*a*.

2. *Sayings of the Fathers* (ed. C. Taylor), v. 12–15. See also *Sabbath*, 32 *seq.*, and *Mechilta* (ed. Friedman), 95*b*. *Arachin*, 16*a*.

3. See *Mechilta*, 25*a*, 32*b*. *Gen. Rabbah*, ch. 48, and *Tossephta Sotah*, iv. 7, and parallels.

4. *Taanith*, 21*a*.

5. *Sayings of the Fathers*, iv. 5.

6. *Baba Bathra*, 9*b*.

7. *Yoma*, 39*a*.

8. *Berachoth*, 33*a*.
9. *Sabbath*, 13*b*.
10. *Berachoth*, 7*a*.
11. See *Mechilta*, 68*b*, and parallels. *Siphra*, 112*b*. *Pessikta* of R. Kahana, 167*b*. Cp. *Sanhedrin*, 44*a*.
12. *Aboth* de R. Nathan, 40*a*, 59*b*, and 62*b*.
13. *Baba Bathra*, 10*a*.
14. *Eccles. Rabbah*, ix. 7.
15. 5*a*.
16. 7*b*.
17. See *Mechilta*, 95*b*, and parallels.
18. See *Kiddushin*, 40*b*. *Mechilta*, 63*b*. *Lev. Rabbah*, iv.
19. See *Sabbath*, 54*a*.
20. *Exodus Rabbah*, c. 35, and parallels.
21. See *Negaim*, ii. 1.
22. *Exod. Rabbah*, c. 46.
23. *Taanith*, 11*a*.
24. See *Berachoth*, 5*a*.
25. *Tanchuma*, כי תשא, § 2. Cp. *Mechilta*, 72*b*.
26. *Siphré*, 73*b*, and parallels.
27. *Taanith*, 8*a*.
28. *Arachin*, 16*b*.
29. *Sayings of the Fathers*, iv. 15.
30. See *Chagigah*, 5*a*.
31. *Sabbath*, 55*a*.
32. *Menachoth*, 29*b*.
33. *Taanith*, 25*a*.
34. *Gen. Rabbah*, xxvii.; *Pessikta*, 136*b*; *Sanhedrin*, vi. 5; *Berachoth*, 7*a*.
35. *Sayings of the Fathers*, i. 3, p. 27, ed. Taylor. See also note 8.
36. *Abodah Zarah*, 19*a*; *Siphré*, 79*b*.
37. *Berachoth*, 58*b*.
38. See *Exod. R.*, 30, and parallels.
39. See ראשית חכמה, i. 9.
40. See רמתים צופים, 33*b*.
41. See *Sabbath*, 55*b*, and *Siphra*, 27*a*.

IX. THE LAW AND RECENT CRITICISM

1. *Judaism and Christianity, a Sketch of the Progress of Thought from Old Testament to New Testament*, by C. H. Toy, Professor in Harvard University. London, 1890.

2. See *Pessikta* of R. Kahana, 61*b*, and parallels, and *Erubin*, 13*b*.

3. Tal. Jer., *Sabbath*, 5*b*.

4. מטטרון, the name of an angel, already found in the Talmud, but playing a more important part in the *Book of Chambers*, where he is identified with Enoch. The etymology of the word is doubtful, some authors considering it to be of Persian origin (*Mithra*) ; others again deriving it from the Greek μετὰ τύραννον, or μετὰ θρόνον.

5. ספירות.

6. מימרא, "The Word," sometimes substituted for God. See J. Levy's *Chaldäisches Wörterbuch, s.v.*

7. אדם קדמון, כתר.

8. *Mechilta*, 104*a*.

9. See Tal. Jer., *Yoma*, 45*b*. Cf. Maimonides, *Mishneh Torah*, הלכות שבת פ״ב ה״ג.

10. *Tosephta Berachoth*, iii. 7.

11. *Sabbath*, 10*b*. The name of the Rabbi is not given, but the fact that R. Simeon b. Gamaliel (160 A.C.) already refers to this interpretation makes it clear that its anonymous author must have lived at least a generation before.

12. כוס של קדוש.

13. See *Midrash* to the Psalms xcii. and *Deut. Rabbah* iii. The Rabbis perceived in the words וקראת לשבת ענג (Isa. lviii. 13), a command to make the Sabbath a day of pleasure, whilst the word חפצך was understood by them to mean "needs," "wants," or "business" (*not* "pleasure"). Cf. *Sabbath*, 113*a* and *b*.

14. See *Gen. Rabbah*, xi. (and parallels), and *Sabbath*, 119*a*.

15. See *Maaseh Torah* (ed. Schönblum) and *Deut. Rabbah*, i.

16. *Sabbath*, 25*b* and 119*a*.

17. *Betsah*, 16*a*. Cf. Baer's notes in his *Prayer-Book*, p. 203 *seq.*

18. See *Sabbath*, 119*b*, and *Gen. Rabbah*, xi.

19. See *Sabbath,* 10*b*, and *Gen. Rabbah, ibid.*
20. תפלין.
21. *Nazir,* 23*b*.

X. THE HEBREW COLLECTION OF THE BRITISH MUSEUM

1. אור זרוע by R. Isaac b. Moses of Vienna (thirteenth century), mostly on legal subjects.
2. יוחסין, Yuchasin.
3. מכלל, Miklal.
4. מועד, זרעים, the former treating of the agricultural laws of the Bible, the latter of those relating to the Sabbath, Passover, and other festivals.
5. מחזור, "Cycle," containing the liturgy for the festivals.
6. Since then edited by the Mekize Nirdamim.
7. Eve of the last day of the Feast of Tabernacles.

XI. TITLES OF JEWISH BOOKS

1. ש"ס. ששה סדרים.
2. ברייתא.
3. פאה.
4. ילקוט, Yalkut.
5. חזית.
6. שוחר טוב.
7. ויסעו.
8. ילמדנו, והזהיר.
9. רעיא מהימנא.
10. שער המלך, משנה תורה, מניד משנה, משנה למלך, עמק המלך.
11. חיים שאל.
12. חד גריא לא ישראל.
13. ש"לה. שני לוחות הברית.

XII. THE CHILD IN JEWISH LITERATURE

1. The main authorities on the subjects of this essay are *Die Lebensalter*, by Dr. Leopold Löw; *The Jewish Rite of Circumcision*, by Dr. Asher; an article by Dr. Perles in the Graetz *Jubelschrift*, p. 23 *seq.*; *Merkwürdigkeiten der Juden*, by Schudt; the מקורי המנהגים and other works on ritual customs; Güdemann's *Geschichte des Erziehungswesens und der Cultur der Juden*; and *Das Kind in Brauch und Sitte der Völker*, by Dr. Ploss.

2. אמת, אמתי.

3. לילית, Is. xxxiv. 14.

4. See above, note 39 to Nachmanides.

5. ברית מילה, "Covenant of Circumcision." This is the usual expression in Hebrew literature for the rite of circumcision.

6. שלום זכר.

7. מוהל, גוזר.

8. פריון הבן.

9. חקת התורה, on educational matters.

10. סחורה, "business," or "wares."

11. I am indebted for the English adaptation to Mrs. Henry Lucas.

12. *Bereshith Rabbah*, chapter xx. For another reading see ראשית חכמה (ed. Cracow), p. 374.

13. *Abodah Zarah*, 3*b*.

14. This is the way in which Deut. xxxi. 10–12 was explained.

15. סופרים, "Scribes"; treating of the regulations concerning the writing of the Law, but containing also much liturgical matter.

16. ספרדים, by which name the Jews of the Spanish rite are designated.

17. נצחון ישן, a controversial work published by Wagenseil. See above, p. 203, for another victory.

18. סנדלפון, who is probably known to the English reader from Longfellow's poem.

19. בר מצוה.

20. קידוש, "Sanctification" — "benediction" — on the eve of Sabbath, which is pronounced over a cup of wine.

21. שמחת תורה, on the 23rd of Tishri, when the last portion from the Pentateuch is read.

22. הלל, "Praise," *i.e.* Ps. cxiii.–cxviii.

23. קריש, the name of a prayer commencing יתגדל ויתקדש, "Magnified and sanctified be," etc.

24. Prayer beginning ברכו, "Bless ye," etc.

25. ברוך שאמר, beginning of a prayer, "Blessed be He," etc.

26. See Schürer's *Die Gemeindeverfassung der Juden in Rom*, p. 24. Cf. *Hebräische Bibliographie*, xix. p. 79.

XIII. WOMAN IN TEMPLE AND SYNAGOGUE

1. צְבָאֹת.

2. תחנות.

XIV. THE EARLIEST JEWISH COMMUNITY IN EUROPE

1. מעבר יבק.

2. יעמור. In olden times the weekly lesson from the Law used to be read by seven members of the congregation who were "called up" for this purpose; the Priest and the Levite took precedence of laymen for this honour. At the present day, the members of the congregation are still called up, but the actual reading is performed by an official.

INDEX

This Index contains the most important names of persons, titles of books, technical terms and Hebrew words occurring in the text. In the notes to the text, commencing with p. 415, the Hebrew words are for the most part given also in Hebrew characters.